365 Gr[eat]
Chocolate Desserts

Other books in this series are:

365 Great Chocolate Desserts

Natalie Haughton

A JOHN BOSWELL ASSOCIATES BOOK

HarperCollins*Publishers*

Dear Reader:

We welcome your recommendations for future 365
Ways books. Send your suggestions and a recipe, if
you'd like, to Cookbook Editor, HarperCollins
Publishers, 10 East 53rd Street, New York, NY 10022.
If we choose your title suggestion or your recipe we
will acknowledge you in the book and send you a free
copy.

Thank you for your support.

Sincerely yours,
The Editor

Reissued in 1996.

Series Editor: Susan Wyler
Design: Nigel Rollings
Index: Maro Riofrancos

Library of Congress Catalog Card Number 90-56355
ISBN 0-06-018665-8

96 97 98 99 00 DT/HC 10 9 8 7 6 5 4 3 2 1

For my children, Alexis and Grant, and chocophiles everywhere. Enjoy!

Acknowledgments

"*Chocolate is my life,*" is painted on a little sign that graces a corner of my kitchen; it says a lot. I'm always willing to sample a delicious chocolate dessert on a moment's notice. So writing this book was a dream come true.

A million thanks to my husband, Fred, and my children, Alexis and Grant, for always being there and for their love, faith, confidence, and discriminating tastebuds.

Special thanks also to the following: my parents, Phyllis and Andrew Hartanov, for all those wonderful childhood chocolate dessert memories (among them chocolate bread pudding, chocolate chiffon pie, and Frango Mints); to friends, relatives, colleagues, good cooks, and chefs who have shared their special chocolate creations and secrets with me over the years; to Hershey Chocolate U.S.A., Guittard Chocolate Co., and Lindt & Sprungli, Inc., for their advice and assistance; to Susan Wyler, my editor, who gave me an opportunity to share my passion for chocolate; to Mike Sievers for his invaluable computer expertise; and to all those chocolate taste testers who happily sacrificed their diets for a good cause.

Special gratitude and appreciation to the talented Patti Gray for her encouragement and spirited recipe inspirations and to my sister, Tammie Coronado, for her help with recipe testing.

Contents

You'll want to pull out your best cake stand for these cakes and tortes of all descriptions, whether it's a simple dark, moist Blackout Cake, frosted with creamy Chocolate Ganache, or a gorgeous Chocolate Blitz Torte, layered with strawberries and whipped cream.

An entire chapter devoted to one of the easiest and most popular desserts—and all the recipes are chocolate. Choose from flavors like Chocolate Raspberry Truffle Cheesecake, Mocha Chocolate Chip Cheesecake, Easy Chocolate Chunk Cheesecake, and Peanut Butter Cup Cheesecake.

Here are pies and tarts to fill a dessert cart. Family-style favorites, Chocolate Buttermilk Walnut Pie and Easy Chocolate-Coffee Mousse Pie, and company creations, like Chocolate Coconut Pecan Pie and Chocolate Hazelnut Tart.

These are the showstoppers you'll be proud to serve. Drop-dead favorites, like Caramel Turtle Truffle Tart, Triple Chocolate Napoleons with Raspberry Sauce, and Flourless Bittersweet Apricot-Walnut Torte, and whimsical, dressy desserts, such as Chocolate-Cinnamon Dessert Nachos and Dessert Spring Rolls.

When there's no time to fuss, but you want to serve a homemade dessert, this chapter comes to the rescue with easy-as-pie recipes like Rocky Road Refrigerator Cake, made with fudge brownie mix, Chocolate Café au Lait Cake, made with packaged devil's food cake mix and graham cracker crumbs, and Quick Kahlua Chocolate Cream Pie.

Here are all those wonderful ice cream cakes and frozen pies and tortes that you can make well ahead and pull out on a moment's notice. Plus recipes for some of the best homemade chocolate ice creams ever, with flavors like Orange Chocolate Flake, Chocolate Chocolate Chunk, and White Chocolate Raspberry.

For Love of Chocolate

There's something almost magical about chocolate. It brings a smile to everyone's face. Decadent, divine, heavenly, voluptuous, ultimate, exquisite, luscious, wicked, luxurious, enticing, tempting, irresistible: these are just a few of the words used to describe chocolate. Ask a person what he or she would like for dessert, and more often than not, the answer is "something chocolate."

While the Swiss, who are the world's leading chocolate-eaters, eat almost twice as much chocolate per capita as we do in the United States—a whopping 19.9 pounds per person—chocolate is America's favorite flavor. I know it certainly is mine.

While testing the recipes for this book, I found that semisweet chocolate chips, which are often more economical than blocks of semisweet chocolate, can be used very successfully in most recipes. They melt easily in the microwave and require no cutting or chopping. Very delicate recipes, such as mousses and truffles, which showcase the chocolate and call for only a couple of other ingredients, may require an exceptionally high-quality imported variety, but I found that the semisweet chips work well in most baking recipes and in recipes that use chocolate in combination with a number of other ingredients.

For my testing, I used good domestic chocolate brands, such as Hershey's, Baker's, Nestle, Guittard, and Ghirardelli; all worked well and tasted delicious. Of course, if you prefer to use a more expensive chocolate, by all means go ahead. Callebaut, Tobler, and Lindt are excellent imports.

Because of the technical nature of recipes for cakes, pies, pastries, and the like, many of which are as exact as chemical formulas, be aware that slight changes in proportions, ingredient substitutions (beyond the chocolate mentioned above), and inaccurate measurements may alter the finished results. Never attempt, for example, to use sugar substitute in place of sugar or to substitute honey for sugar.

In recipes calling for flour, either bleached or unbleached all-purpose can be used. All flour in this book is unsifted, unless otherwise specified. For best results, measure flour by spooning straight from the bag or canister into a graduated dry-ingredient measuring cup. Level with the straight edge of a knife. Cake flour is used in a few cake recipes to yield a more delicate, tender crumb and a lighter product. Use solid vegetable shortening for greasing pans, unless the recipe designates butter.

There is no substitute for the rich flavor butter imparts to chocolate desserts. I'd rather eat dessert only once a week and go all out than compromise on flavor and texture. While I find little difference between salted and unsalted butter in many recipes—and specify unsalted, or sweet, butter only where it will make a difference in a delicate dessert—feel free to use whatever type of butter you have on hand.

Recipes in this book were tested with large eggs. Use size grade AA or A eggs with clean, uncracked shells that have been stored under refrigeration. For the recipes in this book it's not necessary to bring eggs to room temperature before using them. I have severely limited the number of recipes that use raw or lightly cooked eggs since they can harbor salmonella, a bacteria that causes food poisoning. While I did include some traditional mousses and chiffons that use raw or lightly cooked eggs or egg whites, all such recipes are flagged with a warning. Please read the paragraph of caution carefully and only make these recipes at your own risk.

Most of the following desserts are foolproof. However, keep in mind that high heat is the enemy of chocolate. It destroys flavor and texture. To ensure success when baking, always preheat your oven at least 10 to 15 minutes ahead. Check the temperature with a good oven thermometer. A variance of 25 or 50 degrees can mean the difference between success and failure.

When melting chocolate, it is also critical to watch closely to avoid scorching. I favor the microwave method, which you'll find used extensively throughout this book. Not only is it fast, but there's less chance of the chocolate coming in contact with water or moisture, which will cause the chocolate to seize or thicken to a tight, congealed lump that's hard to work with.

To melt chocolate in the microwave oven, place it in a glass measuring cup, custard cup, or bowl—do not cover—and heat on High 1 to 2 minutes, or according to the time specified in an individual recipe. Watch carefully and always try the minimum time first. The chocolate will not look melted; in fact, it will retain its shape. When the appearance of the chocolate changes from dull to shiny, stir until smooth and melted. If a few lumps remain, return it to the microwave for a few seconds. White chocolate can also be melted in the microwave, but it is so delicate that Medium heat must be used instead of High power.

If you do not have a microwave, or it is inconvenient to use it, chop the chocolate into small pieces and melt in the top of a double boiler over hot—not even simmering—water, stirring often. Be sure to avoid allowing water or steam, even on a spoon, to come into contact with the chocolate, or it will tighten up, as mentioned above.

While it's best to use the type of chocolate specified in a recipe, if you're in a pinch and need to substitute unsweetened cocoa powder for chocolate, use 3 tablespoons cocoa and 1 tablespoon shortening—butter, margarine, or oil—for each ounce of unsweetened chocolate. Keep in mind, though, that the results will not be as rich and velvety.

What follows is a glossary of the different types of chocolate available for cooking. The varieties are determined by the amounts of chocolate liquor (not an alcohol, but the essence of the cocoa bean), cocoa butter, sugar, and flavorings they contain. Manufacturers vary the amounts to create their own special blends.

Unsweetened Chocolate:
Also referred to as baking or bitter chocolate, this is hardened chocolate liquor. It contains no sugar. Unsweetened chocolate, which is usually packaged in eight (one-ounce) blocks, is the simplest form of chocolate available. According to the U.S. Standard of Identity, it must contain between 50 and 58 percent cocoa butter.

Bittersweet Chocolate:
This chocolate is slightly sweetened. The amount of sugar used depends on the manufacturer. This chocolate, which must contain at least 35 percent chocolate liquor, should be used when intense chocolate taste is desired. Bittersweet and semisweet can be used interchangeably in cooking and baking.

Semisweet Chocolate:
This all-purpose chocolate, which must also contain at least 35 percent chocolate liquor, is prepared by blending chocolate liquor with varying amounts of sweeteners and sometimes flavorings. Semisweet chocolate is available in bar form as well as chips and pieces. The different forms can be used interchangeably in recipes.

Sweet Cooking Chocolate:
This must contain 15 percent chocolate liquor. It often has a higher sugar content than semisweet chocolate does. It's available in four-ounce bars.

Milk Chocolate:
This mild-flavored chocolate can contain as little as 10 percent chocolate liquor, but must have 12 percent milk solids. It is used widely for candy bars but rarely, except for milk chocolate chips, in cooking. Don't substitute this for other kinds of chocolate in recipes.

Unsweetened Cocoa Powder:

This is powdered chocolate from which a portion of the cocoa butter has been removed. Fat content can vary from 10 to 21 percent. Cocoa will keep indefinitely in a cool place. Dutch-processed cocoa, called European-style by one domestic manufacturer, is made by treating the chocolate liquor with an alkaline solution, which makes a cocoa that is darker in color and more mellow. Recipes note when Dutch-processed cocoa is preferred. While regular cocoa can be used, the flavor and texture of the end product may vary.

White Chocolate:

Although technically not chocolate according to the U.S. Standard of Identity, because it contains no chocolate liquor, white chocolate is made from cocoa butter, sugar, flavorings, and fresh or dried milk. You'll find it labeled white baking bar or chips, Swiss white chocolate, or confectionery bars. White chocolate is actually ivory-colored, not white. Follow specific recipes designed to use white chocolate; do not substitute for other types of chocolate called for in recipes.

Compound Chocolate or Confectioners' Coating Chocolate:

This is also referred to as "summer coating," artificial, or imitation chocolate. Some or all of the cocoa butter has been replaced by other fats, such as coconut oil or palm oil, to prevent it from melting at high temperatures. Available at cake decorating and candymaking supply stores, it's economical and easy to use (it sets up faster, doesn't discolor, doesn't have to be tempered, and dries shiny) for dipping and molding, though the taste and texture is not the same as true chocolate.

Commercial Coating Chocolate:

Called couverture, this is the chocolate professional candymakers use for dipping and making chocolate curls, ruffles, and the like. It is not readily available to consumers (except through a baker's supply house or specialty mail order source), but European chocolate with a high cocoa butter content can be used in its place.

Chocolate keeps well, but it is best stored in a cool, dry place between 60°F and 75°F and at less than 50 percent relative humidity. Chocolate can be refrigerated (it becomes very hard and brittle when cold), but it must be wrapped tightly in moistureproof wrap and in a moistureproof container to avoid absorption of odors and to prevent condensation of moisture on it when removed from the refrigerator. There are varying opinions about whether chocolate can be frozen. Some say you can freeze it as long as three to four months without a change in flavor, texture, or appearance and others avoid freezing altogether.

Occasionally you may have noticed a grayish-white dull film on the surface of some chocolate. This "bloom" develops when chocolate is exposed to fluctuating hot and cold temperatures. The gray film or discoloration is softened cocoa butter that has seeped to the surface and solidified when the chocolate cooled. Although bloom is unattractive, it is perfectly safe to eat, and the chocolate will regain its rich brown color when melted or used in cooking.

With the exception of several of the showier recipes in the Chocolate Entertains chapter, which take a bit more time and patience, most of the following desserts have been designed with busy cooks in mind. Taste and ease of preparation are my main concerns. While I've included decorating suggestions at the end of many recipes, I've left some plain for simplicity's sake. But by all means, for entertaining, keep in mind that whipped cream, shaved chocolate, nuts, berries, even chopped candy, will dress up any chocolate dessert with professional aplomb.

With the variety that follows, I'm sure you'll find your own favorites. Now is the time to head into the kitchen and whip up the grandest finale of all—a great chocolate dessert. To chocolate dessert lovers everywhere, enjoy!

Chapter 1

Chocolate on a Pedestal

Chocolate cakes and tortes come in all sizes, shapes, and flavors. Some are plain, others are lavish—but all of those in this collection are tantalizing. Who doesn't love chocolate cake? For many it evokes fond childhood memories. At our house, chocolate cake was a must for birthdays and any special occasion. Vanilla-flavored cakes would never do.

When it comes to cake baking, follow the recipes here which have been formulated for success. Don't tamper with the amounts of ingredients, or you might end up with a disaster. Unlike other types of cooking where measurements may not be crucial, baking is a more exact science. Also, follow recipe directions for greasing and flouring pans for easy unmolding.

When baking, be sure to measure ingredients accurately, using dry measures for dry ingredients and liquid measures for liquids. Recipes use either all-purpose or cake flour. In some cases cake flour yields a lighter product, but if cake flour is not available, substitute 1 cup less 2 tablespoons all-purpose flour for every cup of cake flour called for in the recipe. Do not attempt to substitute other kinds of flour, such as whole wheat flour for all-purpose, in cake recipes. You will be disappointed with the results, which may be heavy and unappealing. An electric mixer is an asset for preparing cake batters and does an excellent job of creaming together ingredients. For best results, be sure not to overwork the cake batters once the last ingredients have been added.

An accurate oven is important as well. If you do lots of baking an oven thermometer is a wise investment. To tell if a cake is completely baked, insert a wooden pick or cake tester in the center of the cake; if it comes out clean it's done. Be sure cakes are cooled completely before frosting.

The only problem you'll have with these recipes is deciding which one to make first. Chocolate is teamed with a wide spectrum of flavors in these delectable variations. There's Peanut Butter Fudge Cake, Chocolate Cranberry Cake, Chocolate Apple Cake, Chocolate Buttermilk Layer Cake, and Chocolate Peanut Butter Bundt Cake among them. The Red Devil's Food Cake is unusual (it contains tomato sauce and red wine vinegar) but moist and delicious.

For those fond of cake rolls, you'll be jazzed about the Orange Chocolate Cake Roll and Mocha-Filled Chocolate Cake Roll. Also included are some fabulous fruitcakes come holiday time—Chocolate Zucchini Fruitcake, White Chocolate Orange Fruitcake, and Almond Chocolate Fruitcake Loaf. All rated tops with tasters.

1   BLACKOUT CAKE

Prep: 30 minutes   Cook: 35 to 40 minutes   Serves: 12 to 16

This is one of my all-time favorite cakes—moist, dark, and chocolate through and through. It's always a hit, no matter where and when it's served. My children adore this for birthdays, special occasions, or whenever they can talk me into making it. To make it especially festive, garnish the cake with piped whipped cream and shaved chocolate.

1½ sticks (6 ounces) butter,
       softened
3 cups sugar
3 eggs
2 teaspoons vanilla extract
4 (1-ounce) squares
       unsweetened chocolate,
       melted
3 cups flour

3 teaspoons baking soda
½ teaspoon salt
¾ cup buttermilk
1⅓ cups boiling water
       Chocolate Ganache (recipe
       follows)
¾ to 1 cup diced roasted
       almonds

1. Preheat oven to 350°F. Grease two 9-inch round cake pans. Dust with flour; tap out excess.

2. In a large bowl, beat together butter and sugar with an electric mixer on medium speed until light and fluffy, 1 to 2 minutes. Add eggs and vanilla and beat until well blended. Add chocolate and beat 1 to 2 minutes.

3. Mix together flour, baking soda, and salt. Add to chocolate mixture in two additions alternately with buttermilk. Beat until well blended. With mixer on low speed, add boiling water and beat until smooth (batter will be thin). Pour batter into prepared pans.

4. Bake 35 to 40 minutes, or until a cake tester inserted in center comes out clean. Let cool in pans 10 to 15 minutes, then unmold onto racks and let cool completely.

5. Cover a cake layer with a little more than one third of Chocolate Ganache. Set second cake layer on top. Frost top and sides of cake with remaining ganache. Press almonds into side of cake. Refrigerate cake 3 to 4 hours, or until ganache is firm, before serving.

2   CHOCOLATE GANACHE

Prep: 5 minutes   Cook: 3 minutes   Chill: 1 to 1½ hours
Makes: enough to fill and frost a 2-layer 9-inch cake

This is an ideal frosting and filling for a large variety of cakes. And it's a breeze to prepare with a little help from the microwave oven.

18 ounces semisweet chocolate
      chips or semisweet or
      bittersweet chocolate,
      chopped (3 cups)

1½ cups heavy cream
  2 tablespoons butter, cut up
  1 teaspoon vanilla extract

1. In a 2-quart glass measure, combine chocolate chips and heavy cream. Heat in a microwave oven on High 3 minutes, or until melted and smooth when stirred. Stir in butter and vanilla.

2. Cover and refrigerate 1 to 1½ hours, or until ganache holds its shape and is thick enough to spread on cake.

3   ORANGE CHOCOLATE YOGURT CAKE

Prep: 20 minutes   Cook: 35 to 40 minutes   Serves: 12

  1 stick (4 ounces) butter,
      softened
1½ cups sugar
  4 (1-ounce) squares
      unsweetened chocolate,
      melted
  3 eggs
  1 tablespoon grated orange
      zest
      Juice of 1 large orange
      (⅓ to ½ cup)

  1 teaspoon orange extract
1½ cups plain yogurt
2¼ cups flour
  1 teaspoon baking soda
  1 teaspoon baking powder
  ½ teaspoon salt
  3 tablespoons orange
      marmalade

1. Preheat oven to 325°F. Grease a 9 x 13-inch baking pan. Dust with flour; tap out excess.

2. In a large bowl, beat together butter and sugar with an electric mixer on medium speed until light and fluffy, 1 to 2 minutes. Beat in melted chocolate. Add eggs, one at a time, beating well after each addition. Beat in orange zest, orange juice, orange extract, and 1 cup yogurt until well blended.

3. Sift together flour, baking soda, baking powder, and salt. With mixer on low speed, beat into chocolate mixture just until combined. Scrape batter into prepared pan and spread evenly.

4. Bake 35 to 40 minutes, or until a cake tester inserted in center comes out clean. Let cake cool in pan, then cut into squares. Mix remaining ½ cup yogurt with marmalade. Spoon a dollop on top of each cake square.

4 MOCHA-NUT PUDDING CAKE
Prep: 10 minutes   Cook: 35 to 40 minutes   Serves: 6 to 8

In this old-fashioned dessert, the pudding layer ends up on the bottom of the pan with the cake on top.

1   cup flour
¾   cup granulated sugar
¼   cup plus 3 tablespoons
      unsweetened cocoa
      powder
2   teaspoons baking powder
¼   teaspoon salt
½   cup milk
2   tablespoons butter, melted

1   teaspoon vanilla extract
¾   cup packed light brown
      sugar
¾   cup chopped walnuts or
      pecans
1¾   cups very hot brewed coffee
      Vanilla ice cream or
      whipped cream

1. Preheat oven to 350°F. In a medium bowl, combine flour, granulated sugar, 3 tablespoons cocoa, baking powder, and salt; mix to blend. Stir in milk, butter, and vanilla, blending well. Scrape batter into a buttered 9-inch square baking pan and spread evenly.

2. In a medium bowl, mix together brown sugar, walnuts, and remaining ¼ cup cocoa. Sprinkle over batter in pan. Gently pour hot coffee evenly over all.

3. Bake 35 to 40 minutes, or until cake is firm to the touch. Let cool slightly. Cut into squares and serve with sauce from bottom of pan. Top with vanilla ice cream or whipped cream.

5 CHOCOLATE COFFEE-NUT CAKE
Prep: 20 minutes   Cook: 55 to 60 minutes   Serves: 10 to 12

This is a versatile cake that totes well to picnics or potlucks. It's fine with just a sprinkling of powdered sugar on top, but you can gussy it up with your favorite frosting, if you prefer.

1   cup boiling brewed coffee
4   (1-ounce) squares
       unsweetened chocolate,
       chopped
1   stick (4 ounces) butter,
       softened
1⅔   cups packed brown sugar
2   teaspoons vanilla extract

2   eggs
2   cups flour
1   teaspoon baking soda
1   teaspoon ground cinnamon
½   teaspoon salt
½   cup sour cream
¾   cup chopped pecans
       Powdered sugar

1. Preheat oven to 325°F. Grease a 9-inch springform pan. Dust with flour; tap out excess.

2. In a small bowl, pour boiling coffee over chocolate and stir until melted and smooth. In a large bowl, beat together butter, brown sugar, and vanilla with an electric mixer on medium speed until light and fluffy, 1 to 2 minutes. Beat in eggs until well blended, then beat in chocolate mixture.

3. Sift flour with baking soda, cinnamon, and salt. Add to chocolate mixture alternately with sour cream, beating only until blended. Stir in nuts. Turn batter into prepared pan.

4. Bake 55 to 60 minutes, or until a cake tester inserted in center comes out clean. Let cake cool in pan. Run sharp knife around edges to loosen. Remove springform side. Sift powdered sugar over top.

---

6   PEANUT BUTTER FUDGE CAKE
Prep: 25 minutes   Cook: 50 to 55 minutes   Serves: 12

This scratch fudge cake contains semisweet and peanut butter chips and is topped with a chocolate-peanut butter glaze.

1   stick (4 ounces) plus
    3 tablespoons butter or
    margarine, softened
	3 cups flour
	1½ teaspoons baking soda
	1 teaspoon baking powder

2   cups sugar
2   eggs
2   teaspoons vanilla extract
	6 ounces semisweet chocolate
	    chips (1 cup)
	6 ounces peanut butter-
	    flavored chips (1 cup)

4   (1-ounce) squares
    unsweetened chocolate,
    melted
	Chocolate Peanut Butter
	    Glaze (page 83)

1. Preheat oven to 350°F. In a large bowl, beat together butter and sugar with an electric mixer on medium speed until light and fluffy, 1 to 2 minutes. Beat in eggs, vanilla, and melted chocolate until well mixed.

2. Combine flour, baking soda, and baking powder. With mixer on low speed, add dry ingredients to chocolate mixture alternately with 2 cups warm water, beating until well blended. Stir in chocolate chips and peanut butter chips.

3. Turn batter into a well-greased 12-cup bundt pan. Bake 50 to 55 minutes, or until a cake tester inserted in center comes out clean. Let cake cool in pan 15 minutes, then unmold onto a plate and let cool completely. Spoon Chocolate Peanut Butter Glaze over cake. Refrigerate until glaze is firm.

7 THREE LAYER COCOA CAKE
Prep: 30 minutes   Cook: 30 to 35 minutes   Serves: 10 to 12

A high and lovely cake, frosted and filled with an orange cream cheese frosting.

1½ cups hot brewed coffee
1 cup boiling water
1¼ cups firmly packed
    unsweetened cocoa
    powder
1 cup corn oil
2½ cups sugar
4 eggs

2 teaspoons vanilla extract
3 cups flour
2 teaspoons baking soda
2 teaspoons baking powder
½ teaspoon salt
   Orange Cocoa Cream
    Cheese Frosting (recipe
    follows)

1. Preheat oven to 350°F. Grease three 9-inch round cake pans. Dust with flour; tap out excess.

2. In a medium bowl, pour hot coffee and boiling water over cocoa. Whisk or stir to combine; set aside to let cool.

3. In a large bowl, beat together oil and sugar with an electric mixer on low speed until well blended, 1 to 2 minutes. Add eggs and vanilla; beat on medium speed 30 seconds.

4. Sift flour with baking soda, baking powder, and salt. With mixer on low speed, alternately add flour mixture and chocolate liquid to oil mixture, beating just until combined. Scrape batter into prepared pans and spread evenly.

5. Bake 30 to 35 minutes, or until a cake tester inserted in center of cakes comes out clean. Let cakes cool in pans 10 to 15 minutes, then unmold onto racks and let cool completely.

6. Stack cooled cake layers and fill with about half of Orange Cocoa Cream Cheese Frosting in between. Cover top and sides of cake with remaining frosting.

8 ORANGE COCOA CREAM CHEESE FROSTING
Prep: 5 minutes   Cook: none   Makes: enough to fill and frost a 3-layer 9-inch cake

4 tablespoons butter, softened
1 (8-ounce) package cream
    cheese, softened
1 teaspoon orange extract
¼ cup Triple Sec or other
    orange-flavored liqueur

¾ cup unsweetened cocoa
    powder
3½ cups powdered sugar

In a medium bowl, beat together butter and cream cheese with an electric mixer on low speed until smooth. Add orange extract, Triple Sec, and cocoa; beat until smooth. Add powdered sugar and beat on high speed until smooth and fluffy.

---

9 CHOCOLATE BANANA SPLIT STREUSEL CAKE
Prep: 30 minutes   Cook: 50 to 55 minutes   Serves: 12

1 stick (4 ounces) butter or margarine, softened
1½ cups granulated sugar
2 large ripe bananas, peeled and mashed
½ cup firmly packed unsweetened cocoa powder
1 teaspoon vanilla extract

4 eggs
2 cups flour
1 teaspoon baking powder
1 teaspoon baking soda
½ teaspoon salt
½ cup sour cream
Chocolate Streusel Filling (recipe follows)
Powdered sugar

1. Preheat oven to 350°F. In a large bowl, beat together butter and granulated sugar with an electric mixer on medium speed until well mixed, 1 to 2 minutes. With mixer on low, beat in bananas, cocoa, and vanilla until well blended. With mixer on medium, add eggs one at a time, beating well after each addition.

2. Sift together flour, baking powder, baking soda, and salt. Beat into chocolate mixture alternately with sour cream just until combined.

3. Spread one third of batter evenly in well-greased 12-cup bundt pan. Top with half of Chocolate Streusel Filling. Carefully spread half of remaining batter over filling. Top with remaining streusel, then remaining batter, spreading evenly.

4. Bake 50 to 55 minutes, or until a cake tester inserted in center comes out clean. Let cool in pan 15 minutes, then unmold onto a rack and let cool completely. Sift powdered sugar over top.

CHOCOLATE STREUSEL FILLING

4 tablespoons butter, melted and cooled
½ cup packed brown sugar
½ cup flour

6 ounces semisweet chocolate chips (1 cup)
1 cup chopped pecans
½ teaspoon ground allspice

In a medium bowl, combine butter, brown sugar, flour, chocolate chips, pecans, and allspice. Mix until thoroughly combined.

10   TUNNEL OF FUDGE CAKE
Prep: 20 minutes   Cook: 58 to 62 minutes   Serves: 14 to 16

In 1966 a chocolate cake called the Tunnel of Fudge Cake, made with a boxed frosting mix, won the Pillsbury BAKE-OFF® Contest. Although the frosting mix was discontinued, Pillsbury continued to receive so many requests for the cake that the company developed a scratch recipe to simulate the original. Here it is.

3½ sticks (14 ounces) margarine
     or butter, softened
1¾ cups granulated sugar
  6 eggs
2¾ cups powdered sugar
2¼ cups flour

1 cup unsweetened cocoa
     powder
2 cups chopped walnuts*
     (8 ounces)
1½ to 2 tablespoons milk

1. Preheat oven to 350°F. Grease a 12-cup bundt pan or 10-inch angel food tube pan. Dust with flower; tap out excess.

2. In a large bowl, beat together margarine and granulated sugar with an electric mixer on medium speed until light and fluffy, 1 to 2 minutes. Add eggs, one at a time, beating well after each addition. Gradually add 2 cups powdered sugar, beating until well blended. By hand, stir in flour, ¾ cup cocoa, and nuts; mix until well blended. Spoon batter into prepared pan and spread evenly.

3. Bake 58 to 62 minutes. (Since this cake has a soft tunnel of fudge, ordinary doneness test cannot be used. Accurate oven temperature and baking time are critical.) Let cake cool upright in pan on a rack 1 hour; then invert onto serving plate and let cool completely.

4. To make glaze, in a small bowl, combine remaining ¾ cup powdered sugar, remaining ¼ cup cocoa, and milk. Mix until well blended. Spoon glaze over top of cool cake, allowing some to run down sides. Store cake tightly covered.

* Nuts are essential for the success of this recipe.

11   CHOCOLATE BUTTERMILK LAYER CAKE
Prep: 20 minutes   Cook: 35 to 40 minutes   Serves: 8 to 12

2 sticks (8 ounces) butter,
     softened
2 cups sugar
3 eggs
2½ cups cake flour
 ¾ cup firmly packed
     unsweetened cocoa
     powder

2 teaspoons baking soda
1 teaspoon baking powder
½ teaspoon salt
1½ cups buttermilk
     Buttermilk Chocolate
     Frosting (recipe follows)

1. Preheat oven to 350°F. Grease two 9-inch round cake pans. Dust with flour; tap out excess.

2. In a large bowl, beat together butter and sugar with an electric mixer on medium speed until light and fluffy, 1 to 2 minutes. Beat in eggs just until combined.

3. Sift together cake flour, cocoa, baking soda, baking powder, and salt. Add buttermilk and flour mixture alternately to butter mixture, beating just until blended. Divide batter between prepared pans.

4. Bake 35 to 40 minutes, or until a cake tester inserted in center comes out clean. Let cakes cool in pans 10 minutes, then unmold onto racks and let cool completely. Fill and frost cake with Buttermilk Chocolate Frosting. Refrigerate until serving time.

---

12   BUTTERMILK CHOCOLATE FROSTING
Prep: 5 minutes   Cook: none   Makes: enough to fill and frost a 2-layer 9-inch cake

4 tablespoons butter, softened	½ cup buttermilk
½ cup unsweetened cocoa powder	4 cups powdered sugar

In a medium bowl, beat together butter and cocoa with an electric mixer on low speed until smooth, 1 to 2 minutes. Add buttermilk and powdered sugar and beat on high speed until smooth and fluffy, 1 to 2 minutes.

---

13   EASY SOUR CREAM CHOCOLATE CHIP CAKE
Prep: 10 minutes   Cook: 45 to 55 minutes   Serves: 12 to 14

Great to serve with morning, afternoon, or evening coffee or for brunch or dessert anytime.

1 stick (4 ounces) butter, softened	1 teaspoon baking powder
1¼ cups sugar	½ teaspoon baking soda
2 eggs	Dash of salt
1 cup sour cream	1 cup chopped walnuts or pecans
2 teaspoons vanilla extract	1½ cups semisweet chocolate chips (9 ounces)
2 cups flour	

1. Preheat oven to 350°F. In a large bowl, beat together butter, sugar, and eggs with an electric mixer on medium speed until light and fluffy, 3 to 4 minutes. Beat in sour cream and vanilla until well blended. Add flour, baking powder, baking soda, and salt; beat until well mixed. Stir in nuts and chocolate chips. Turn batter into a well-greased 12-cup bundt pan.

2. Bake 45 to 55 minutes, or until golden and a cake tester inserted in center comes out clean. Let cake cool in pan 15 minutes, then unmold onto a serving plate to cool completely.

14 CHOCOLATE GINGERBREAD

Prep: 25 minutes   Cook: 35 to 40 minutes   Serves: 12

1½ sticks (6 ounces) butter	2 teaspoons baking powder
1 cup packed brown sugar	1½ teaspoons baking soda
2 teaspoons grated lemon zest	4 teaspoons ground ginger
1 cup granulated sugar	2 teaspoons ground cinnamon
½ cup firmly packed	½ teaspoon ground cloves
unsweetened cocoa	½ teaspoon grated nutmeg
powder	1¼ cups buttermilk
3 eggs	½ cup currants or raisins
2 cups flour	Powdered sugar

1. Preheat oven to 350°F. Grease a 9 x 13-inch baking pan.

2. In a large bowl, beat together butter and brown sugar with an electric mixer on medium speed until fluffy, 1 to 2 minutes.

3. In a food processor or blender, process lemon zest and granulated sugar until lemon zest is very finely grated. Add to butter mixture and beat until well blended. Beat in cocoa. Add eggs, one at a time, beating well after each addition.

4. Sift together flour, baking powder, baking soda, ginger, cinnamon, cloves, and nutmeg. Add to chocolate mixture alternately with buttermilk, beating just enough to combine. Fold in currants. Turn batter into prepared pan.

5. Bake 35 to 40 minutes, or until a cake tester inserted in center comes out clean. Serve warm, with a dusting of powdered sugar.

15 BORDER GRILL OAXACAN CHOCOLATE MOCHA CAKE

*Prep: 20 minutes   Cook: 15 minutes   Chill: 6 hours
Serves: 10 to 14*

Susan Feniger and Mary Sue Milliken, co-owners of Border Grill in Santa Monica, California, and City restaurant in Los Angeles gave me this recipe. Mary Sue's mother, Ruth Milliken, the pastry chef at the Border Grill, helped dream up this chocolate creation.

18 ounces bittersweet	1 cup heavy cream
chocolate, cut up	2 tablespoons powdered
2 sticks (8 ounces) unsalted	sugar
butter	¼ cup sour cream
6 eggs	1 teaspoon vanilla extract
2 tablespoons instant espresso	1 cup toasted pecan halves
coffee powder	

1. Preheat oven to 425°F. Grease one 9-inch round cake pan. Line bottom with a round of parchment or wax paper.

2. In a 2-quart glass bowl, combine 16 ounces chocolate and the butter. Heat in a microwave oven on High 1½ to 2½ minutes, stirring once or twice, until melted and smooth.

3. In a large bowl, beat eggs with an electric mixer on high speed until slightly thickened and lemon colored, 5 to 7 minutes. Fold one third of eggs into chocolate mixture. Fold in remaining eggs until well blended. Fold in espresso powder.

4. Turn batter into prepared pan. Set in another larger pan and add water to reach one third way up side of cake pan. Bake 5 minutes. Cover pan with foil. Bake 10 minutes longer. Remove cake pan from water bath, uncover, and let cake cool on a rack 45 minutes. Refrigerate at least 6 hours or overnight. With a sharp knife, loosen sides of cake from pan. Turn out onto a serving plate.

5. An hour or so before serving, in a medium bowl, beat together heavy cream and powdered sugar with an electric mixer on high speed until soft peaks form. Add sour cream and vanilla and beat until well mixed and peaks hold their shape. Spread over top and sides of cooled cake. Arrange pecans around edge of cake. Melt remaining 2 ounces chocolate and drizzle with a fork over top of cake in a decorative pattern. Refrigerate until serving time.

---

16   CHOCOLATE PEACH AND BERRY SHORTCAKE

Prep: 15 minutes   Cook: 15 to 16 minutes   Serves: 7 to 8

When it's shortcake season, here's an irresistible chocolate version to accompany fresh fruits.

1¾ cups flour	1 egg
½ cup sugar	¾ cup milk
¼ cup plus 2 tablespoons unsweetened cocoa powder	½ cup semisweet chocolate chips
2 teaspoons baking powder	1½ cups heavy cream, whipped
½ teaspoon baking soda	8 cups cut up fresh peaches, strawberries, and raspberries
1 stick (4 ounces) butter or margarine	

1. Preheat oven to 450°F. In a medium bowl, combine flour, sugar, cocoa, baking powder, and baking soda. Cut in butter until mixture resembles coarse crumbs. Stir in egg, milk, and chocolate chips just until moistened.

2. Spread dough in a greased 9-inch round cake pan. Bake 15 to 16 minutes, or until a cake tester inserted in center comes out clean; do not overbake. Let cool in pan until barely warm.

3. To serve, cut warm shortcake into wedges. Split each wedge horizontally in half. Place bottom halves on individual serving plates. Top with a little whipped cream and a generous spoonful of fruit. Replace top of shortcake. Top with more fruit and whipped cream. Serve immediately.

17   PECAN FUDGE TORTE
Prep: 25 minutes   Cook: 32 to 34 minutes   Serves: 10

A variation of this stylish single-layer fudge nut cake has been found on numerous restaurant menus over the years. A thick chocolate glaze adds the finishing touch.

1 stick (4 ounces) butter	¾ cup flour
10 ounces bittersweet or semisweet chocolate, cut up	½ teaspoon baking powder
	¼ teaspoon salt
	1 cup chopped pecans
¾ cup sugar	Fudgy Glaze (recipe follows)
4 eggs	
1 teaspoon vanilla extract	Whipped cream

1. Preheat oven to 350°F. In a large 2-quart glass bowl, combine butter and chocolate. Heat in a microwave oven on High, stirring once or twice, 1½ to 2 minutes, or until chocolate is melted and mixture is smooth. Whisk in sugar, eggs, and vanilla until well blended. Add flour, baking powder, and salt and mix well. Stir in chopped pecans.

2. Spread batter evenly in a buttered 9-inch springform pan. Bake 30 to 32 minutes, or until a toothpick inserted in center comes out slightly moist. Let cool in pan.

3. Pour Fudgy Glaze onto middle of cake and spread over top using a spatula. Refrigerate 1 hour, or until set. Cover and store in refrigerator until serving time. Run sharp knife around edges to loosen cake from pan; remove springform side. Serve slices topped with a dollop of whipped cream, if desired.

18   FUDGY GLAZE
Prep: 5 minutes   Cook: 1½ to 2 minutes   Makes: about ¾ cup

4 tablespoons butter	Dash of salt
3 tablespoons light corn syrup	6 ounces semisweet chocolate chips (1 cup)
1 tablespoon Cognac, Grand Marnier, or other liqueur	
1 teaspoon instant coffee or espresso powder	

1. In a 1-quart glass bowl, combine butter, corn syrup, brandy, coffee powder, salt, and 2 tablespoons water. Heat in a microwave oven on High 1½ to 2 minutes, until boiling and butter is melted when stirred.

2. Add chocolate chips; let stand 1 minute. Whisk until chocolate is melted and mixture is smooth. Refrigerate until glaze is cool and of spreading consistency, but not too hard.

19 CHOCOLATE COCONUT CAKE

Prep: 25 minutes   Cook: 30 to 33 minutes   Serves: 8 to 10

Team coconut and chocolate in this dense cake for a special flavor treat. The cream cheese-based frosting sets it off perfectly.

- 2 sticks (8 ounces) butter or margarine, softened
- 2 cups sugar
- 1 teaspoon coconut extract
- ½ cup firmly packed unsweetened cocoa powder
- 5 eggs
- 2½ cups cake flour
- 1 teaspoon baking powder
- 1 teaspoon baking soda
- 1 cup buttermilk
- 2½ cups flaked coconut
- Coconut-Cream Cheese Frosting (recipe follows)

1. Preheat oven to 350°F. Grease two 9-inch round cake pans. Dust with flour; tap out excess.

2. In a large bowl, beat together butter and sugar with an electric mixer on medium speed until light and fluffy, 1 to 2 minutes. Add coconut extract and cocoa; beat until well blended. Add eggs, one at a time, beating well after each addition.

3. Sift together flour, baking powder, and baking soda. With mixer on low speed, add to chocolate mixture alternately with buttermilk, beating only until combined. Stir in 1½ cups coconut. Divide batter between 2 prepared pans.

4. Bake 30 to 33 minutes, or until a cake tester inserted in center of cake comes out clean. Let cool in pans 15 minutes, then unmold onto racks to cool completely.

5. Meanwhile toast remaining 1 cup coconut in 300°F oven 6 to 8 minutes, or until golden brown; let cool. Fill cake layers with about one third of Coconut-Cream Cheese Frosting. Cover top and sides of cake with remaining frosting. Sprinkle toasted coconut over top and press gently into side of cake. Refrigerate until serving time.

COCONUT-CREAM CHEESE FROSTING

- 4 tablespoons butter or margarine, softened
- 1 (8-ounce) package cream cheese, softened
- ½ teaspoon coconut extract
- 4½ cups powdered sugar
- 1 tablespoon buttermilk

In a medium bowl, beat together butter, cream cheese, and coconut extract with an electric mixer on medium speed until well blended. Add powdered sugar and buttermilk and beat on high speed until thoroughly blended and very smooth.

20   ORANGE CHOCOLATE CAKE ROLL

Prep: 45 minutes   Cook: 20 minutes   Chill: 6 hours   Serves: 8 to 10

4   eggs
⅔   cup plus 1 tablespoon sugar
4   tablespoons butter, melted
¾   cup flour
¼   cup firmly packed
       unsweetened cocoa
       powder
1   tablespoon grated orange
       zest

Orange Curd Filling (recipe
       follows)
2   (1-ounce) squares semisweet
       chocolate, cut up
¼   cup heavy cream
1   tablespoon Grand Marnier

1. Preheat oven to 350°F. Grease a 10 x 15-inch jelly-roll pan and line with parchment or wax paper. Lightly grease parchment.

2. In a large bowl, beat together eggs and ⅔ cup sugar with an electric mixer on high speed until light and fluffy, about 3 minutes. Beat in melted butter. Sift together flour and cocoa and fold into egg mixture along with orange zest. Spread batter evenly in prepared pan.

3. Bake 15 minutes, or until cake springs back when touched in center. Immediately turn cake out onto a large sheet of wax paper sprinkled with remaining 1 tablespoon sugar. Peel off parchment. Starting at one short end, gently roll up cake in wax paper with paper inside cake. Let cake cool rolled up, then unroll cake and spread Orange Curd Filling to within 2 inches of edges. Roll up cake gently from short side, jelly-roll fashion (without paper). Wrap in plastic wrap and refrigerate 6 hours or overnight.

4. In a small glass bowl, combine chocolate and cream. Heat in a microwave oven on High 40 to 60 seconds, or until melted and smooth when stirred. Stir in Grand Marnier. Just before serving, drizzle chocolate Grand Marnier sauce on top of the cake.

ORANGE CURD FILLING

¼   cup orange juice
4   eggs
2   sticks (8 ounces) butter, cut
       into tablespoons
¼   cup sugar

1   tablespoon grated orange
       zest
6   ounces cream cheese,
       softened

In a small saucepan, combine orange juice, eggs, butter, sugar, and orange zest. Cook over medium-low heat, stirring constantly, until mixture thickens, about 10 minutes. Do not boil. Whisk in cream cheese. Cover and refrigerate until chilled before spreading on cake roll.

21 CHOCOLATE APPLESAUCE CAKE
Prep: 20 minutes   Cook: 40 to 45 minutes   Serves: 12

This old-fashioned cake is reminiscent of the kind grandma used to make. A chocolate caramel nut frosting adds the finishing touch.

1 stick (4 ounces) butter or margarine, softened	2 cups cake flour
1¼ cups sugar	2 teaspoons baking soda
1 cup unsweetened applesauce	1 teaspoon baking powder
	¼ teaspoon salt
4 (1-ounce) squares unsweetened chocolate, melted	½ cup buttermilk
	6 ounces semisweet chocolate chips (1 cup)
1 teaspoon ground cinnamon	⅓ cup coarsely chopped blanched almonds
1½ teaspoons vanilla extract	Chocolate Caramel Nut Frosting (recipe follows)
3 eggs	

1. Preheat oven to 350°F. Grease a 9 x 13-inch baking pan. Dust with flour; tap out excess.

2. In a large bowl, beat together butter and sugar with an electric mixer on medium speed until fluffy, 1 to 2 minutes. With mixer on low speed, beat in applesauce, melted chocolate, cinnamon, and vanilla until well mixed. Add eggs, one at a time, beating well after each addition.

3. Sift together flour, baking soda, baking powder, and salt. With mixer on low speed, alternately add buttermilk and flour mixture to chocolate mixture, beating only until blended. Stir in chocolate chips and almonds. Turn batter into prepared pan.

4. Bake 35 to 40 minutes, or until a cake tester inserted in center comes out clean. Let cool completely in pan. Spread Chocolate Caramel Nut Frosting over top of cake. To serve, cut into squares.

---

22 CHOCOLATE CARAMEL NUT FROSTING
Prep: 5 minutes   Cook: 3 minutes   Makes: enough to frost a 9 by 13-inch cake

1 cup packed brown sugar	⅓ cup coarsely chopped blanched almonds
4 tablespoons butter	6 ounces semisweet chocolate chips (1 cup)
½ cup heavy cream	

1. In a medium saucepan, combine brown sugar, butter, and cream. Bring to a boil, stirring often, over medium heat. Reduce heat to low and simmer 3 minutes. Stir in nuts.

2. Let cool completely. Stir in chocolate chips; frosting will be chunky.

23   CHOCOLATE CARROT CAKE

Prep: 35 minutes   Cook: 45 to 50 minutes   Serves: 12

This fabulous cake with grated carrots, raisins, chocolate chips, and orange flavoring is high and dense.

1 stick (4 ounces) butter, softened	1 cup sour cream
½ cup corn oil	2½ cups flour
2 cups sugar	1 tablespoon baking powder
4 eggs	2 teaspoons baking soda
4 (1-ounce) squares unsweetened chocolate, melted	1 teaspoon salt
	2 cups finely grated carrots (about 2 large)
1 tablespoon grated orange zest	1 cup dark raisins
Juice from 1 large orange (about ⅓ to ½ cup)	6 ounces semisweet chocolate chips (1 cup)
	Orange Cream Cheese Frosting (recipe follows)

1. Preheat oven to 350°F. Grease two 8-inch square baking pans. Dust with flour; tap out excess.

2. In a large bowl, beat together butter, oil, and sugar with an electric mixer on medium speed until light and fluffy, 1 to 2 minutes. Add eggs, one at a time, beating well after each addition. Beat in melted chocolate, orange zest, orange juice, and sour cream.

3. Sift together flour, baking powder, baking soda, and salt. Add to chocolate mixture, beating just enough to combine. Stir in carrots, raisins, and chocolate chips. Divide batter between prepared pans.

4. Bake 45 to 50 minutes, or until a cake tester inserted in center comes out clean. Let cakes cool in pans 10 minutes, then unmold onto racks to cool completely. Fill and frost cake with Orange Cream Cheese Frosting. Refrigerate until serving time.

ORANGE CREAM CHEESE FROSTING

1 (8-ounce) package cream cheese, softened	1 teaspoon orange extract
	4 cups powdered sugar
1 stick (4 ounces) butter, softened	1 tablespoon buttermilk

In a medium bowl, beat together cream cheese, butter, and orange extract with an electric mixer on medium speed until smooth and fluffy, 1 to 2 minutes. Gradually beat in powdered sugar and buttermilk until blended, then beat on high speed until smooth and fluffy.

24   UPDATED CHOCOLATE MAYONNAISE CAKE

Prep: 25 minutes   Cook: 25 to 30 minutes   Serves: 8

Reduced-calorie mayonnaise updates the famous recipe classic, while still providing the richness and moistness it always did.

1 cup boiling water
½ cup firmly packed unsweetened cocoa powder
1 cup reduced-calorie mayonnaise
1¼ cups sugar
1 teaspoon almond extract

2¼ cups flour
2 teaspoons baking soda
¼ teaspoon salt
Cocoa Mayo Icing (recipe follows)
¾ cup chopped roasted sliced almonds

1. Preheat oven to 350°F. Grease two 8-inch round cake pans. Dust with flour; tap out excess.

2. In a medium bowl, pour boiling water over cocoa; set aside to cool. In a large bowl, beat together mayonnaise and sugar with an electric mixer on medium speed until light and fluffy, about 1 minute. Beat in almond extract and dissolved cocoa. Sift together flour, baking soda, and salt. With mixer on low speed, gradually beat into chocolate mixture just until combined. Divide batter evenly between 2 prepared pans.

3. Bake 25 to 30 minutes, or until a cake tester inserted in center comes out clean. Let cool in pans 10 minutes, then unmold onto racks and let cool completely. Fill and frost cake with Cocoa Mayo Icing. Sprinkle almonds over top and gently press into sides of cake. Refrigerate until serving time.

COCOA MAYO ICING

½ cup reduced-calorie mayonnaise
½ cup firmly packed unsweetened cocoa powder

½ teaspoon almond extract
2½ to 3 cups powdered sugar
1 tablespoon milk

In a medium bowl, beat together mayonnaise, cocoa, and almond extract with an electric mixer on medium speed until smooth. Add powdered sugar and milk and beat on high speed until smooth and fluffy.

25   CHOCOLATE ESPRESSO CREAM CUPCAKES

Prep: 20 minutes   Cook: 30 to 32 minutes   Makes: 20

These are a takeoff of the popular black bottom cupcakes. A coffee-flavored cream filling is at the center of each little cake.

1¼ cups flour
1⅓ cups sugar
½   cup unsweetened cocoa
     powder
¾   teaspoon baking soda
½   teaspoon plus ⅛ teaspoon
     salt
1   cup buttermilk
2   eggs

⅓   cup vegetable oil
2   teaspoons vanilla extract
1   (8-ounce) package cream
     cheese, softened
1   tablespoon instant espresso
     powder
½   cup miniature semisweet
     chocolate chips

1. Preheat oven to 350°F. In a large bowl, beat together flour, 1 cup sugar, cocoa, baking soda, and ½ teaspoon salt with an electric mixer on low speed. Add buttermilk, 1 egg, oil, and 1 teaspoon vanilla. Beat on medium speed until thoroughly mixed and smooth.

2. Divide batter evenly among 20 paper-lined muffin cups 2½ inches in diameter.

3. To make filling, in a medium bowl, beat together cream cheese, espresso, powder and remaining ⅓ cup sugar, ⅛ teaspoon salt, 1 egg, and 1 teaspoon vanilla with electric mixer on medium speed until smooth. Stir in chocolate chips.

4. Spoon about 1 tablespoon cream cheese filling onto center of each cupcake. Bake 30 to 32 minutes, or until cupcakes spring back when touched lightly. Let cool in pans 5 minutes, then unmold onto racks to cool completely.

26   CHOCOLATE POUND CAKE

Prep: 20 minutes   Cook: 55 to 60 minutes   Serves: 12

This is a good basic cake. Serve plain or topped with ice cream or assorted fresh fruits and chocolate sauce.

2   sticks (8 ounces) butter,
     softened
2½ cups sugar
1   teaspoon vanilla extract
1   cup firmly packed
     unsweetened cocoa
     powder

5   eggs
2½ cups cake flour
1   teaspoon baking powder
½   teaspoon salt
1   cup buttermilk

1. Preheat oven to 325°F. In a large bowl, beat together butter, sugar, and vanilla with an electric mixer on medium speed until light and fluffy, 1 to 2 minutes. Add cocoa and beat well. Add eggs, one at a time, beating well after each addition.

2. Sift together flour, baking powder, and salt. With mixer on low speed, beat into chocolate mixture alternately with buttermilk just until combined. Turn batter into a well-greased 12-cup bundt pan; smooth top.

3. Bake 55 to 60 minutes, or until a cake tester inserted in center comes out clean. Let cake cool in pan 15 minutes, then unmold onto a wire rack and let cool completely.

---

27   CHOCOLATE FUDGE FRUITCAKE

Prep: 30 minutes   Cook: 2½ hours   Chill: 3 to 4 weeks
Makes: two 9-inch loaves

A chocolate batter surrounds the fruits and nuts in this holiday cake. Bake the cakes ahead, if desired, and tuck in the freezer to ease last-minute baking chores.

1 cup brandy	1½ sticks (6 ounces) butter
1 cup candied pineapple	1½ cups sugar
chunks	6 eggs, separated
½ cup halved candied cherries	2 cups flour
1 cup raisins	1 teaspoon baking powder
4 (1-ounce) squares	3 cups coarsely chopped
unsweetened chocolate	pecans

1. In a medium bowl, pour ½ cup brandy over pineapple chunks, cherries, and raisins. Let stand 2 to 3 hours or overnight. Grease two 9 x 5 x 3-inch loaf pans. Line with brown paper or parchment paper and grease paper. Preheat oven to 250°F.

2. Melt chocolate in a double boiler or in a microwave oven until melted and smooth when stirred. Set aside to let cool.

3. In a large bowl, beat together butter and 1 cup sugar with an electric mixer on medium speed until light and fluffy, about 2 minutes. Beat in egg yolks, 2 at a time, beating well after each addition. Beat in cooled chocolate until well blended.

4. Sift together flour and baking powder. Add to chocolate mixture along with ¼ cup brandy. Mix well. Stir in pecans and brandied fruit mixture with its liquid.

5. In a large bowl, beat egg whites with clean, dry beaters on high speed until almost stiff. Gradually beat in remaining ½ cup sugar. Beat until soft peaks form. Fold into chocolate batter. Turn batter into prepared pans, dividing evenly and smoothing tops.

6. Place pans in oven. Set a shallow pan of water on a rack below pans. Bake 2½ hours (replenishing water as necessary), until a cake tester inserted in center comes out clean. Let cakes stand 15 minutes; then unmold. Pour 2 tablespoons remaining brandy over each cake. Let cool completely. Wrap cakes in plastic wrap, then overwrap in foil. Store in refrigerator 3 to 4 weeks, sprinkling with additional brandy 2 or 3 times during aging period.

28 CHOCOLATE FROSTED QUICK-FIX POUND CAKE

Prep: 15 minutes   Cook: 20 minutes   Chill: 30 minutes   Serves: 10

Here's a good way to embellish a pound cake and turn out a dessert fast when unexpected guests drop by.

¾ cup sugar
3 teaspoons cornstarch
  Dash of salt
2 (1-ounce) squares
  unsweetened chocolate,
  cut up
1 cup boiling water

3 tablespoons butter
1½ teaspoons vanilla extract
1 (16-ounce) pound cake loaf
2 (1.4-ounce) milk chocolate
  crisp butter toffee candy
  bars (such as Skor Bar),
  chopped

1. In a medium saucepan, whisk together sugar, cornstarch, and salt. Stir in chocolate and boiling water. Cook over medium heat, whisking constantly, until mixture bubbles and thickens. Boil, whisking, 20 to 30 seconds.

2. Remove from heat and stir in butter and vanilla until well blended. Set frosting aside to cool 5 minutes.

3. Meanwhile, cut pound cake horizontally into 4 equal layers. Place bottom layer on a serving plate and cover with a thin layer of chocolate frosting. Set another cake layer on top and cover with more frosting. Repeat with the third layer and more frosting. Top with remaining cake layer and frost top and side of cake with remaining frosting. Sprinkle toffee candy over top of cake. Refrigerate at least 30 minutes, or until frosting is set, before serving.

29 CHOCOLATE CANDY BAR CAKE

Prep: 30 minutes   Cook: 26½ to 30 minutes   Serves: 12 to 14

My son, Grant, loves this. It's a Snickers bar devotee's dream come true.

3 cups flour
2 cups sugar
¼ cup plus 2 tablespoons
  unsweetened cocoa
  powder
2 teaspoons baking soda
½ teaspoon salt
¾ cup vegetable oil
2 tablespoons vinegar

1 tablespoon vanilla extract
1 cup heavy cream
6 ounces semisweet chocolate
  chips (1 cup)
1 cup milk chocolate chips
15 snack-size Snickers candy
  bars, cut into thin slices
½ cup chopped peanuts

1. Preheat oven to 350°F. In a large bowl, mix together flour, sugar, cocoa, baking soda, and salt. Whisk in oil, vinegar, 2 teaspoons vanilla, and 2 cups cold water until well blended.

2. Pour into 2 greased 9-inch round cake pans, dividing evenly. Bake 25 to 28 minutes, or until a cake tester inserted in center of cakes comes out clean. Let cakes cool in pans 15 to 20 minutes, then unmold onto racks to cool completely.

3. Meanwhile, in a 2-quart bowl, combine cream, semisweet chocolate chips, and milk chocolate chips. Heat in a microwave oven on High 1½ to 2 minutes, or until melted and smooth when stirred. Stir in remaining 1 teaspoon vanilla.

4. Remove ¾ cup chocolate mixture and set aside to let cool. While remaining mixture is still warm—but not hot—add Snickers pieces and stir until combined (some of the pieces will remain chunky; some will melt). Set aside to let cool.

5. When firm enough to spread, fill stacked cake layers with half of Snickers mixture. Spread remaining mixture evenly over top of cake. Frost sides of cake with some of reserved ¾ cup chocolate mixture and spread remaining chocolate mixture over top of cake. Sprinkle peanuts around top edge of cake to make a border. Refrigerate cake until 1 hour before serving.

30   CHOCOLATE APPLE CAKE
Prep: 35 minutes   Cook: 55 to 60 minutes   Serves: 12

For those who like chocolate and apples, try this moist cake. It sports a cinnamon sugar glaze zipped up with a splash of brandy.

¾ cup corn oil	5 eggs
1 stick (4 ounces) butter or margarine, softened	2½ cups cake flour
	1 teaspoon baking soda
2¼ cups granulated sugar	1 teaspoon salt
½ cup firmly packed unsweetened cocoa powder	3 cups diced (½-inch) peeled green apples
	½ cup currants or raisins
2 teaspoons ground cinnamon	1 cup powdered sugar
½ teaspoon grated nutmeg	¼ cup brandy
½ teaspoon ground allspice	

1. Preheat oven to 350°F. Generously grease a 12-cup bundt pan.

2. In a large bowl, beat together oil, butter, and granulated sugar with an electric mixer on medium speed until well blended, about 2 minutes. With mixer on low speed, beat in cocoa, 1 teaspoon cinnamon, nutmeg, and allspice. With mixer on medium, add eggs, one at a time, beating well after each addition.

3. Sift together flour, baking soda, and salt. Add to chocolate mixture, beating only enough to combine. Stir in apples and currants. Turn batter into prepared pan and spread evenly.

4. Bake 55 to 60 minutes, or until a cake tester inserted in center comes out clean. Let cool in pan 20 minutes, then unmold onto a rack to cool completely.

5. Meanwhile, prepare glaze: In a small bowl, whisk together powdered sugar, remaining 1 teaspoon cinnamon, and brandy until smooth. Drizzle over cool cake, letting some run down side. Serve warm or at room temperature.

31   WHITE CHOCOLATE ORANGE FRUITCAKE

Prep: 30 minutes   Marinate: 3 hours   Cook: 80 to 90 minutes
Chill: 2 to 3 days   Serves: 12 to 15

Slices of this lovely fruitcake are flecked with golden fruits and pecans. Top with a white chocolate topping for a special finishing touch. Be sure to age at least a few days before serving for best slicing and mellow flavor.

4 cups diced mixed dried
      fruits (nectarines,
      peaches, pears, apricots,
      apples only; do not use
      figs, dates, or raisins)
1 cup Grand Marnier or other
      orange-flavored liqueur
1 stick (4 ounces) butter
½ cup packed light brown
      sugar
4 eggs
1 teaspoon vanilla extract

1 teaspoon grated orange zest
½ teaspoon cinnamon
8 ounces imported white
      chocolate, melted and
      cooled slightly
1 cup plus 2 tablespoons flour
1½ cups chopped pecans
      White Chocolate Topping
      (recipe follows)
      Apricot halves and chopped
      pecans

1. In a medium bowl, combine dried fruits and ⅔ cup Grand Marnier. Let stand several hours or overnight.

2. Preheat oven to 325°F. Line a 9-inch springform pan with a round of waxed paper cut to fit the bottom. Butter bottom and sides of pan. Dust with flour; tap out excess.

3. To make batter, in a large bowl, beat together butter and brown sugar with an electric mixer on medium speed until light and fluffy, 1 to 2 minutes. Beat in eggs, one at a time, beating well after each addition. Beat in vanilla, orange zest, and cinnamon. Add white chocolate and beat until mixture is light and fluffy, 3 to 4 minutes. Add 1 cup flour and beat until well blended.

4. Add remaining 2 tablespoons flour and 1½ cups chopped pecans to fruit mixture and toss to coat well. Add to batter and mix thoroughly. Turn batter into prepared pan and smooth top. Set springform pan in a larger baking pan and add enough hot water to reach 1 inch up side of springform pan.

5. Bake 1 hour and 20 to 30 minutes, until a cake tester inserted in center of cake comes out clean. If top is browning too quickly, cover springform with foil the last ½ hour of baking.

6. Remove springform pan from water bath. Sprinkle remaining ⅓ cup Grand Marnier over top of cake and let cool in pan. When completely cool, run a sharp knife around edges of pan to loosen cake. Remove springform side of pan. Carefully remove cake from bottom of pan; peel off wax paper. Wrap cake in plastic wrap; then wrap in foil. Refrigerate at least 2 to 3 days or up to 2 weeks before serving. For longer storage, freeze cake.

7. An hour before serving time, unwrap cake and frost evenly with White Chocolate Topping. Garnish edge of top of cake with apricot halves. Sprinkle additional chopped pecans over center of cake. Return to refrigerator until serving time.

WHITE CHOCOLATE TOPPING

⅓ cup heavy cream
6 ounces imported white
   chocolate, cut up

2 teaspoons Grand Marnier

1. In a 1-quart glass bowl, heat cream in a microwave oven on High 30 to 45 seconds, or until very hot. Stir in white chocolate, mixing well. Return to microwave and heat on Medium 30 to 60 seconds, or until chocolate is melted when stirred. Stir in Grand Marnier.

2. Cover and refrigerate until glaze thickens to spreading consistency.

---

32 TRIPLE CHOCOLATE ZUCCHINI CAKE
Prep: 35 minutes   Cook: 60 to 65 minutes   Serves: 12

This cake sports a triple dose of chocolate. Zucchini keeps it moist.

2 sticks (8 ounces) butter,
   softened
1 cup granulated sugar
1 cup packed brown sugar
1 (8-ounce) package cream
   cheese, softened
3 (1-ounce) squares
   unsweetened chocolate,
   melted
¼ cup unsweetened cocoa
   powder
6 eggs
1 tablespoon grated orange
   zest

Juice of 1 large orange (⅓ to
   ½ cup)
2¾ cups flour
1 teaspoon salt
1 teaspoon baking powder
1 teaspoon baking soda
12 ounces semisweet chocolate
   chips (2 cups)
3 cups grated zucchini (about
   3 medium)
Powdered sugar

1. Preheat oven to 350°F. Grease a 12-cup bundt pan.

2. In a large bowl, beat together butter, granulated sugar, and brown sugar with an electric mixer on medium speed until light and fluffy, 1 to 2 minutes. Add cream cheese, melted chocolate, and cocoa and continue beating 2 minutes. Add eggs, one at a time, beating well after each addition. Beat in orange zest and orange juice.

3. Sift together flour, salt, baking powder, and baking soda. With mixer on low speed, gently beat into chocolate mixture. Stir in chocolate chips and zucchini. Turn into prepared pan.

4. Bake 60 to 65 minutes, or until a cake tester inserted in center comes out clean. Let cool in pan 15 minutes, then unmold onto a rack and let cool completely. Sift powdered sugar over top of cake before serving.

33 CHOCOLATE TEA CAKE
Prep: 15 minutes   Cook: 30 to 35 minutes   Makes: 16 squares

Trump's is a chic Los Angeles restaurant that serves afternoon tea. Once a month, all of the desserts are chocolate, and this is one of executive chef Michael Roberts's popular offerings.

1½ sticks (6 ounces) butter,
    softened
¾ cup granulated sugar
8 ounces bittersweet or
    semisweet chocolate,
    melted and cooled

4 eggs
½ cup flour
Powdered sugar or
    unsweetened cocoa
    powder

1. Preheat oven to 350° F. In a medium bowl, beat together butter and sugar with an electric mixer on high speed until light and fluffy, 2 to 3 minutes. Beat in melted chocolate. Add eggs, one at a time, beating well after each addition. Mix in flour just until incorporated. Turn batter into a foil- or parchment-lined 9-inch square baking pan.

2. Bake 30 to 35 minutes, or until cake puffs and a toothpick inserted in center comes out clean. Cake will rise slightly, then sink. Let cake cool in pan.

3. Invert cool cake to unmold onto a serving plate; peel off foil. Sift powdered sugar or cocoa over top. Cut into 16 squares.

34 CHOCOLATE MALTED CAKE
Prep: 30 minutes   Cook: 35 to 40 minutes   Serves: 8 to 10

This cake, which has malted milk powder in both the cake and frosting, is designed especially for malted milk fans. Garnish the cake with malted milk candy balls, if desired.

1 stick (4 ounces) butter,
    softened
1⅓ cups sugar
1 cup instant malted milk
    powder
¾ cup firmly packed
    unsweetened cocoa
    powder

4 eggs
2 cups flour
3 teaspoons baking powder
½ teaspoon salt
1¼ cups half-and-half
Chocolate Malted Frosting
    (recipe follows)

1. Preheat oven to 350°F. In a large bowl, beat together butter and sugar with an electric mixer on medium speed until light and fluffy, 1 to 2 minutes. Add malted milk powder and cocoa and beat just until mixed. Add eggs, beating until incorporated.

2. Sift together flour, baking powder, and salt. Add to chocolate mixture alternately with half-and-half. Beat on medium speed 30 seconds. Spread evenly in a well-greased and floured 9 x 13-inch baking pan.

3. Bake 35 to 40 minutes, or until a cake tester inserted in center comes out clean. Let cool in pan completely. Spread Chocolate Malted Frosting on top of cake. Let stand at room temperature until serving time.

CHOCOLATE MALTED FROSTING

½ cup half-and-half
½ cup instant malted milk
     powder
 1 stick (4 ounces) butter,
     softened

½ cup firmly packed
     unsweetened cocoa
     powder
2½ cups powdered sugar

1. In a medium bowl, pour half-and-half over malted milk powder. Stir to combine and let stand 15 minutes to dissolve milk powder.

2. In a medium bowl, beat together butter and cocoa with an electric mixer on low speed until well blended. Add malted milk mixture and beat to mix. Add powdered sugar and beat on high speed until light and fluffy.

---

35 CHOCOLATE IRISH POTATO CAKE
Prep: 20 minutes   Cook: 45 to 50 minutes   Serves: 12

Leftover mashed potatoes keep this cake moist. Use the real thing—not instant mashed potatoes, which will alter the taste. The generous amount of Irish cream liqueur imparts an intriguing flavor to this special cake.

 2 sticks (8 ounces) butter,
     softened
1½ cups granulated sugar
 4 (1-ounce) squares
     unsweetened chocolate,
     melted
 1 cup mashed potatoes
 1 tablespoon instant coffee or
     espresso powder

 4 eggs
1¾ cups flour
 2 teaspoons baking powder
½ teaspoon salt
 1 cup Irish cream liqueur
     Powdered sugar

1. Preheat oven to 350°F. In a large bowl, beat together butter and granulated sugar with an electric mixer on medium speed until light and fluffy, 1 to 2 minutes. Beat in melted chocolate, mashed potatoes, and coffee powder until well blended. Add eggs, one at a time, beating well after each addition.

2. Sift together flour, baking powder, and salt. Beat into chocolate mixture alternately with Irish liqueur just until combined. Turn batter into well-greased 12-cup bundt pan.

3. Bake 45 to 50 minutes, or until a cake tester inserted in center comes out clean. Let cake cool in pan 15 minutes, then unmold onto a wire rack and let cool completely. Sift powdered sugar over top of cake before serving.

36   CHOCOLATE BLITZ TORTE

Prep: 30 minutes   Cook: 30 to 32 minutes   Serves: 12

This is a dessert that dates back years. It was one of my grandmother's favorites. This version sports meringue-covered chocolate cake stacked together with strawberries and whipped cream in between.

1 stick (4 ounces) butter, softened	½ teaspoon baking soda
1¼ cups granulated sugar	⅓ cup milk
1 teaspoon vanilla extract	½ cup sliced blanched almonds
4 eggs, separated	1½ cups heavy cream
Dash of salt	2 tablespoons powdered sugar
⅓ cup unsweetened cocoa powder	1 pint basket fresh strawberries, sliced
1 cup flour	
1 teaspoon baking powder	

1. Preheat oven to 325°F. Grease two 9-inch round cake pans. Dust with flour; tap out excess.

2. In a medium bowl, beat together butter, ½ cup granulated sugar, vanilla, egg yolks, and salt with an electric mixer on medium speed until light and fluffy, 2 to 3 minutes. Add cocoa and beat until well blended. Sift together flour with baking powder and baking soda. Add to chocolate mixture alternately with milk. Beat just until combined. Divide batter evenly between prepared pans, spreading and smoothing tops.

3. In a medium bowl, beat egg whites with electric mixer with clean, dry beaters on medium speed until foamy. Gradually add remaining ¾ cup granulated sugar and beat with mixer on high speed until stiff peaks form. Divide meringue between 2 pans, carefully spreading evenly over cake batter. Sprinkle almonds on top.

4. Bake 30 to 32 minutes, or until golden brown. Let cakes cool 5 to 10 minutes in pans, then unmold onto racks, meringue sides up, and let cool completely.

5. In a medium bowl, beat together heavy cream and powdered sugar with an electric mixer on high speed until stiff.

6. To assemble cake, place one cake layer, meringue side down, on a serving plate. Cover with two thirds of whipped cream and top with strawberry slices. Place remaining cake layer, meringue side up, on top of strawberries. Frost side of cake with remaining whipped cream. Refrigerate at least 1 hour before serving. Cake is best prepared and served within a day of baking.

37 CHOCOLATE PEANUT BUTTER BUNDT CAKE

Prep: 20 minutes   Cook: 55 to 60 minutes   Serves: 12

This cake is irresistible for peanut butter and chocolate devotees.

2 sticks (8 ounces) butter or margarine, softened
2 cups sugar
½ cup chunky peanut butter
4 (1-ounce) squares unsweetened chocolate, melted
6 eggs
2 cups flour

2 teaspoons baking powder
½ teaspoon baking soda
⅓ cup milk
6 ounces semisweet chocolate chips (1 cup)
Quick Chocolate Frosting (recipe follows)
⅓ cup chopped peanuts

1. Preheat oven to 350°F. Butter a 12-cup bundt pan.

2. In a large bowl, beat together butter and sugar with an electric mixer on medium speed until light and fluffy, 1 to 2 minutes. Add peanut butter and melted chocolate and beat until well blended. Add eggs, one at a time, beating well after each addition.

3. Sift together flour, baking powder, and baking soda. Beat into chocolate mixture alternately with milk just until combined. Stir in chocolate chips. Turn batter into prepared pan.

4. Bake 55 to 60 minutes, or until a cake tester inserted in center comes out clean. Let cool in pan 15 minutes, then unmold onto a rack and let cool completely.

5. Frost cake all over with Quick Chocolate Frosting. Sprinkle peanuts on top.

38 QUICK CHOCOLATE FROSTING

Prep: 2 minutes   Cook: 1 to 1½ minutes   Makes: about 1½ cups

6 ounces semisweet chocolate chips (1 cup)
2 tablespoons butter

2 cups powdered sugar
6 tablespoons milk

1. In a 1-quart glass bowl, combine chocolate chips and butter. Heat in a microwave oven on High 1 to 1½ minutes, or until melted and smooth when stirred.

2. Beat in powdered sugar and milk.

39   CHOCOLATE CRANBERRY CAKE

Prep: 20 minutes   Cook: 45 to 50 minutes   Serves: 12

¾ cup corn oil
1½ cups granulated sugar
¾ cup firmly packed
    unsweetened cocoa
    powder
1 (16-ounce) can jellied
   cranberry sauce
   Juice of 1 large orange (⅓ to
   ½ cup)
1 tablespoon grated orange
   zest

6 eggs
2½ cups flour
2 teaspoons baking powder
1 teaspoon baking soda
½ teaspoon salt
6 ounces semisweet chocolate
   chips (1 cup)
½ cup chopped pecans
   Powdered sugar

1. Preheat oven to 350°F. In a large bowl, beat together corn oil and granulated sugar with an electric mixer on high speed until well blended. Add cocoa, cranberry sauce, orange juice, and orange zest. Beat until well blended. Add eggs, one at a time, beating well after each addition.

2. Sift together flour, baking powder, baking soda, and salt. Add to cranberry mixture and beat on low speed just until combined. Stir in chocolate chips and pecans. Turn batter into a well-greased 12-cup bundt pan, spreading evenly.

3. Bake 45 to 50 minutes, or until a cake tester inserted in center comes out clean. Let cake cool in pan 20 to 30 minutes, then unmold onto a rack and let cool completely. Dust top with a sifting of powdered sugar before serving.

40   ANGEL FOOD CAKE DESSERT

Prep: 20 minutes   Cook: 30 minutes   Chill: 6 hours   Serves: 6 to 8

This is irresistible—how can you miss with whipped cream, cake, Heath Bars, and fudge sauce?

1 envelope unflavored gelatin
2 cups heavy cream
1 tablespoon powdered sugar
2 (5-ounce) packages
   miniature Heath Bars or
   other milk chocolate–
   covered toffee bars,
   chopped into ¼-inch
   pieces

1 (10-ounce) angel food cake
1 (11¾-ounce) jar hot fudge
   sauce or Dark Chocolate
   Fudge Sauce (page 206),
   warmed

1. In a small glass bowl, stir together gelatin and 2 tablespoons water. Cook in microwave oven on High 30 seconds. Let stand 2 minutes, then stir in ¼ cup cream; let stand 5 minutes, or until mixture cools to room temperature.

2. In a medium bowl, beat together remaining 1¾ cups cream and powdered sugar with an electric mixer on high speed until soft peaks form. Beat in gelatin mixture; continue to beat until stiff. Fold in candy bar pieces.

3. Slice angel food cake horizontally into 3 equal layers. Fill and frost cake with whipped cream mixture. Refrigerate 6 hours or overnight, until set.

4. To serve, cut cake into wedges with a sharp serrated knife. Drizzle a little fudge sauce on top. Serve immediately.

---

41 CHOCOLATE PANFORTE
Prep: 20 minutes   Cook: 43 to 45 minutes   Serves: 12 to 16

This dense, chewy Italian fruitcake is a traditional Christmas favorite in Siena, Italy, where it has been enjoyed for ages. Traditionally, *panforte*, which means "strong bread" in Italian, contains citron. This version does not. A nonchocolate panforte sampled at a casual San Francisco restaurant, Sputino, was the inspiration for this version, though the restaurant uses dried sweet cherries rather than the apricots called for here. Chocolate has been added to this rendition as well.

1 cup hazelnuts	1¼ teaspoons ground cinnamon
1 cup whole blanched almonds	¼ teaspoon ground cloves
1 cup chopped dried apricots	¼ teaspoon ground nutmeg
1 cup chopped candied orange peel	Dash of pepper
⅓ cup flour	½ cup granulated sugar
½ cup unsweetened cocoa powder	½ cup honey
	2 tablespoons butter
	Sifted powdered sugar or cocoa powder

1. Preheat oven to 325°F. Butter a 9-inch springform pan. Line bottom with a round of parchment or wax paper. Line sides of pan with a strip of paper cut to fit.

2. Spread out hazelnuts and almonds on 2 separate baking sheets. Place in oven and bake until almonds are lightly toasted, about 5 minutes; transfer almonds to a plate to cool. Continue baking hazelnuts until nuts are lightly browned and dark skins are cracked. Rub warm hazelnuts in a terrycloth towel to remove as much of skins as possible.

3. In a large bowl, combine hazelnuts, almonds, apricots, orange peel, and flour; mix well.Stir in cocoa, cinnamon, cloves, nutmeg, and pepper.

4. In a 1½-quart saucepan, combine granulated sugar, honey, and butter. Heat to boiling over medium heat, stirring often. Boil, stirring constantly, 5 minutes, or until mixture reaches 248°F on a candy thermometer.

5. Working quickly, pour boiling syrup over nut-fruit mixture, mixing until thoroughly incorporated and evenly coated. Turn into prepared springform pan. Smooth top with spatula. Bake 35 minutes. Do not overbake. (The panforte will harden as it cools.) Remove cake from oven and let cool completely in pan. Run a sharp knife around edges of pan to loosen cake. Remove springform side of pan. Peel off parchment paper and wrap cake well in plastic wrap; then wrap in foil. Store at room temperature 3 weeks or freeze 2 to 3 months. Just before serving, sift powdered sugar on top.

42 MOCHA-FILLED CHOCOLATE CAKE ROLL

Prep: 30 minutes   Cook: 13 to 15 minutes   Chill: 6 hours
Serves: 8 to 10

This delicate, light, and airy cake roll is filled with a light updated mocha buttercream made with egg whites rather than egg yolks. A sprinkling of powdered sugar is all that's needed to finish off the cake.

4 whole eggs
2 egg yolks
⅔ cup plus 1 tablespoon
   granulated sugar
⅓ cup firmly packed
   unsweetened cocoa
   powder

½ cup cake flour
2 tablespoons cornstarch
¼ teaspoon salt
½ cup finely ground pecans
Mocha Butter Cream (recipe
   follows)
Powdered sugar

1. Preheat oven to 350°F. Grease a 10 x 15-inch jelly-roll pan and line with parchment or wax paper. Lightly grease parchment paper.

2. In a large bowl, beat whole eggs, egg yolks, and ⅔ cup granulated sugar with an electric mixer on high speed until very light and fluffy, about 5 minutes. In a medium bowl, sift together cocoa, cake flour, cornstarch, and salt. Fold into egg mixture until well blended. Gently fold in pecans. Spread into prepared pan.

3. Bake 13 to 15 minutes, or until cake begins to pull away from sides of pan and springs back when touched lightly. Immediately flip pan over onto a large sheet of wax paper sprinkled with remaining 1 tablespoon granulated sugar. Remove pan and peel off parchment paper. Starting on one long side, gently roll cake up jelly-roll fashion with wax paper in between. Allow cake to cool rolled up.

4. Unroll cake and spread Mocha Butter Cream to within 2 inches of edges. Roll again from long side jelly-roll fashion, this time without paper. Wrap in plastic wrap and refrigerate 6 hours or overnight. Just before serving, trim ends of cake and sift powdered sugar on top.

43 MOCHA BUTTER CREAM

Prep: 10 minutes   Cook: none   Makes: about 3 cups

6 (1-ounce) squares semisweet
   chocolate
1 cup heavy cream
2 egg whites *

⅓ cup powdered sugar
1 tablespoon instant espresso
   powder

1. Melt chocolate over low heat or in microwave oven until smooth when stirred. Set aside and let cool.

2. In a medium bowl, whip cream with an electric mixer on high speed until stiff.

3. In a separate medium bowl with clean, dry beaters, beat egg whites on high until stiff but not dry. Beat in powdered sugar and espresso powder until blended. Fold in melted chocolate until well mixed; then fold in whipped cream. Cover and refrigerate until chilled and spreadable before using.

* **CAUTION:** *Because of the possible threat of salmonella—a bacteria that causes food poisoning—from raw eggs, U.S. Government officials recommend that the very young, the elderly, pregnant women, and people with serious illnesses or weakened immune systems not eat raw or lightly cooked eggs. Keep this in mind and consume raw or lightly cooked eggs at your own risk.*

---

44 CHOCOLATE ZUCCHINI FRUITCAKE
Prep: 35 minutes   Cook: 60 to 65 minutes   Chill: 1 to 2 weeks
Makes: two 9-inch loaves

This novel cake, abundant with zucchini, raisins, dried apricots, dates, brandy, nuts, and chocolate, is a winner. Make it when the summer zucchini crop is prolific and freeze, well wrapped, for the holiday season.

1 (12-ounce) box raisins (2 cups)
1 (6-ounce) package dried apricots, chopped
1 cup chopped pitted dates
1 cup brandy
1 cup vegetable oil
3 eggs
2 cups packed brown sugar
1 tablespoon vanilla extract
3 cups flour
½ cup unsweetened cocoa powder
1 tablespoon ground cinnamon
2 teaspoons baking soda
2 teaspoons ground allspice
1 teaspoon ground nutmeg
1 teaspoon ground cloves
¾ teaspoon salt
¾ teaspoon baking powder
2 cups grated zucchini (about 2 medium)
2 cups coarsely chopped walnuts

1. Preheat oven to 325°F. Grease two 9 x 5 x 3-inch loaf pans. Dust with flour and tap out excess; or line with parchment paper.

2. In a 2-quart glass bowl, combine raisins, apricots, dates, and ½ cup brandy. Heat in a microwave oven on High for 2 minutes, until most of liquid is absorbed; stir and set aside.

3. In a large bowl, beat together oil, eggs, brown sugar, and vanilla with an electric mixer on medium speed until well blended, 2 to 3 minutes.

4. Add flour, cocoa, cinnamon, baking soda, allspice, nutmeg, cloves, salt, and baking powder. Beat until well blended. Stir in zucchini, walnuts, and reserved fruit mixture and its liquid.

5. Spoon batter into prepared pans. Bake 60 to 65 minutes, or until a cake tester inserted in center comes out clean. Do not overbake. Sprinkle remaining ½ cup brandy over warm cakes. Let cool in pans on racks, then loosen sides of cake carefully with a sharp knife and unmold. Wrap cakes well in plastic wrap; then wrap in aluminum foil. Store in refrigerator or freezer. Allow refrigerated cakes to age at least 1 to 2 weeks before serving.

45   RED DEVIL'S FOOD CAKE

Prep: 30 minutes   Cook: 35 to 40 minutes   Serves: 10

Bet your friends and family will never guess the unusual secret ingredients—tomato sauce and red wine vinegar—in this moist, yummy cake.

2   sticks (8 ounces) butter or margarine, softened
2   cups sugar
¾   cup firmly packed unsweetened cocoa powder (preferably Dutch-processed)
4   eggs

1   (6-ounce) can tomato juice
1   tablespoon red wine vinegar
2½   cups cake flour
1½   teaspoons baking soda
     Fudge Frosting (recipe follows)
½   cup chopped walnuts

1. Preheat oven to 350°F. Grease two 9-inch round cake pans. Dust with flour; tap out excess.

2. In a large bowl, beat together butter and sugar with an electric mixer on medium speed until light and fluffy, 1 to 2 minutes. With mixer on low speed, beat in cocoa until well blended. Return speed to medium and add eggs, one at a time, beating well after each addition.

3. Mix together tomato juice and vinegar. Sift together flour and baking soda. With mixer on low speed, beat into chocolate mixture alternately with tomato juice mixture just until combined. Turn batter into prepared pans.

4. Bake 35 to 40 minutes, or until a cake tester inserted in center comes out clean. Let cakes cool in pans 10 minutes, then unmold onto racks and let cool completely.

5. Fill and frost cake with Fudge Frosting. Sprinkle walnuts over top and press into side of cake.

46   FUDGE FROSTING

Prep: 10 minutes   Cook: none   Makes: enough to fill and frost a 2-layer 9-inch cake

1   stick (4 ounces) butter or margarine, softened
6   ounces bittersweet chocolate, melted

½   cup heavy cream
4½   cups powdered sugar
1   teaspoon vanilla extract

1. In a medium bowl, beat together butter and melted chocolate with an electric mixer on medium speed until combined, 1 minute. Beat in cream.

2. Add powdered sugar and vanilla and beat on high speed until frosting is smooth and fluffy.

47   ALMOND CHOCOLATE FRUITCAKE LOAF
Prep: 40 minutes   Cook: 1 hour   Chill: 2 days   Makes: 1 long loaf

This fruitcake, prepared with an almond paste cake base, is studded with chocolate chips, three different kinds of nuts, and just a few candied fruits for color. It tastes a lot like chocolate-covered marzipan. Be sure to refrigerate it a couple of days prior to serving for easy slicing.

1 cup hazelnuts	½ teaspoon baking powder
1 stick (4 ounces) butter, softened	6 ounces miniature semisweet chocolate chips (1 cup)
7 ounces almond paste	½ cup semisweet chocolate chips
½ cup sugar	
3 tablespoons dark or amber rum	1 cup chopped assorted candied cherry-pineapple mix (red cherries and red, green, and yellow pineapple)
1 teaspoon vanilla extract	
1 tablespoon grated orange zest	
1 tablespoon grated lemon zest	1½ cups chopped pecans
3 eggs	1 cup coarsely chopped walnuts
½ cup flour	

1. Preheat oven to 325°F. Grease a 4½ x 12½-inch long loaf pan and line completely with waxed paper; grease the paper.

2. Spread out hazelnuts on a small baking sheet. Toast in oven 10 to 12 minutes, or until nuts are lightly browned and dark skins are cracked. Rub warm nuts in a terrycloth towel to remove as much skin as possible.

3. In a large bowl, beat together butter, almond paste, and sugar with an electric mixer on medium speed until well blended. Beat in rum, vanilla, orange zest, and lemon zest. Add eggs, one at a time, beating well after each addition. Add flour and baking powder and beat until combined. Stir in chocolate chips, candied fruits, pecans, and walnuts until well mixed. Scrape batter into prepared loaf pan.

4. Bake about 1 hour, or until cake springs back when touched lightly and top is golden brown. Let cake cool in pan 30 to 40 minutes, then unmold cake by lifting with wax paper onto a wire rack and let cool completely. Carefully peel off wax paper. Wrap cake in plastic wrap and then in aluminum foil. Refrigerate at least 2 days or up to 2 weeks before serving.

NOTE: *Loaf is best cut into ½-inch or thicker slices for serving. Cut each slice in half or thirds. Loaf also freezes well. For ease in handling and serving, cut loaf into 2 or 3 horizontal pieces and wrap each piece individually.*

Chapter 2

The Cheesecake Stands Alone

Culinary fashions come and go, but cheesecakes never go out of style. They always seem to be in vogue on the trendiest as well as the most nondescript restaurant menus. One California restaurant, which opened more than a decade ago, offers more than 40 different cheesecake flavor varieties, and the list keeps growing in response to customer demand.

It's no wonder. Cheesecake—in a class by itself with its velvety smooth texture—has universal appeal. Who can resist indulging in a piece of this decadent creation? And if it's chocolate, watch out!

While cheesecake connoisseurs and aficionados abound, personal styles vary. Some people prefer their cheesecake creamy, light, and airy, while others favor a drier, heavier texture. Topping preferences vary from plain to fancy and to anything in between.

No matter how much you like your cheesecake, this chapter is devoted to smashing variations redolent with chocolate in all its forms—from white chocolate to semisweet to bittersweet—and with numerous other flavorings and ingredients: raspberry, orange, candy bars, nuts, peanut butter, rocky road, coffee, and more.

The common denominator in all these cakes is cream cheese and a springform pan. A springform pan, which is used for desserts that are not inverted, consists of a metal ring with a spring release and a base that is clamped on. If you don't have a springform pan, invest in one and add it to your list of equipment basics. It's a versatile pan and great for many other desserts as well as cheesecakes, including tortes, truffle-style cakes, and frozen creations. A nine-inch springform is the size most often called for in recipes, but the pan is also available in sizes ranging from eight to eleven or twelve inches in diameter.

Most often, cheesecakes have some type of crust, usually prepared from cookie crumbs. Try all kinds of cookie crumbs—chocolate wafer, peanut butter, coconut macaroons, chocolate chip, and whatever else strikes your fancy. Pastry dough can also be used. Whenever lining the springform pan with crumbs or dough, press at least one inch up the sides of the pan to avoid leakage of the cheesecake mixture. You'll end up with a more attractive-looking cake.

I find that baking cheesecakes a short time at a high oven temperature at first and then reducing the temperature for the longest baking period generally yields the best results with fewer cracks and less browning.

One of the most appealing attributes of cheese-cakes is that they can and must be prepared well in advance of serving time, freeing the cook for other last-minute tasks. Also, cheesecakes are difficult to ruin. And if the top of your cake does by chance look like the Grand Canyon, simply cover it with whipped cream and garnish with one of the ingredients, such as chopped-up candy bars or nuts, that are used in the cake.

None of these cheesecakes are difficult or tricky to make, although some take more time than others. Now bring on the Chocolate Chantilly Cheesecake, Rocky Road Cheese-cake Deluxe, Chocolate Peanut Butter Cheesecake, White Chocolate Raspberry Cheesecake, Peanut Butter Cup Cheese-cake, Chocolate Pecan Cheesecake, and more. The most difficult chore will be deciding which one to make first.

---

48   MOCHA CHOCOLATE CHIP CHEESECAKE

Prep: 15 minutes   Cook: 40 to 45 minutes   Chill: 6 hours
Serves: 12 to 14

This cheesecake is rich and smooth and flavored with coffee and chocolate chips.

1½ cups chocolate wafer cookie crumbs	3 eggs
½ cup finely chopped pecans	1 teaspoon vanilla extract
4 tablespoons butter	4 teaspoons instant espresso powder
3 (8-ounce) packages cream cheese, softened	2 tablespoons flour
1 cup packed light brown sugar	1 cup sour cream
	1½ cups semisweet chocolate chips (9 ounces)

1. Preheat oven to 400°F. To make crust, in a medium bowl, combine chocolate crumbs, pecans, and butter; mix well. Press into bottom and halfway up sides of a 9-inch springform pan.

2. To make filling, in a large bowl with an electric mixer on medium speed, beat together cream cheese and sugar until fluffy, 1 to 2 minutes. Beat in eggs, vanilla, and espresso until smooth and well blended, about 2 minutes. Add flour and sour cream and beat until smooth. Stir in chocolate chips. Scrape filling into prepared crust; smooth top.

3. Bake 15 minutes. Reduce oven temperature to 300° and continue baking 25 to 30 minutes, or until cheesecake is set around edges but still jiggles slightly in center. Let cake cool 2 to 3 hours, then refrigerate until well chilled, 6 hours or overnight. An hour before serving, run a knife around edge of pan to loosen cake and remove springform side of pan.

49   HEATH BAR MOCHA CHEESECAKE

Prep: 20 minutes   Cook: 75 to 80 minutes   Chill: 6 hours
Serves: 12 to 14

This is a winner—with Heath candy bars inside the cheesecake and on top. A milk chocolate topping offsets the coffee-flavored cheesecake perfectly.

8 (1 ³/₁₆-ounce) original Heath English Toffee candy bars
1 (9-ounce) package chocolate wafer cookies
3 tablespoons butter, melted
1⅓ cups heavy cream
5 tablespoons instant coffee crystals

3 (8-ounce) packages cream cheese, softened
1 cup sugar
4 eggs
1 tablespoon vanilla extract
1 (11.5-ounce) package milk chocolate chips (2 cups)

1. Preheat oven to 325°F. Coarsely chop 4 Heath bars. Finely chop remaining 4 bars. Reserve separately.

2. Make crust: In a food processor, grind cookies into fine crumbs. Add melted butter and process until mixed. Press into bottom and about 1 inch up sides of a 9½-inch springform pan. Sprinkle coarsely chopped Heath bars over crust. Refrigerate while preparing filling.

3. In a 1-cup glass measure, combine ½ cup cream and coffee crystals. Heat in a microwave oven on High 40 to 60 seconds, or until coffee dissolves when stirred. Refrigerate until cool, about 15 minutes.

4. In a large bowl, beat together cream cheese and sugar with an electric mixer on medium speed until smooth, 1 to 2 minutes. Beat in ½ cup cream, eggs, and vanilla until well mixed, 1 to 2 minutes. With mixer on low speed, beat in chilled coffee-cream mixture; continue beating 5 minutes. Turn into prepared crust.

5. Bake 1 hour and 15 to 20 minutes, or until cheesecake looks set around edges and center still jiggles slightly. Let cake cool; then refrigerate.

6. When cake is cool, in top of a double boiler, heat together chocolate chips and remaining ⅓ cup cream, stirring often, until melted and smooth. Let cool in refrigerator until slightly thickened. Spread topping over cheesecake. Sprinkle finely chopped candy bars on top. Refrigerate until chocolate layer is set and cake is well chilled, 6 hours. Run a knife around edge of pan to loosen cake and remove springform side of pan.

50 ROCKY ROAD CHEESECAKE DELUXE

Prep: 30 minutes   Cook: 50 to 60 minutes   Chill: 8 hours
Serves: 8 to 10

A rocky road topping, loaded with shredded coconut, marshmallows, chopped toasted almonds, and chocolate pieces, is what makes this cheesecake special. A final glazing of chocolate covers the top and sides of the cake.

1   **(9-inch) Chocolate Wafer Crust (page 135)**
2   **(8-ounce) packages cream cheese, softened**
1   **cup sugar**
4   **eggs**
2   **teaspoons vanilla extract**

1½   **cups semisweet chocolate chips (9 ounces), melted and cooled**
     Rocky Road Topping (recipe follows)
1   **cup chopped toasted almonds**

1. Prepare Chocolate Wafer Crust recipe as directed, pressing crumb mixture into bottom and about 1 inch up sides of a 9-inch springform pan. Preheat oven to 325°F.

2. In a food processor, combine cream cheese, sugar, eggs, and vanilla. Turn machine quickly on and off in short spurts to combine, then process continually until smooth. Add melted chocolate and process until well blended.

3. Turn filling into Chocolate Wafer Crust, spreading evenly. Bake 50 to 60 minutes, or until set. Let cool, then refrigerate until chilled, 6 hours or overnight.

4. Spoon Rocky Road Topping evenly over cheesecake, mounding center higher than sides. Refrigerate until firm, about 2 hours. Run a sharp knife around edge of pan to loosen cake and remove springform side of pan. Spread top and sides with reserved chocolate from Rocky Road Topping recipe. Press almonds lightly onto sides of cake. Refrigerate until serving time.

ROCKY ROAD TOPPING

1   **cup heavy cream**
1⅓   **cups plus ¼ cup semisweet chocolate chips**
1   **tablespoon butter**
1   **tablespoon light corn syrup**

1   **cup shredded coconut**
3   **to 3½ cups miniature marshmallows**
½   **cup chopped toasted almonds**

1. In a 2-quart glass bowl, combine cream and 1⅓ cups chocolate chips. Heat in a microwave oven on High 1½ to 2½ minutes, or until chocolate is melted and mixture is smooth when stirred. Transfer 1 cup of the mixture to a small bowl and set aside remainder. Add butter and corn syrup to chocolate mixture in small bowl and stir until smooth. Refrigerate until thickened to spreading consistency, 20 to 25 minutes. Reserve to use for spreading on top and sides of cake.

2. To reserved chocolate mixture in 2-quart bowl, add coconut, marshmallows, almonds, and remaining ¼ cup chocolate chips. Mix well.

---

51 SNICKERS BAR CHEESECAKE
Prep: 30 minutes   Cook: 75 to 85 minutes   Chill: 4 to 5 hours
Serves: 12 to 14

1 (9-ounce) package chocolate
   wafer cookies
4 tablespoons butter, melted
3 (8-ounce) packages cream
   cheese, softened
1 cup sugar
4 eggs

1 tablespoon vanilla extract
2 cups heavy cream
1½ pounds snack-size Snickers
   bars, each bar cut into
   sixths
Yummy Fudge Topping
   (recipe follows)

1. Preheat oven to 325°F. In a food processor, grind cookies into fine crumbs. Add butter and process until well blended. Press into bottom and about 1 inch up sides of a 9½- or 10-inch springform pan.

2. In a large bowl, beat together cream cheese and sugar with an electric mixer on medium speed until smooth, 1 to 2 minutes. Beat in eggs, one at a time. Beat in vanilla and 1 cup cream; beat 3 to 4 minutes. Fold in 1½ cups cut-up Snickers pieces.

3. Turn into crumb-lined pan. Bake 1 hour and 15 to 25 minutes, or until cheesecake is almost set but center still jiggles slightly. Let cool to room temperature. Sprinkle remaining candy pieces over top of cheesecake. Refrigerate at least 4 to 5 hours before serving. Run a knife around edge of pan to loosen cake and remove springform side of pan. Just before serving, drizzle Yummy Fudge Topping over cake. Whip remaining 1 cup cream until stiff and spoon a dollop over each slice.

YUMMY FUDGE TOPPING

2 (1-ounce) squares
   unsweetened chocolate
2 tablespoons butter

⅓ cup boiling water
¾ cup sugar
3 tablespoons light corn syrup

In a heavy, medium saucepan, melt chocolate and butter over low heat, stirring often, about 2 minutes. Stir in boiling water, sugar, and corn syrup; mix until smooth. Increase heat to medium and cook until mixture starts to boil. Boil gently 5 minutes without stirring. Remove from heat and let cool until lukewarm, 20 to 30 minutes.

52 PEANUT BUTTER CUP CHEESECAKE

Prep: 20 minutes   Cook: 55 to 65 minutes   Chill: 6 hours
Serves: 12

1 (9-ounce) package chocolate
    wafer cookies
4 tablespoons butter, melted
4 (8-ounce) packages cream
    cheese, softened
1 cup sugar
4 eggs

3 tablespoons flour
⅓ cup milk
1½ teaspoons vanilla extract
6 (1.8-ounce) packages peanut
    butter cups (2 per
    package), chopped
1 cup heavy cream, whipped

1. Preheat oven to 425°F. In a food processor, grind cookies into fine crumbs. Add melted butter and process until well mixed. Press crumb mixture into bottom and two thirds up sides of a 9-inch springform pan.

2. In a large bowl, beat together cream cheese and sugar with an electric mixer on medium speed until light, fluffy, and smooth, 2 to 3 minutes. Beat in eggs, one at a time, beating well after each addition. Beat in flour, milk, and vanilla. Beat until well blended and smooth, about 4 minutes.

3. Sprinkle 4 packages of chopped peanut butter cups evenly over bottom of chocolate crust. Carefully pour cheesecake mixture over all; spread evenly.

4. Bake 15 minutes. Reduce oven temperature to 250°F and bake 40 to 50 minutes longer, or until edges are set and cake jiggles only slightly in center.

5. Let cheesecake cool to room temperature, then refrigerate until well chilled, 6 hours or overnight. Run a knife around edge of pan to loosen cake and remove springform side of pan. Shortly before serving, garnish with whipped cream and sprinkle remaining 2 packages chopped peanut butter cups on top.

53 PEANUT CHOCOLATE CHIP CHEESECAKE SQUARES

Prep: 20 minutes   Cook: 33 minutes   Makes: 48

1 (9-ounce) package chocolate
    wafer cookies
5 tablespoons butter, melted
1 (8-ounce) package cream
    cheese, softened
½ cup powdered sugar

1 egg
2 teaspoons vanilla extract
1½ cups dry roasted unsalted
    peanuts
6 ounces semisweet chocolate
    chips (1 cup)

1. Preheat oven to 350°F. In a food processor, grind cookies into fine crumbs. Add melted butter and process until well blended. Press mixture evenly into bottom of an ungreased 9 x 13-inch baking pan. Bake crust 8 minutes.

2. In a medium bowl, beat together cream cheese, powdered sugar, egg, and vanilla with an electric mixer on medium speed until smooth, about 2 minutes. Spread evenly over baked crust. Sprinkle peanuts and chocolate chips over cream cheese filling; press in lightly.

3. Bake 25 minutes, or until set. Let cool in pan before cutting into 48 (1½-inch) squares. Store, tightly wrapped, in refrigerator.

Variation: **CHOCOLATE-WALNUT ORANGE CHEESECAKE SQUARES**

Add 1 tablespoon grated orange zest to cream cheese filling. Use 1½ cups chopped walnuts instead of peanuts and proceed with recipe as directed above.

---

54 CHOCOLATE PEANUT BUTTER CHEESECAKE

Prep: 30 minutes   Cook: 1 hour   Chill: 8 hours   Serves: 14 to 16

This rich and creamy creation is reminiscent of a sophisticated peanut butter cup candy.

2 cups creme-filled peanut butter cookie crumbs (½ of a 15½-ounce package)	1½ cups sugar
	6 eggs
	2 teaspoons vanilla extract
5 tablespoons butter, melted	10 ounces semisweet chocolate, melted
2¼ pounds cream cheese, softened	1 cup smooth or crunchy peanut butter

1. Preheat oven to 350°F. In a medium bowl, mix together cookie crumbs and butter until well blended. Press into bottom and 1 inch up sides of a 10-inch springform pan. Bake crust 10 minutes. Let cool.

2. Reduce oven temperature to 300°F. In a large bowl, beat together cream cheese and sugar with an electric mixer on medium speed until light and fluffy, 2 to 3 minutes. Gradually beat in eggs and vanilla and beat until smooth, about 2 minutes.

3. Transfer one third of batter to another bowl and set aside. Beat melted chocolate into remaining batter. Turn chocolate mixture into cooled crust. With mixer on medium speed, beat peanut butter into remaining one third batter until thoroughly mixed. Carefully spoon peanut butter mixture on top of chocolate cheese mixture in pan. Using the long handle of a wooden spoon, swirl the two flavors together.

4. Bake about 1 hour, or until cheesecake is set around edges and puffed but still jiggles slightly in the center. Let cake cool 2 hours, then refrigerate until well chilled, 8 hours or overnight. Run a knife around edge of pan to loosen cake and remove springform side of pan.

55   CHOCOLATE CHANTILLY CHEESECAKE

Prep: 45 minutes   Cook: 1 hour   Chill: 10 hours   Serves: 12 to 16

This dessert combines two favorites—cheesecake and chocolate mousse —in a single creation.

1½ cups chocolate wafer cookie crumbs	2 teaspoons vanilla extract
3 tablespoons butter, melted	¼ cup Grand Marnier or Orange Curaçao
2 (8-ounce) packages cream cheese, cut into cubes and softened	6 ounces semisweet chocolate chips (1 cup)
1 cup sugar	1 tablespoon grated orange zest
4 eggs	1½ cups heavy cream, whipped

1. Preheat oven to 325°F. Make crust: In a medium bowl, mix together cookie crumbs and melted butter. Press into bottom and about 1 inch up sides of a 9-inch springform pan.

2. To make cheesecake layer, in a food processor, combine cream cheese and sugar; process until smooth. Add eggs and vanilla and process until well blended. Pour filling into prepared crust. Bake about 1 hour, or until set. Let cake cool, then refrigerate until chilled, about 6 hours.

3. When cheesecake is cold, prepare chocolate mousse layer: In a small glass bowl, combine Grand Marnier and chocolate chips. Heat in a microwave oven on High 1 to 1½ minutes, stirring once or twice, or until chocolate is melted. Stir in orange zest. Let cool.

4. Fold cooled chocolate mixture into whipped cream until well blended. Spread evenly over cold cheesecake layer and refrigerate 4 hours or overnight. Run a sharp knife around edge of pan to loosen cake and remove springform side of pan.

56   CHOCOLATE CHIP CHEESECAKE

Prep: 15 minutes   Cook: 70 to 75 minutes   Chill: 6 hours Serves: 8 to 10

1½ cups chocolate wafer cookie crumbs	4 eggs
1 cup plus 1 tablespoon sugar	2 teaspoons vanilla extract
3 tablespoons butter, melted	¾ cup miniature semisweet chocolate chips
2 (8-ounce) packages cream cheese, cubed and softened	

1. Preheat oven to 325°F. To make crust, in a medium bowl, mix together chocolate crumbs, 1 tablespoon sugar, and melted butter until well mixed. Press into bottom and about 1 inch up sides of an 8-inch springform pan.

2. To make filling, in a food processor, combine cream cheese, remaining 1 cup sugar, eggs, and vanilla. Turn machine quickly on and off in short spurts to combine, then process continuously until smooth. Turn filling into prepared crust.

3. Sprinkle chocolate chips on top of cake. Bake 70 to 75 minutes, or until a toothpick inserted in center comes out clean. Let cake cool to room temperature, then refrigerate until well chilled, at least 6 hours. Run a knife around edge of pan to loosen cake and remove springform side of pan.

Variation: **CHOCOLATE CHOCOLATE CHIP ESPRESSO CHEESECAKE**

Melt 6 (1-ounce) squares semisweet chocolate, cool slightly, and add to cream cheese mixture along with 2 teaspoons instant espresso powder or instant coffee powder and blend until smooth. Turn filling into chocolate crust and proceed as recipe directs above.

---

57   EASY CHOCOLATE CHUNK CHEESECAKE

Prep: 15 minutes   Cook: 40 to 50 minutes   Chill: 6 to 8 hours
Serves: 10 to 12

This is a simple recipe I've been making for years, long before chocolate cheesecake came into vogue. It's still delicious.

1 cup chocolate wafer cookie crumbs	6 ounces semisweet chocolate chips (1 cup)
1 cup finely chopped pecans	¼ cup Grand Marnier or Orange Curaçao
4 tablespoons butter, melted	2 teaspoons grated orange zest
1 cup sugar	6 ounces bittersweet chocolate, chopped into ½-inch chunks
2 (8-ounce) packages cream cheese, softened	
4 eggs	

1. Preheat oven to 350°F. To make crust, in a medium bowl, mix together cookie crumbs, pecans, and melted butter. Press into bottom and halfway up sides of a 9-inch springform pan.

2. In a medium bowl, beat together sugar and cream cheese with an electric mixer on medium speed until light and fluffy, 2 to 3 minutes. Beat in eggs, one at a time, beating well after addition.

3. In a 1-quart glass cup, combine chocolate chips and Grand Marnier. Heat in a microwave oven on High 1¼ to 1½ minutes, or until smooth and melted when stirred. Beat into cream cheese mixture, along with orange zest, until well blended. Stir in bittersweet chocolate chunks. Turn into prepared crust.

4. Bake 40 to 50 minutes, or until cheesecake is set 1 inch from center. Let cake cool, then refrigerate until well chilled, 6 to 8 hours or overnight. Run a knife around edge of pan to loosen cake and remove springform side of pan.

58   RICOTTA CHOCOLATE CHIP ORANGE CHEESECAKE

Prep: 20 minutes   Cook: 60 to 70 minutes   Chill: 4 to 5 hours
Serves: 10 to 12

Try this different and refreshing cheesecake for a change of pace.

2 **pounds ricotta cheese**
6 **eggs**
1¼ **cups granulated sugar**
2 **teaspoons vanilla extract**
⅓ **cup heavy cream**
1½ **tablespoons grated orange zest**

1 **(12-ounce) package miniature semisweet chocolate chips (2 cups)**
½ **cup chopped blanched almonds**
   Powdered sugar

1. Preheat oven to 375°F. In a large bowl, beat together ricotta cheese, eggs, granulated sugar, and vanilla with an electric mixer on medium speed until fluffy, about 3 to 4 minutes. Beat in cream and orange zest. Stir in chocolate chips.

2. Turn batter into a buttered 9-inch springform pan. Sprinkle almonds over top. Bake 60 to 70 minutes or until golden and set. Let cheesecake cool to room temperature, then refrigerate until well chilled, 4 to 5 hours. Run a knife around edge of pan to loosen cake and remove springform side of pan. Before serving, sift powdered sugar over top, if desired.

---

59   CHOCOLATE RASPBERRY TRUFFLE CHEESECAKE

Prep: 30 minutes   Cook: 1¼ to 1½ hours   Chill: 6 hours
Serves: 12 to 16

This cake is rich, loaded with chocolate and raspberry jam. Serve small slices—a little goes a long way.

1 **(9-ounce) package chocolate wafer cookies**
3 **tablespoons butter, melted**
12 **ounces semisweet chocolate chips (2 cups)**
1½ **cups heavy cream**
¾ **cup seedless red raspberry jam**

2 **(8-ounce) packages cream cheese, softened**
¾ **cup sugar**
4 **eggs**
2 **teaspoons vanilla extract**

1. Preheat oven to 325°F. In a food processor, grind cookies into fine crumbs. Add melted butter and process until thoroughly mixed. Press into bottom and about 1 inch up sides of a 9-inch springform pan. Refrigerate crust while preparing filling.

2. In a 2-quart glass bowl, combine chocolate chips and 1 cup cream. Heat in a microwave oven on High 3 to 4 minutes, or until mixture is smooth, stirring twice. Mix in jam and stir until dissolved. Let cool 10 minutes.

3. In a large bowl, beat together cream cheese and sugar with an electric mixer on medium speed until smooth, 1 to 2 minutes. Add eggs, one at a time, beating well after each addition. Add vanilla and chocolate-raspberry mixture and beat 5 minutes. Pour mixture into chilled crust.

4. Bake 1¼ to 1½ hours, or until cheesecake is set around edges but still jiggles slightly in center. Let cake cool, then refrigerate until well chilled, 6 hours or overnight.

5. When ready to serve, run a knife around edge of pan to loosen cake and remove springform side of pan. Whip remaining ½ cup cream and, using a pastry bag fitted with a ½-inch star tip, pipe a border around edges of cheesecake.

---

60   WHITE CHOCOLATE RASPBERRY CHEESECAKE

Prep: 25 minutes   Cook: 64 to 70 minutes   Chill: 6 hours
Serves: 12

This cheesecake is best served within a day or two of making.

Chocolate Pastry Crust (page 57)
4 (8-ounce) packages cream cheese, softened
¾ cup sugar
4 eggs
¾ cup sour cream
2 teaspoons vanilla extract

1 tablespoon cornstarch
8 ounces imported white chocolate, cut into ½- to ¾-inch pieces
⅔ cup seedless red raspberry jam, melted

1. Preheat oven to 400°F. Prepare Chocolate Pastry Crust, but do not refrigerate. Press evenly into bottom and three quarters way up sides of a 9-inch springform pan. Refrigerate 15 minutes.

2. Bake crust 9 to 10 minutes. Let cool.

3. Meanwhile, prepare filling. In a large bowl, beat together cream cheese and sugar with an electric mixer on medium speed until light and fluffy, 1 to 2 minutes. Beat in eggs, one at a time, until thoroughly blended. Beat in sour cream, vanilla, and cornstarch until blended. Beat 3 to 4 minutes longer.

4. Arrange white chocolate pieces in a single layer over bottom of cooled crust. Spoon two thirds of cream cheese filling over white chocolate. Drop teaspoonfuls of jam over surface of cream cheese filling. Top with remaining cream cheese filling; spread evenly. Run a knife gently across and through jam and cream cheese mixture for a swirled or marbled effect.

5. Bake 15 minutes. Reduce oven temperature to 275°F and bake 40 to 45 minutes longer, or until cheesecake is set around edges but still jiggles slightly in center. Let cake cool completely to room temperature, then refrigerate until chilled, 6 hours or overnight. Run a sharp knife around edge of pan to loosen cake and remove springform side of pan.

61   WHITE CHOCOLATE CHEESECAKE

Prep: 15 minutes   Cook: 60 to 65 minutes   Chill: 6 hours
Serves: 8 to 10

For a truly dramatic presentation, garnish with rosettes of whipped cream and white or dark chocolate leaves before serving.

1½ cups chocolate wafer cookie
       crumbs
2 tablespoons butter, melted
3 (8-ounce) packages cream
       cheese, softened
½ cup sugar

5 eggs
1 tablespoon vanilla extract
14 ounces imported white
       chocolate, melted and
       cooled

1. Preheat oven to 325°F. To prepare crust, in a medium bowl, combine cookie crumbs and butter; mix until well blended. Press into bottom and halfway up sides of a greased 8½- or 9-inch springform pan. Line outside of pan with a double thickness of aluminum foil, bringing foil up around sides to prevent butter from leaking out of pan.

2. In a large bowl, beat together cream cheese and sugar with an electric mixer on medium speed until light and fluffy, about 2 minutes. Beat in eggs and vanilla until smooth, about 2 minutes. Then beat in white chocolate until smooth. Pour filling into prepared crust.

3. Bake 60 to 65 minutes, or until cake barely jiggles in center. Let cake cool, then refrigerate until chilled, 6 hours or overnight. Run a sharp knife around edge of pan to loosen cake and remove springform side of pan.

62   PEANUT BUTTER 'N' CHOCOLATE CHEESECAKE SQUARES

Prep: 20 minutes   Cook: 30 to 35 minutes   Makes: 50

These have been designed to serve as bar-type cookies and make plenty for a crowd. If you want to serve larger squares, don't hesitate. Peanut butter fans will cheer!

1 (20-ounce) package
       refrigerated chocolate
       chocolate chip cookie
       dough
3 (8-ounce) packages cream
       cheese, softened

1 cup sugar
¾ cup smooth or crunchy
       peanut butter
4 eggs
½ cup heavy cream

1. Preheat oven to 350°F. Line a 10 x 15-inch jelly-roll pan with foil and grease well. Cut cookie dough into 4 lengthwise pieces and place on foil-lined pan. Press with heel of hand to evenly spread over bottom of pan to make a crust. Smooth with a table knife. Bake 8 minutes.

2. Meanwhile, prepare cheesecake filling. In a large bowl, beat together cream cheese, sugar, and peanut butter with an electric mixer on medium speed until light and fluffy, 2 to 3 minutes. Add eggs and cream and beat on high 4 minutes.

3. Spread filling evenly over prebaked crust. Bake 22 to 27 minutes, or until just set. Cool to room temperature, then refrigerate until chilled. To serve, cut into 50 squares; carefully remove foil from bottom of squares.

63 CHOCOLATE PECAN CHEESECAKE
Prep: 45 minutes   Cook: 80 to 85 minutes   Chill: 6 hours
Serves: 12 to 14

This dessert has two layers—the bottom is similar to chocolate pecan pie and the top is plain cheesecake. To speed preparation time, use a packaged refrigerator-type pie crust. Or if you like, substitute a chocolate cookie-type crust. This cheesecake freezes well.

1 prepared unbaked refrigerated 9-inch pie crust
1 heaping teaspoon flour
1 stick (4 ounces) butter, melted
⅓ cup unsweetened cocoa powder
½ cup heavy cream
½ cup corn syrup

1½ cups sugar
2½ cups chopped pecans
2 (8-ounce) packages cream cheese, softened
3 eggs
2 teaspoons vanilla extract
Whipped cream, pecan halves, and chocolate curls

1. Remove pie crust from package and let stand at room temperature 15 to 20 minutes to soften slightly. Preheat oven to 400°F. Unfold crust. Peel off one plastic sheet. Press out fold lines and repair any cracks by pushing dough together with fingers and water if necessary. Sprinkle flour over crust, spreading over entire surface to edges. Place crust, floured side down, in a 9½-inch springform pan. Peel off plastic sheet. Ease crust into pan, pressing firmly against bottom and partway up sides of pan. Place a piece of aluminum foil over crust; press in gently. Bake 8 to 10 minutes. Remove foil and bake 5 minutes longer.

2. Meanwhile, in a medium bowl, mix together melted butter, cocoa, cream, corn syrup, and ¾ cup sugar until well blended. Stir in pecans. Spoon into prebaked pie shell. Bake 15 minutes.

3. Meanwhile, in a large bowl, beat together cream cheese, eggs, vanilla, and remaining ¾ cup sugar with an electric mixer on medium speed until light and fluffy, 2 to 3 minutes. Pour over pecan layer.

4. Reduce oven temperature to 325°F. Bake 50 to 55 minutes, or until cake barely jiggles in center. Let cake cool to room temperature, then refrigerate 6 hours or overnight. Run a sharp knife around edge of pan to loosen cake and remove springform side of pan. Before serving, decorate cake with whipped cream, pecans, and chocolate curls, if desired.

Chapter 3

Chocolate in a Crust

Mention the word pie, and some cooks turn the other way. More than likely they fear making the crust, which really isn't that difficult. In fact, modern cooks are blessed with a commercial product known as all-ready pie crusts, which are available in the refrigerated deli sections of most supermarkets. The crusts are rolled out and ready to go into a pie pan or tart pan. Quality and texture-wise they are head and shoulders above their frozen counterparts. And in fact, when I've used them, which is often these days, people ask for my pie crust recipe! I've shared my secret with many an excellent baker!

So pie-making need no longer be intimidating. This chapter offers a wealth of terrific filling options bursting with chocolate flavor. The pies go together in a jiffy too. Besides the traditional pastry crust, crusts here run the gamut from chocolate pastry to various flavor cookie crumbs to butter cookie crusts to meringues. Crumb crusts made with store-bought cookies are the easiest and most popular of all. For best results, crush the cookies in a food processor and then add melted butter (to bind the mixture), processing until well blended. If using a 9-ounce box of chocolate wafer cookie crumbs, you can figure that it will yield about 2⅓ cups crumbs. If you opt to make your own pie pastry from scratch, use chilled fat so that it remains firm during mixing.

If you plan to make tarts, which by their very nature are shallower than pies, invest in a round fluted metal tart pan with a removable bottom. The sizes most often called for in recipes are 9½ and 11 inches in diameter. Most of these pie recipes call for a 9-inch pie pan. Very little other equipment is needed for these desserts.

This chapter includes fast-fix no-bake pies as well as many that are baked. In addition, several tarts, some laden with beautiful, fresh seasonal fruits, are offered. Here's a rundown of some of my favorites that may become yours too: Chocolate Macadamia Pie, Chocolate Angel Pie, Strawberry Chocolate Cream Cheese Pie, Easy Chocolate-Coffee Mousse Pie, Quick Crustless Fudge Pie, and Chocolate Pecan Pie.

64   CHOCOLATE CHIP PECAN PIE

Prep: 15 minutes   Cook: 40 to 50 minutes   Serves: 6 to 7

This is best served slightly warm topped with a dollop of whipped cream.

3 eggs
⅔ cup sugar
½ teaspoon salt
5 tablespoons butter, melted
1 cup dark corn syrup
1⅓ cups chopped pecans

6 ounces semisweet chocolate chips (1 cup)
1 (9-inch) unbaked pastry crust (store-bought or homemade)
Whipped cream

1. Preheat oven to 375°F. In a medium bowl, whisk together eggs, sugar, salt, melted butter, and corn syrup until well mixed. Stir in pecans and chocolate chips.

2. Turn into unbaked crust. Bake 40 to 50 minutes, or until browned. Serve warm, topped with whipped cream.

65   STRAWBERRY CHOCOLATE CREAM CHEESE PIE

Prep: 20 minutes   Cook: none   Chill: 2 hours   Serves: 8

When strawberries are in season, here's a good way for chocolate lovers to enjoy them.

1 (8-ounce) package cream cheese, softened
½ cup powdered sugar
2 tablespoons Cointreau or orange juice
6 ounces semisweet chocolate chips (1 cup), melted
1 cup heavy cream, whipped

1 (9-inch) baked, cooled Chocolate Pastry Crust (recipe follows) or regular pastry crust
2 pints fresh whole strawberries
3 to 4 tablespoons orange marmalade or apricot jam

1. In a medium bowl, mix together cream cheese, powdered sugar, and Cointreau until smooth. Add melted chocolate and stir until well blended. Fold in whipped cream. Spread evenly in baked crust. Refrigerate until chilled, 2 to 3 hours or overnight.

2. Rinse and hull strawberries; drain on paper towels. Set berries, pointed side up, on top of pie, covering entire surface.

3. Warm marmalade in microwave oven or over low heat until melted. Brush over strawberries. Refrigerate for up to 5 hours before serving.

NOTE: *A 21-ounce can cherry pie topping and filling can be used instead of strawberries and marmalade to top pie.*

66   CHOCOLATE PASTRY CRUST

Prep: 15 minutes   Cook: 10 to 12 minutes
Makes: a single 9-inch crust

Any time you desire a chocolate pie crust, try this versatile one. Bake and fill as desired.

1 cup flour	1 stick (4 ounces) cold butter,
⅓ cup unsweetened cocoa	cut up
powder	1 teaspoon vanilla extract
¼ cup sugar	

1. In food processor, combine flour, cocoa, and sugar. Process until well blended, about 15 to 20 seconds. Add butter; turn machine quickly on and off until mixture is in fine crumbs.

2. With machine on, add vanilla and 2 tablespoons cold water through feed tube. Process just until dough forms ball. Wrap dough in plastic wrap and flatten into a round disc. Refrigerate 15 to 20 minutes.

3. Roll out dough on a floured surface into a 12-inch circle. Fold in half and ease gently into a lightly greased 9-inch pie pan. Unfold dough, trim, and flute edge. Prick with fork at ½-inch intervals. Refrigerate or freeze 15 minutes.

4. Preheat oven to 400°F. Bake 10 to 12 minutes or until set. Cool before filling.

67   CHOCOLATE ANGEL PIE

Prep: 15 minutes   Cook: 60 to 70 minutes   Chill: 2 to 3 hours
Serves: 6 to 8

This is a classic—light and easy. Whenever you have extra egg whites on hand, reach for this recipe. The filling is a rich mousse-like chocolate chantilly, made without eggs.

4 egg whites	1 teaspoon vanilla extract
¼ teaspoon cream of tartar	Chocolate Chantilly (recipe
¼ teaspoon salt	follows)
1 cup sugar	

1. Preheat oven to 275°F. In a medium bowl, beat egg whites with cream of tartar and salt with an electric mixer on medium speed until soft peaks form. Turn mixer to high and gradually beat in sugar. Add vanilla and beat until glossy, stiff peaks form.

2. Spread meringue in a greased 9-inch pie pan, building up the sides. Bake 60 to 70 minutes, until meringue is cream colored. Turn oven off; leave in oven with door ajar 1 hour. Remove from oven and let cool to room temperature.

3. When shell is cool, fill with Chocolate Chantilly. Refrigerate until chilled, 2 to 3 hours.

68 CHOCOLATE CHANTILLY
Prep: 10 minutes   Cook: 1½ minutes   Chill: 2 to 3 hours   Serves: 6

This is rich and mousse-like but it's made without eggs—a boon these days, when there is so much concern about salmonella in raw eggs. Use it as a pie or cake filling, or simply serve it in stemmed glasses like a chocolate mousse. This is one idea you'll want to add to your "basics" recipe repertoire.

½ cup sugar
4 (1-ounce) squares
    unsweetened chocolate,
    cut up

1 teaspoon vanilla extract
1 cup heavy cream

1. In a 1-quart bowl, combine sugar, chocolate, and ¼ cup water. Heat in a microwave oven on High about 1½ minutes, or until chocolate is melted and mixture is smooth when stirred. Stir in vanilla. Let cool.

2. Whip cream until it forms soft peaks. Fold into cooled chocolate mixture. Spoon chantilly into a large meringue shell, individual meringue shells, or stemmed glasses or dessert dishes. Cover and refrigerate until set, 2 to 3 hours.

69 GERMAN'S CHOCOLATE PIE
Prep: 15 minutes   Cook: 30 to 35 minutes   Serves: 6 to 8

This classic is a favorite with those who like the flavors of coconut, pecans, and chocolate.

1 (4-ounce) bar German's
    sweet baking chocolate,
    broken up
1 cup heavy cream
4 tablespoons butter
2 eggs
1 teaspoon vanilla extract
⅛ teaspoon salt

¾ cup sugar
3 tablespoons cornstarch
1 cup chopped pecans
1 (9-inch) unbaked pastry
    shell
1⅓ cups flaked or shredded
    coconut
Whipped cream

1. Preheat oven to 375°F. In a 1-quart glass bowl, combine chocolate, cream, and butter. Heat in a microwave oven on High 2 to 2½ minutes, or until chocolate is melted and mixture is smooth when stirred.

2. In a medium bowl, whisk together eggs, vanilla, salt, and sugar until well blended. Whisk in cornstarch until thoroughly mixed. Whisk egg mixture into chocolate mixture until well blended. Stir in pecans. Turn into unbaked pastry shell. Sprinkle coconut on top and, using a knife, swirl into chocolate filling.

3. Bake 30 to 35 minutes, or until almost set and golden brown. Let cool. Garnish with whipped cream, if desired.

70   QUICK CHOCOLATE CHANTILLY PIE

Prep: 20 minutes   Cook: 12 to 14 minutes   Chill: 3 hours
Serves: 8 to 10

1 cup flour
¼ cup unsweetened cocoa
     powder
¼ cup sugar
1 stick (4 ounces) butter,
     softened
¼ cup finely chopped walnuts,
     almonds, or pecans
½ teaspoon vanilla extract

6 ounces semisweet or
     bittersweet chocolate, cut
     up
½ cup brewed coffee
2 tablespoons brandy
2 cups heavy cream
     Raspberry Sauce (recipe
     follows) or ½ pint fresh
     raspberries

1. Preheat oven to 400°F. Make crust: In a medium bowl, combine flour, cocoa, sugar, butter, nuts, and vanilla. Blend with a fork until mixture is in fine crumbs. Knead until dough holds together. Press into bottom and up sides of deep-dish 9-inch pie dish. Bake 12 to 14 minutes, or until set. Let crust cool.

2. To make filling, in a 1-quart glass bowl, combine chocolate and coffee. Heat in microwave oven on High 1 minute; stir. Cook 1 minute longer, or until chocolate is melted and smooth when stirred. Stir in brandy. Let stand until cool.

3. In a medium bowl, whip cream with an electric mixer on high speed until stiff peaks form. Add cool chocolate mixture and beat on medium speed until well blended. Turn into cooled crust. Swirl top with the back of a spoon.

4. Refrigerate until set, several hours or overnight. Serve with Raspberry Sauce or top with fresh raspberries, if desired.

RASPBERRY SAUCE

This sauce is great to serve over chocolate truffle cakes, terrines, and mousses and to line dessert plates.

2 (12-ounce) bags frozen
     unsweetened red
     raspberries, thawed
¾ cup powdered sugar

2 tablespoons Grand Marnier,
     raspberry-flavored
     liqueur, or other liqueur
     of your choice

1. In a food processor, combine thawed raspberries and powdered sugar. Process until smooth. Add Grand Marnier and process to blend well.

2. To remove seeds, press puree through a wire strainer placed over a non-reactive bowl. Using a rubber spatula, scrape underside of strainer. Discard seeds. Serve immediately or cover and refrigerate up to 2 days. Mix before serving.

71   YOSEMITE MUD BAVARIAN PIE
Prep: 40 minutes   Cook: about 3 minutes   Chill: 6 hours
Serves: 6 to 8

This fabulous pie sports a chocolate coconut crust, a chocolate Bavarian filling, and a rocky road-style topping—enough to send chocolate lovers into ecstasy.

1 envelope unflavored gelatin
½ cup brewed strong coffee, at room temperature
⅔ cup sugar
¾ cup milk
½ cup firmly packed unsweetened cocoa powder
1 cup plus 1 tablespoon heavy cream

Chocolate Coconut Crust (recipe follows)
1½ cups miniature marshmallows
1 cup toasted walnut pieces
¼ cup semisweet chocolate chips
2 tablespoons butter

1. To make Bavarian filling, in a glass measure, sprinkle gelatin over coffee to soften; set aside. In a medium saucepan, whisk together sugar, milk, and cocoa. Bring to a simmer over medium heat. Reduce heat to low and cook 2 minutes. Remove from heat; stir in reserved gelatin mixture and refrigerate until mixture holds its shape.

2. Whip 1 cup cream until stiff and fold into gelatin mixture until no streaks of white remain. Turn into chilled Chocolate Coconut Crust. Sprinkle marshmallows and walnuts over top. Refrigerate 6 hours or overnight.

3. Just before serving, make topping: In a small glass bowl, melt chocolate chips and butter in a microwave oven on High 30 to 40 seconds, or until melted and smooth when stirred. Stir in remaining 1 tablespoon cream. Let cool for 5 minutes, then drizzle over pie and serve.

72   CHOCOLATE COCONUT CRUST
Prep: 2 minutes   Cook: 2 to 3 minutes   Makes: a single 9-inch crust

3 tablespoons butter
½ cup semisweet chocolate chips

1½ cups flaked coconut
½ cup chopped walnuts

In a medium-size heavy saucepan, melt butter and chocolate over low heat, stirring occasionally, 2 to 3 minutes. Stir in coconut and walnuts, mixing well. Press mixture into bottom and up sides of a lightly buttered 9-inch pie pan. Refrigerate until ready to use.

73   CHOCOLATE DEVIL PIE
Prep: 10 minutes   Cook: 32 to 37 minutes   Serves: 10

This is a cross between a chocolate truffle and a brownie pie. It's wonderfully rich but light.

5   (1-ounce) squares
    unsweetened chocolate,
    cut up
1½ sticks (6 ounces) butter
2   cups sugar
4   eggs

⅓   cup heavy cream
2   teaspoons vanilla extract
1   unbaked 10-inch deep-dish
    pastry crust
    Whipped cream

1. Preheat oven to 350°F. In a 2-quart glass bowl, melt chocolate and butter in a microwave oven on High 1½ to 2 minutes, stirring once or twice until smooth and blended.

2. Add sugar, eggs, cream, and vanilla. Whisk until well blended. Turn into crust.

3. Bake 30 to 35 minutes, or until set. Cover edges of crust with foil during last 10 minutes of baking time, if necessary, to prevent burning. Serve warm or at room temperature, topped with whipped cream.

74   CHOCOLATE MACADAMIA PIE
Prep: 15 minutes   Cook: 30 to 35 minutes   Chill: 2 hours
Serves: 6 to 7

This is a cinch to prepare and special enough for guests. Serve topped with whipped cream or vanilla ice cream.

1   cup packed brown sugar
1   tablespoon flour
2   eggs
5   tablespoons butter, melted
2   tablespoons milk
2   teaspoons vanilla extract
1   (7-ounce) jar dry-roasted
    macadamia nuts (about
    1½ cups)

6   ounces semisweet chocolate
    chips (1 cup)
1   cup shredded or flaked
    coconut
1   (9-inch) unbaked pie crust

1. Preheat oven to 350°F. In a large bowl, combine brown sugar and flour. With a fork or wooden spoon (not an electric mixer), beat in eggs, butter, milk, and vanilla. Stir in nuts, chocolate chips, and coconut until well mixed.

2. Turn into pie crust. Bake 30 to 35 minutes, until just barely set. Let pie cool, then refrigerate until set, at least 2 hours.

75   EASY AS PIE BLACK AND WHITE CHOCOLATE PIE
Prep: 15 minutes   Cook: 35 minutes   Serves: 8

This crustless pie, filled with bittersweet and white chocolate chunks, can be thrown together in a jiffy with a stick of pie crust mix.

4 tablespoons butter, softened
¾ cup packed brown sugar
3 eggs
1 teaspoon vanilla extract
1 teaspoon grated orange zest
3 ounces bittersweet chocolate, cut into ½-inch chunks
½ cup white chocolate chunks (½-inch pieces)
⅔ cup chopped pecans
1 stick pie-crust mix (½ of an 11-ounce package)
Whipped cream

1. Preheat oven to 325°F. In a medium bowl, beat together butter and brown sugar with an electric mixer on medium speed until creamy. Beat in eggs, vanilla, and orange zest until well blended; mixture may look slightly curdled. Stir in bittersweet and white chocolate chunks and pecans. Crumble pie-crust mix on top, stirring with a fork until well blended.

2. Turn into a greased 9-inch pie plate. Bake 35 minutes, or until set. Let pie cool before serving, topped with whipped cream.

76   FABULOUS COFFEE-CHOCOLATE PIE
Prep: 30 minutes   Cook: none   Chill: 4 hours   Serves: 8

No chocolate book would be complete without this pie, better known as Blum's Coffee-Toffee Pie, and credited to the San Francisco confectionery and dessert shop. The dessert shop no longer exists, but the pie, which has been around for years, lives on, and is one I've made often. It's rich, but it always rates raves. Here's my rendition, which includes a couple of minor changes from the original.

1 stick (4 ounces) butter, softened
2 (1-ounce) squares unsweetened chocolate, melted and cooled
¾ cup packed light brown sugar
1 tablespoon plus 2 teaspoons instant coffee powder
2 eggs*
Easy Chocolate Walnut Crust (recipe follows)
1 cup heavy cream
¼ cup powdered sugar
Chocolate curls

1. In a medium bowl, beat together butter, chocolate, brown sugar, and 2 teaspoons coffee powder with an electric mixer on medium speed until fluffy, about 2 minutes. Beat in eggs, one at a time, beating 3 to 4 minutes after each addition.

2. Turn into cold Easy Chocolate Walnut Crust, spreading evenly. Refrigerate at least 4 hours or overnight.

3. Up to 2 hours before serving, make topping: In a medium bowl, beat cream with remaining 1 tablespoon coffee powder and powdered sugar until stiff. Decorate top of pie with swirls of cream or pipe through a pastry bag fitted with a large star tip. Garnish with chocolate curls. Refrigerate until serving time. Use sharp knife to cut through crust and into slices to serve.

   * CAUTION: *Because of the possible threat of salmonella—a bacteria that causes food poisoning—from raw eggs, U.S. Government officials recommend that the very young, the elderly, pregnant women, and people with serious illnesses or weakened immune systems not eat raw or lightly cooked eggs. Keep this in mind and consume raw or lightly cooked eggs at your own risk.*

---

77 EASY CHOCOLATE WALNUT CRUST
Prep: 10 minutes   Cook: 14 to 15 minutes   Makes: a single 9-inch crust

1 (1-ounce) square
  unsweetened chocolate,
  cut up
1 stick pie-crust mix (½ of an
  11-ounce package)

¼ cup packed light brown
  sugar
¾ cup finely chopped walnuts
1 teaspoon vanilla extract

1. Preheat oven to 375°F. In a food processor, grate chocolate.

2. Crumble pie-crust stick into a medium bowl. Stir in grated chocolate, brown sugar, and nuts. Drizzle vanilla and 1 tablespoon cold water over mixture and mix with a fork until well blended. Dough will be crumbly.

3. Turn into a well-greased deep 9-inch pie plate and press evenly over bottom and up sides. Bake in center of oven 14 to 15 minutes. Let cool, then refrigerate until chilled.

---

78 CHOCOLATE BUTTERMILK WALNUT PIE
Prep: 15 minutes   Cook: 40 to 45 minutes   Serves: 8

1⅔ cups sugar
1 cup buttermilk
½ cup buttermilk baking mix
  (such as Bisquick)
½ cup unsweetened cocoa
  powder

4 tablespoons butter or
  margarine, melted
3 eggs
2 teaspoons vanilla extract
1 cup chopped walnuts
  Vanilla or coffee ice cream

1. Preheat oven to 350°F. In a food processor, combine sugar, buttermilk, baking mix, cocoa, melted butter, eggs, and vanilla. Process until smooth and well blended, scraping down sides of bowl once or twice, 1 to 2 minutes.

2. Pour filling into a well-greased 9-inch pie pan. Sprinkle walnuts on top. Bake 40 to 45 minutes, or until set. Serve pie warm or cold, topped with scoops of ice cream.

79   QUICK CRUSTLESS FUDGE PIE
Prep: 15 minutes   Cook: 25 to 30 minutes   Serves: 8

This is one of those in-a-hurry creation to whip up on last-minute notice when friends or relatives are stopping by for coffee, dinner, or dessert.

4 tablespoons butter	¾ cup packed brown sugar
12 ounces semisweet chocolate chips (2 cups)	3 eggs
	¼ cup flour
¼ cup dark or amber rum	1½ cups coarsely chopped
2 teaspoons instant coffee powder	walnuts
	Whipped cream

1. Preheat oven to 350°F. In a 2-quart glass bowl, combine butter and chocolate. Heat in a microwave oven on High 1¼ to 1¾ minutes, until mixture is melted and smooth when stirred. Stir in rum, coffee powder, brown sugar, eggs, and flour; mix until smooth and well blended. Stir in 1 cup nuts.

2. Turn into a greased 9-inch glass pie plate. Sprinkle remaining ½ cup nuts on top. Bake 25 to 30 minutes or until puffed (pie should still be moist inside). Do not overbake. Let pie cool to room temperature before serving, topped with whipped cream.

---

80   CHOCOLATE MOUSSE PIE
Prep: 45 minutes   Cook: about 15 minutes   Chill: 4 hours
Serves: 12

My friend Harriet Part, who is a terrific cook, shared this recipe with me. Although it's a bit involved, the results are worth the lengthy preparation time. This dessert has always been a favorite with all who taste it.

1 cup sugar	⅓ cup dark rum
3 egg whites	2 cups heavy cream, whipped
Dash of salt	Chocolate Crumb Crust
⅛ teaspoon cream of tartar	(recipe follows)
½ teaspoon vanilla extract	Chocolate leaves or shaved
12 ounces semisweet or bittersweet chocolate, cut up	chocolate and whipped cream
3 (1-ounce) squares unsweetened chocolate, cut up	

1. In a medium saucepan, combine sugar and ⅓ cup water. Cook over medium-high heat, swirling pan slowly—not stirring—until syrup comes to a boil. Continue swirling until mixture turns from cloudy to clear. Cover pan, reduce heat to low, and simmer while beating egg whites.

2. In a large bowl, beat egg whites with an electric mixer on medium speed for 30 seconds. Add salt and cream of tartar, and beat with mixer on high speed until egg whites form stiff peaks. Beat in vanilla.

3. Remove cover from sugar syrup pan, increase heat to medium-high, and boil until syrup reaches 238°F on a candy thermometer or forms a soft ball.

4. Resume beating egg whites with mixer on medium speed while gradually pouring in boiling syrup in a thin stream. Beat until meringue cools and stiff peaks form, 8 to 10 minutes.

5. In a 1-quart glass bowl, combine semisweet and unsweetened chocolate and rum. Heat in microwave oven on High 1½ to 2 minutes, or until chocolate is melted and smooth when stirred. Let cool.

6. Using electric mixer on medium speed, beat chocolate mixture into meringue. Let cool. Fold in whipped cream. Spoon filling evenly into chilled Chocolate Crumb Crust. Refrigerate until firm, 4 hours or overnight. Or freeze up to 4 weeks, then thaw in refrigerator 8 to 10 hours before serving. Garnish as desired with chocolate leaves and additional whipped cream.

CHOCOLATE CRUMB CRUST

2 cups chocolate wafer cookie crumbs	1½ tablespoons sugar 5 tablespoons butter, melted

Preheat oven to 350°F. In a medium bowl, combine cookie crumbs, sugar, and butter; mix well. Press into bottom and partway up sides of a 10-inch springform pan. Bake 10 to 12 minutes. Let cool.

---

81   NO-BAKE CHOCOLATE RICOTTA PIE
Prep: 10 minutes   Cook: none   Chill: 3 hours   Serves: 6 to 8

Here's a fast-fix dessert that's not overly sweet.

1 (15- or 16-ounce) container low-fat ricotta cheese	½ cup chopped pistachio nuts
¼ cup powdered sugar	1 (9-inch) baked Chocolate Wafer Crust (page 135)
1 teaspoon vanilla extract	Whipped cream and shaved chocolate
2 tablespoons heavy cream	
6 ounces semisweet chocolate chips (1 cup), melted	

1. In a medium bowl, beat together ricotta cheese, powdered sugar, vanilla, and cream with an electric mixer on medium speed until light and fluffy, 2 to 3 minutes. Beat in melted chocolate until well blended. Stir in pistachio nuts.

2. Turn into Chocolate Wafer Crust. Refrigerate until set, several hours or overnight. Decorate top with whipped cream and shaved chocolate.

82   CHOCOLATE PECAN PIE
Prep: 15 minutes   Cook: 36 to 41 minutes   Serves: 8 to 10

This is based on a recipe my mother picked up years ago, when we lived in Virginia. I've added chocolate, and it's terrific.

4 (1-ounce) squares unsweetened chocolate
4 tablespoons butter
2 cups packed brown sugar
2 eggs
¼ cup milk
1 teaspoon vanilla extract
¼ teaspoon salt
3 tablespoons flour

2 cups coarsely chopped pecans (8 ounces)
1 (9-inch) unbaked pastry shell
3 ounces bittersweet or semisweet chocolate, cut into ½-inch chunks
Whipped cream

1. Preheat oven to 375°F. In a 1-quart glass bowl, combine unsweetened chocolate and butter. Heat in a microwave oven on High 1 minute, or until melted and smooth when stirred. Add brown sugar, eggs, milk, vanilla, salt, and flour and mix until well blended.

2. Spread pecans over bottom of unbaked pastry shell. Sprinkle bittersweet chocolate pieces over nuts. Top with filling.

3. Bake 35 to 40 minutes, or until set. Cover edges of pie crust with foil during last 15 minutes of baking time if necessary, to prevent overbrowning. Serve warm or chilled, with whipped cream on the side.

83   CHOCOLATE CHIFFON PIE
Prep: 25 minutes   Cook: about 5 minutes   Chill: 3 hours   Serves: 6 to 8

This was one of my very favorite childhood desserts. Whenever my mother made it for company, she always made an extra pie for us children for dessert. It tastes as good today as I remember it did then. Her secret was the orange zest in the chiffon mixture.

1 envelope unflavored gelatin
½ cup boiling water
2 (1-ounce) squares unsweetened chocolate
1 cup sugar
3 eggs,* separated
¼ teaspoon salt

½ teaspoon vanilla extract
2 teaspoons grated orange zest
1 (9-inch) baked, cooled pastry shell
¾ cup heavy cream, whipped
⅓ cup chopped roasted almonds

1. In a 1-cup glass measure, sprinkle gelatin over ¼ cup cold water to soften. Let stand 5 minutes. In a medium saucepan, combine boiling water and chocolate. Heat together over medium-low heat, whisking constantly, until chocolate is melted and smooth. Remove from heat. Stir gelatin mixture and add to hot chocolate mixture. Whisk until gelatin is dissolved. Whisk in ½ cup sugar until blended, then whisk in egg yolks quickly along with salt, vanilla, and orange zest. Cover and refrigerate until partially set.

2. In a medium bowl, beat egg whites with an electric mixer on medium speed until stiff enough to mound when beater is raised. Gradually add remaining ½ cup sugar. Beat on high speed until stiff peaks form. Fold egg whites into partially set chocolate mixture until well blended.

3. Turn filling into pastry shell. Refrigerate until set, several hours or overnight. Just before serving, spread whipped cream over pie and top with almonds. Refrigerate any leftovers.

   * **CAUTION:** *Because of the possible threat of salmonella—a bacteria that causes food poisoning from raw eggs, U.S. Government officials recommend that the very young, the elderly, pregnant women, and people with serious illnesses or weakened immune systems not eat raw or lightly cooked eggs. Keep this in mind and consume raw or lightly cooked eggs at your own risk.*

84   FRESH FRUIT AND CHOCOLATE TART
Prep: 30 minutes   Cook: 15 to 17 minutes   Chill: 2 hours   Serves: 8

Showcase the season's freshest fruit in this lovely tart with a pecan crust and milk chocolate filling. Serve with whipped cream or crème fraîche on the side for an added fillip.

1¼ cups flour
 1 stick (4 ounces) butter, softened
 3 tablespoons sugar
 1 teaspoon vanilla extract
¼ cup finely chopped pecans or walnuts
 1 cup milk chocolate chips

⅓ cup sour cream
Fresh seasonal fruit, such as peaches, nectarines, cantaloupe, seedless grapes, berries
 3 to 4 tablespoons apricot or seedless raspberry jam

1. Preheat oven to 400°F. To make crust, in a medium bowl, combine flour, butter, sugar, ½ teaspoon vanilla, and pecans. Blend with a fork until mixture resembles fine crumbs. Knead until dough holds together. Press dough firmly and evenly onto bottom and up sides of a 9½-inch fluted metal tart pan with removable bottom. Bake 14 to 16 minutes, or until golden. Let cool.

2. To prepare filling, in a 2-cup glass measuring cup, heat chocolate chips in a microwave oven on High about 1 minute, or until completely melted and smooth when stirred. Stir in sour cream and remaining ½ teaspoon vanilla. Spread filling evenly over cooled crust. Refrigerate 2 to 3 hours, or overnight.

3. About 1 hour before serving, cut peaches, nectarines, or cantaloupe into slices or crescents; drain fruit on paper towels if extremely juicy. Arrange in concentric circles or other design on top of chocolate filling. Fill in with grapes and berries until top of pie is completely covered with fruit. Warm jam in a microwave oven or over low heat until melted. Brush jam over fruit. Refrigerate until serving time.

4. Just before serving, remove side of pan and set tart on a serving dish.

85   FESTIVE MOUSSE PIE

Prep: 45 minutes   Cook: 35 to 40 seconds   Chill: 4 hours
Serves: 10 to 12

This is a specialty of my friend Candi Stern, who traditionally serves it at her big bash on New Year's Day.

1   (9-ounce) package chocolate wafer cookies
1   tablespoon unsweetened cocoa powder
2½   teaspoons instant coffee powder
5   tablespoons unsalted butter, melted
1   envelope unflavored gelatin

1   (8-ounce) package cream cheese, softened
1   cup packed light brown sugar
3   eggs, separated*
6   ounces semisweet chocolate, melted and cooled
1½   teaspoons vanilla extract
3   cups heavy cream, whipped

1. To prepare crust, break up cookies into the bowl of a food processor. Add cocoa and 1½ teaspoons coffee powder. Process into fine crumbs. Add melted butter and process until well mixed. Press into bottom and about 1 inch up sides of a 9½-inch springform pan.

2. To prepare filling, in a 1-cup glass measure, sprinkle gelatin over 2 tablespoons cold water to soften. Let stand 5 minutes. Place in a microwave oven and heat on Medium 35 to 40 seconds, or until liquid is hot and gelatin is dissolved when stirred; set aside.

3. In a large bowl, beat cream cheese with an electric mixer on medium speed until fluffy, about 1 minute. Add ½ cup brown sugar and remaining 1 teaspoon coffee powder and beat until blended. Add egg yolks, one at a time, beating well after each addition. Beat in reserved gelatin; then beat in melted chocolate.

4. In a separate medium bowl, beat egg whites with clean beaters on medium speed until soft peaks form. Turn mixer to high speed and gradually beat in remaining ½ cup brown sugar and vanilla. Beat until stiff, glossy peaks form.

5. Fold egg whites and half of whipped cream into chocolate mixture. Turn into crust. Refrigerate until set, 4 hours or overnight. Or freeze up to 4 weeks, and then thaw in refrigerator 8 to 10 hours before serving. Several hours before serving, top with remaining whipped cream. Return to refrigerator until serving time.

> *** CAUTION:** *Because of the possible threat of salmonella—a bacteria that causes food poisoning—from raw eggs, U.S. Government officials recommend that the very young, the elderly, pregnant women, and people with serious illnesses or weakened immune systems not eat raw or lightly cooked eggs. Keep this in mind and consume raw or lightly cooked eggs at your own risk.*

86   EASY CHOCOLATE-COFFEE MOUSSE PIE
Prep: 30 minutes   Cook: 5 to 6 minutes   Chill: 3 hours   Serves: 12

This is a great ending for a Mexican meal. If you don't want to make a pie, simply spoon the mousse mixture into individual dessert dishes, wine goblets, or parfait glasses. Be sure to chill several hours before serving.

2 cups chocolate wafer cookie crumbs	12 ounces semisweet chocolate chips (2 cups)
1 cup plus 2 tablespoons sugar	⅓ cup coffee-flavored liqueur
5 tablespoons butter, melted	2 teaspoons vanilla extract
2 envelopes unflavored gelatin	2 cups heavy cream, whipped
¼ teaspoon salt	Whipped cream and shaved chocolate
2 cups milk	
1 teaspoon instant coffee powder	

1. To make crust, in a medium bowl, mix together chocolate crumbs, 2 tablespoons sugar, and melted butter. Press into bottom and about 1 inch up sides of a 10-inch springform pan.

2. To make filling, in a medium saucepan, mix together gelatin, remaining 1 cup sugar, and salt. Stir in milk, coffee powder, and chocolate chips. Cook over medium heat, stirring constantly, until chocolate melts and mixture is smooth and well blended. Remove from heat. Stir in liqueur and vanilla.

3. Refrigerate, stirring occasionally, until mixture mounds when dropped from a spoon. Fold in whipped cream. Spoon into prepared crust, spreading evenly. Refrigerate until set, 3 hours or overnight. At serving time, garnish with more whipped cream and shaved chocolate, if desired.

87   CHOCOLATE COCONUT PECAN PIE
Prep: 15 minutes   Cook: 70 to 75 minutes   Serves: 6 to 8

Easy and tasty.

3 eggs	1 cup chopped pecans
⅔ cup sugar	6 ounces semisweet chocolate chips (1 cup)
½ cup light corn syrup	1 (9-inch) unbaked deep-dish pastry crust
½ cup dark corn syrup	Whipped cream
4 tablespoons butter, melted	
1 teaspoon vanilla extract	
1 cup shredded coconut	

1. Preheat oven to 325°F. In a large bowl, whisk together eggs and sugar until well blended. Add light and dark corn syrups, butter, and vanilla. Whisk until combined. Stir in coconut, pecans, and chocolate chips.

2. Turn into pastry crust. Bake 70 to 75 minutes, or until center is almost set. Let cool before serving, topped with whipped cream.

88   IN-A-FLASH CHOCOLATE ORANGE PIE

Prep: 10 minutes   Cook: 1 to 2 minutes   Freeze: 4 hours
Serves: 6 to 8

This no-bake pie couldn't be easier. Keep one in the freezer in case unexpected guests drop by. Just before serving, garnish with dollops of whipped cream and chocolate curls if you think the pie needs dressing up.

6 ounces semisweet chocolate
   chips (1 cup)
⅓ cup milk
4 ounces cream cheese,
   softened
1 tablespoon grated orange
   zest

1 cup heavy cream
1 (8-inch) chocolate cookie
   crumb or graham cracker
   crumb crust (store-bought
   or homemade)

1. In a 1-quart glass bowl, heat chocolate chips and milk in a microwave oven on High 1 to 2 minutes, or until melted and smooth when stirred. Beat in cream cheese and orange zest until smooth. Let cool.

2. Whip cream until stiff. Fold whipped cream into chocolate mixture. Spoon filling into prepared crust. Freeze until firm, about 4 hours.

89   CHOCOLATE HAZELNUT TART

Prep: 25 minutes   Cook: 50 to 56 minutes   Serves: 10 to 12

1¼ cups hazelnuts
1 prepared (unbaked) 9-inch
   refrigerated pie crust
2 tablespoons plus 1½
   teaspoons flour
1 stick (4 ounces) unsalted
   butter
1¼ cups packed light brown
   sugar

3 (1-ounce) squares
   unsweetened chocolate,
   cut up
Dash of salt
2 eggs
1 teaspoon vanilla extract
¼ cup Frangelico hazelnut
   liqueur
1 cup heavy cream

1. Preheat oven to 350°F. Spread out hazelnuts on a small baking sheet. Bake 10 minutes, or until nuts are lightly browned and dark skins are cracked. Rub warm nuts in a terrycloth towel to remove as much of skins as possible. Raise oven temperature to 450°F.

2. Remove pie crust from refrigerator and let stand at room temperature for 15 minutes. Unfold crust. Peel off top plastic sheet. Press out fold lines and repair any cracks by pushing dough together with fingers (wet if necessary). Sprinkle 1½ teaspoons flour over crust, spreading over entire surface to edges. Invert crust, floured side down, in a 9½ x 1-inch fluted tart pan with removable bottom. Peel off plastic sheet, easing crust into pan. Press firmly against bottom and up sides of pan. Prick bottom and sides of crust with a fork. Bake 8 to 9 minutes, or until light golden. Let cool. Reduce oven temperature to 325°F.

3. To make filling, in a 2-quart glass bowl, combine butter, brown sugar, and chocolate. Heat in a microwave oven on High 1½ to 2 minutes, or until smooth when stirred. Whisk in salt, eggs, vanilla, 2 tablespoons Frangelico, and remaining 2 tablespoons flour until well blended.

4. Sprinkle toasted hazelnuts evenly over baked crust. Carefully top with chocolate mixture and spread evenly. Bake 30 to 35 minutes, until filling is set. Do not overbake. Let pie cool thoroughly. Refrigerate until ½ hour before serving time.

5. Up to 2 hours before serving, whip cream until stiff. Beat in remaining 2 tablespoons Frangelico. Serve tart cut into thin slices, topped with hazelnut whipped cream.

---

90   FUDGE TARTLETS
Prep: 25 minutes   Cook: 22 minutes   Makes: 24 tartlets

These tiny tarts are ideal for a dessert buffet, holiday cookie tray, or anytime a special dessert is called for. Make them in advance and freeze to save last-minute work.

4 (1-ounce) squares semisweet chocolate, cut up	1 tablespoon flour Dash of salt
2 tablespoons butter	¾ cup chopped pecans
1 egg	Cream Cheese Pastry (recipe follows)
½ teaspoon rum extract	
3 tablespoons sugar	

1. Preheat oven to 350°F. In a 1-quart glass bowl, combine chocolate and butter. Heat in a microwave oven on High 1½ minutes, or until melted and smooth when stirred. Whisk in egg, rum extract, sugar, flour, and salt until thoroughly blended. Stir in pecans; set aside.

2. Divide Cream Cheese Pastry into 24 equal portions. Press each dough portion evenly in bottom and up sides of an ungreased 2- to 3-inch fluted tartlet pan, preferably with removable bottom. Divide pecan mixture evenly among pastry-lined tartlet pans. Place pans 1 inch apart on baking sheets.

3. Bake about 20 minutes, or until set. Do not overbake. Let tartlets cool in pans 3 to 4 minutes; then use a sharp knife to loosen edges and release tartlets from pans. Transfer to racks and let cool completely.

CREAM CHEESE PASTRY

4 ounces cream cheese, softened	1 teaspoon vanilla extract
1 stick (4 ounces) butter, softened	1 cup flour

In a food processor, combine cream cheese, butter, and vanilla; process until smooth. Add flour and process until well blended and dough begins to cling together in a ball. Wrap dough in plastic wrap and refrigerate 1 to 2 hours.

91   FRESH FRUIT CHOCOLATE FRANGIPANE TART

Prep: 20 minutes   Cook: 15 minutes   Chill: 2 hours   Serves: 8

Arrange fresh seasonal fruits on a butter crust filled with a delicate mixture of blanched almonds, sugar, butter, egg, chocolate, and vanilla. Use a little apricot jam to glaze the fruits.

1 cup blanched whole almonds (4 ounces)	1 teaspoon vanilla extract
¼ cup sugar	Butter Crust (recipe follows)
1 tablespoon flour	1 pint fresh strawberries,
2 (1-ounce) squares semisweet chocolate, melted	sliced, or ½ pint fresh raspberries
2 tablespoons butter, softened	3 tablespoons apricot jam, melted
1 egg	

1. Preheat oven to 350°F. In a food processor, grind almonds until coarsely chopped. Add sugar and flour and process until almonds are finely chopped. Add chocolate and process until blended. Add butter, egg, and vanilla and process until mixture is blended but not smooth.

2. Press Butter Crust into bottom and up sides of a 9½-inch fluted metal tart pan with a removable bottom. Scrape filling into Butter Crust and spread evenly. Bake 15 minutes, or until slightly puffed. Let tart cool in pan. Refrigerate until cold, at least 2 hours.

3. About 1 hour before serving, cover top of chilled tart with strawberries arranged in an attractive design. Brush jam over fruit to glaze. Refrigerate until serving time, then remove side from pan and cut tart into slices.

BUTTER CRUST

1 cup flour	6 tablespoons cold butter
2 tablespoons sugar	1 tablespoon milk
½ teaspoon salt	1 teaspoon vanilla extract

In a food processor, combine flour, sugar, and salt. Cut butter into pieces over flour. Process with about 8 on-and-off turns, until mixture is crumbly. With machine on, add milk and vanilla through feed tube and process just until dough forms a ball and leaves side of bowl.

Chapter 4

Chocolate Entertains

When you want to pull out all the stops and knock guests' socks off, flip through the impressive array of ideas here. Not only are they glamorous, but all taste sensational and are geared for informal as well as elegant entertaining.

These are the kind of desserts that are worth the indulgence and make a meal memorable, regardless of what else is served. Killer chocolate desserts is what I like to call them. Just wait until you try them!

Sprinkled throughout are inspirations shared by chefs, friends, and relatives. Many of these desserts are also personal favorites that have stood the test of time. In addition, several have been developed specifically with special occasions and festivities in mind. As you'll notice, many of these recipes are more complex and require more lengthy preparation time than others elsewhere in the book. But often part of all of the preparation can be done a day or two in advance.

When it comes time to present your grand finale, gussy it up with garnishes, such as whipped cream (pipe it on if you have a pastry bag and feel so inclined), chocolate leaves, shaved chocolate, chocolate curls, chocolate-dipped fresh or dried fruits or nuts, fresh grated orange zest, fresh berries, fresh mint, and the like. Select a flavor used in the cake and use it in the garnish, if possible. For instance, in Flourless Bittersweet Apricot-Walnut Torte, you might garnish the top of the cake with chocolate-dipped apricot and walnut halves.

Remember the old adage that "first we eat with our eyes." And while that's important any time desserts are served, it's crucial when presenting these showstoppers. To dazzle guests, consider Filo Chocolate-Fruit Spectacular, Chocolate Truffle Pecan Tart, Chocolate Mousse Bombe Supreme, Chocolate Almond Torte, Chocolate Ecstasy, Black Bottom Tiramisu, Chocolate Russe Royale, Chocolate Meringue Mousse Torte, and Chocolate Grand Marnier Torte.

For unique and novel conversation-piece desserts that will keep guests talking, present Chocolate-Cinnamon Dessert Nachos, Won Ton Beignets with Chocolate Sauce, Dessert Spring Rolls, Chocolate Orange Quiche, and Raspberry Chocolate Strata. And if you want to try your hand at some restaurant-style desserts shared by chefs, offerings include White Chocolate Raspberry Tart, Chocolate Zuccotto, Nancy's Fabulous Chocolate Terrine, and Triple Chocolate Napoleons with Raspberry Sauce.

So next time you entertain, opt for one of these decadent creations. And get ready for the rave reviews!

92 CARAMEL TURTLE TRUFFLE TART

Prep: 30 minutes   Cook: 28 to 33 minutes   Chill: 1 hour
Serves: 12 to 16

This caramel tart, which tastes almost like a piece of candy, is a breeze to prepare with store-bought caramels. Pile the caramel-pecan mixture on top of a chocolate truffle mixture spread on a butter cookie crust.

1 stick (4 ounces) butter, cut into 8 pieces	1½ cups semisweet chocolate chips (9 ounces)
⅓ cup sugar	½ cup plus ⅓ cup heavy cream
2 teaspoons vanilla extract	1 (14-ounce) package vanilla
1⅓ cups flour	caramels
1 egg	3 cups chopped pecans

1. Preheat oven to 400°F. To make crust, in a food processor, combine butter, sugar, and vanilla. Process 1 minute. Add flour and process to blend. With machine on, add egg through feed tube, and process just until dough forms and leaves sides of bowl.

2. Press dough evenly into bottom and all the way up sides of an 11-inch fluted metal tart pan with a removable bottom. Press a sheet of foil on top of crust and line with pie weights or dried beans. Bake 10 minutes. Remove foil and weights and bake 5 to 7 minutes longer, or until golden. Let cool.

3. Meanwhile, prepare truffle mixture. In a 1-quart glass bowl, combine chocolate chips and ⅓ cup cream. Heat in a microwave oven on High 1 to 1¼ minutes, or until chocolate is melted and smooth when stirred. When crust is cool, spread three-quarters of truffle mixture evenly over bottom of crust. Refrigerate 15 minutes, or until truffle mixture is set.

4. In a large skillet, combine caramels and remaining ½ cup cream. Heat over medium-low heat, stirring often, until caramels are melted and mixture is smooth, about 3 minutes. Stir in pecans. Spread evenly over chilled truffle mixture.

5. Heat remaining chocolate truffle mixture in microwave oven on High 15 to 20 seconds, if necessary, to melt. Drizzle with a fork over top of tart. Refrigerate until filling is set, at least 1 hour. Before serving, remove side of pan and, using a sharp knife, cut tart into slices.

93   RASPBERRY BROWNIE TORTE

Prep: 25 minutes   Cook: 25 minutes   Chill: 3 hours
Serves: 10 to 12

This is an interesting way to serve chocolate mousse with fresh fruit and a brownie.

6 (1-ounce) squares semisweet
    chocolate, cut up
1 (1-ounce) square
    unsweetened chocolate,
    cut up
3 egg yolks*
1 teaspoon vanilla extract
6 tablespoons butter, cut into
    pieces, at room
    temperature

1 cup heavy cream
1 pint fresh raspberries,
    rinsed and well drained
    Brownie Torte Base (recipe
    follows)

1. To prepare mousse topping, in a food processor, combine semisweet and unsweetened chocolate and ⅓ cup hot water. Process until mixture is smooth. With machine on, add egg yolks and vanilla through feed tube; then add butter, a few pieces at a time, processing until well blended.

2. In a medium bowl, whip cream with an electric mixer on high speed until stiff. Fold chocolate mixture into whipped cream. Gently fold in raspberries.

3. Spread mousse mixture evenly over cold Brownie Torte Base in spring-form pan. Cover and refrigerate until firm, several hours or overnight. Or wrap well and freeze; transfer to refrigerator a couple of hours before serving.

    * **CAUTION:** *Because of the possible threat of salmonella—a bacteria that causes food poisoning—from raw eggs, U.S. Government officials recommend that the very young, the elderly, pregnant women, and people with serious illnesses or weakened immune systems not eat raw or lightly cooked eggs. Keep this in mind and consume raw or lightly cooked eggs at your own risk.*

BROWNIE TORTE BASE

2 (1-ounce) squares
    unsweetened chocolate,
    cut up
1 stick (4 ounces) butter

2 eggs
1 cup sugar
1½ teaspoons vanilla extract
½ cup flour

1. Preheat oven to 350°. In a 2-quart glass bowl, combine chocolate and butter. Heat in a microwave oven on High about 1 to 1½ minutes, or until melted and smooth when stirred.

2. With a fork, beat in eggs, sugar, and vanilla until well blended. Add flour and mix well. Spread evenly in a well-buttered 8-inch springform pan.

3. Bake 25 minutes. Brownie should be moist; do not overbake. Let cool in pan.

94   CHOCOLATE RUSSE ROYALE
Prep: 20 minutes   Cook: 5 minutes   Chill: 6 hours   Serves: 6 to 8

This is a lovely creation to serve the most discriminating guests. Make your own chocolate ladyfingers to set it off beautifully.

1   envelope unflavored gelatin
¼   cup brewed strong coffee, at room temperature
1   cup milk
3   egg yolks
½   cup sugar
3   ounces bittersweet chocolate, melted

1   cup heavy cream, whipped
1   recipe Chocolate Ladyfingers (recipe follows)
¼   cup Kahlua or other coffee-flavored liqueur
     Chocolate curls or shavings

1. In a 1-cup glass measure, sprinkle gelatin over coffee to soften; set aside. In a medium saucepan, whisk together milk, egg yolks, and sugar. Bring to a simmer over medium heat, whisking constantly. Reduce heat to low and cook, whisking constantly, 3 minutes; do not boil. Remove from heat and stir in gelatin mixture and chocolate. Refrigerate until mixture begins to hold its shape. Fold in whipped cream.

2. Butter a 9-inch springform pan. Trim ½ inch off one end of each Chocolate Ladyfinger; reserve trimmed pieces. Brush 16 to 18 ladyfingers on both sides with liqueur and use to line pan, standing ladyfingers upright and setting trimmed sides down and rounded sides facing outside of pan. Crumble remaining ladyfingers and trimmed pieces and sprinkle evenly over bottom of pan. Pour in chocolate filling, spreading evenly. Refrigerate 6 hours or overnight.

3. Just before serving, carefully remove springform side of pan and place dessert on a serving plate. Garnish with chocolate curls.

95   CHOCOLATE GRAND MARNIER TORTE
Prep: 15 minutes   Cook: 18 to 21 minutes   Chill: 3 hours
Serves: 12 to 14

Dense and rich, this dessert tastes like chocolate truffle candy, so serve thin slices. Serve with raspberry sauce, crème anglaise, or simply whipped cream and fresh raspberries.

5   eggs
10   ounces semisweet or bittersweet chocolate, cut up
2   (1-ounce) squares unsweetened chocolate, cut up

2   sticks (8 ounces) butter
¼   cup Grand Marnier or other orange-flavored liqueur
     Raspberry Sauce (page 59)
     Whipped cream

1. Preheat oven to 400°F. In a small bowl, cover uncracked eggs with very hot water. Let stand 5 minutes.

2. Meanwhile, in a 2-quart glass bowl, heat semisweet and unsweetened chocolate and butter in a microwave oven on High 2½ to 3 minutes, stirring twice, until melted and smooth. Set aside to let cool slightly.

3. In a large bowl, beat eggs with an electric mixer on high speed, until thick and light yellow, about 5 minutes. Add chocolate mixture and Grand Marnier and beat until well blended.

4. Turn into a buttered, wax paper-lined 8-inch springform pan.

5. Bake 15 to 18 minutes, or until almost set. Let cake cool 1 hour. Then cover with foil and refrigerate several hours or until firm. Remove cake from refrigerator at least 1 hour before serving. Run a sharp knife around sides of cake and remove sides of springform pan. Cut into slices. Serve in a pool of Raspberry Sauce and top with whipped cream.

---

96   CHOCOLATE LINZER TORTE
Prep: 50 minutes   Cook: 40 to 45 minutes   Serves: 10 to 12

Here's a chocolate version of the ever-popular European linzer torte. It's a winner.

½ cup whole blanched
    almonds
1½ cups flour
⅔ cup sugar
2 tablespoons unsweetened
    cocoa powder (preferably
    Dutch-processed)
2 teaspoons cinnamon
½ teaspoon salt

2 sticks (8 ounces) butter,
    cold, cut into tablespoons
2 cups seedless red raspberry
    jam
1 tablespoon grated orange
    zest
6 ounces imported white
    chocolate, chopped into
    ¼-inch pieces

1. In a food processor, finely grind almonds. Add flour, sugar, cocoa, cinnamon, and salt. Process a few seconds to combine. Add butter and turn machine quickly on and off until mixture resembles coarse meal. With machine on, add 3 tablespoons water through feed tube and process until dough forms a ball. Divide dough into 2 equal portions. On a sheet of wax paper, roll out half of dough to a 9 x 11-inch rectangle. Refrigerate 30 minutes. Press remaining dough into an 11-inch fluted metal tart pan with a removable bottom.

2. Preheat oven to 350°F. In a medium bowl, mix together raspberry jam, orange zest, and 4 ounces chopped white chocolate. Spread over crust in tart pan.

3. Cut refrigerated dough into ¾-inch-wide strips and lay in lattice pattern over jam in tart pan, placing half of dough strips horizontally and half vertically about ⅜ inch apart. Bake 40 to 45 minutes, or until top is crispy like a cookie and jam is bubbling. Finely chop remaining 2 ounces white chocolate and sprinkle over tart while hot. Let cool to room temperature before serving.

97   CHOCOLATE LADYFINGERS
Prep: 25 minutes   Cook: 12 to 15 minutes   Makes: 18 to 22

½ cup flour
2 tablespoons unsweetened
   cocoa powder (preferably
   Dutch-processed)

Dash of salt
2 eggs, separated
4 tablespoons sugar

1. Preheat oven to 350°F. Grease 2 cookie sheets and line with parchment paper; grease parchment. In a small bowl, sift together flour, cocoa, and salt; set aside.

2. In a medium bowl, beat egg yolks and 1 tablespoon sugar with an electric mixer on high speed until light and pale colored, 2 to 3 minutes. In a large bowl, beat egg whites and remaining 3 tablespoons sugar with clean beaters on high speed until stiff but not dry, 2 to 3 minutes. Fold egg yolks into egg whites, then fold in reserved flour mixture.

3. Using a rubber spatula, transfer batter into a large pastry bag fitted with a large ½-inch round decorating tip, filling bag half-full at a time. Pipe batter into 18 to 22 strips, each about 2 inches long and 1 inch wide, and spaced 1½ inches apart, onto prepared cookie sheets. Or spoon batter into strips. Bake 12 to 15 minutes. Transfer to a rack and let cool.

98   CHOCOLATE BOURBON CAKE
Prep: 40 minutes   Cook: 68 to 74 minutes   Chill: 3 to 4 hours
Serves: 10 to 12

This cake recipe was shared by Melinda Bugarin, pastry chef at Eureka, Wolfgang Puck's restaurant and brewery in Los Angeles. The dense cake is served with espresso ice cream alongside and sometimes in a pool of bitter-sweet chocolate sauce. Alone or with ice cream, it's yummy and moist!

6 ounces bittersweet
   chocolate, cut up, or 1 cup
   semisweet chocolate
   chips
5 (1-ounce) squares
   unsweetened chocolate,
   cut up
2½ sticks (10 ounces) butter,
   softened

1¾ cups sugar
2 eggs
1 teaspoon vanilla extract
½ cup bourbon
2 cups flour
1 teaspoon baking soda
1½ cups brewed espresso or
   strong coffee
1 tablespoon light corn syrup

1. Preheat oven to 325°F. Grease a 9-inch springform pan (it must be at least 2½ inches high). Line with a round of wax paper cut to fit bottom. Grease waxed paper, dust with cocoa, and tap out any excess. Wrap foil around outside of pan to avoid any leakage of cake into oven during baking.

2. In a 2-quart glass bowl, combine 3 ounces bittersweet chocolate, unsweetened chocolate, and 2 sticks butter. Heat in a microwave oven on High 2 minutes, stirring once, until melted and smooth when stirred. Whisk in sugar, eggs, vanilla, and bourbon until well mixed.

3. Combine flour and baking soda. Add to chocolate mixture in 2 batches alternately with coffee, whisking well after each addition. Batter will be thin.

4. Pour cake batter evenly into prepared pan.

5. Bake 65 to 70 minutes, or until a cake tester inserted in center comes out clean. Let cake cool in pan 1 to 2 hours.

6. Meanwhile, in a 2-cup glass measure, combine remaining bittersweet chocolate and ½ stick butter with corn syrup. Heat in microwave oven on High 1 to 1½ minutes, until melted and smooth when stirred. Let glaze stand until cool but not thickened, about 30 minutes.

7. Unmold and invert cake onto a serving plate. Peel off wax paper and turn cake right side up. Using a spatula or flat knife, spread glaze over top and sides of cake. Refrigerate cake until it is chilled and glaze is set, 3 to 4 hours, or longer.

99 BLACK AND WHITE CHOCOLATE STREUSEL CAKE

Prep: 30 minutes   Cook: 35 to 40 minutes   Serves: 12

Served warm, this is a wonderful choice for a morning coffee get-together, afternoon tea, or Sunday brunch.

1 **stick (4 ounces) butter or margarine, softened**	1 **teaspoon baking soda**
1¼ **cups granulated sugar**	1 **cup sour cream**
½ **cup firmly packed unsweetened cocoa powder (preferably Dutch-processed)**	½ **cup packed brown sugar**
	½ **cup chopped pecans**
	1 **teaspoon cinnamon**
	½ **teaspoon ground allspice**
4 **eggs**	12 **ounces imported white chocolate, cut into ¾-inch chunks**
2 **cups flour**	
2 **teaspoons baking powder**	

1. Preheat oven to 350°F. Generously grease a 9 x 13-inch baking pan. Dust with flour; tap out excess.

2. In a large bowl, beat together butter and granulated sugar with an electric mixer on medium speed until light and fluffy, about 2 minutes. Add cocoa and beat until well mixed. Add eggs, one at a time, beating well after each addition.

3. Stir together flour, baking powder, and baking soda. Add to chocolate mixture alternately with sour cream. In a separate small bowl, mix together brown sugar, pecans, cinnamon, and allspice.

4. Turn half of batter into prepared pan and spread evenly. Sprinkle half of white chocolate chunks and half of brown sugar-nut mixture evenly over batter. Repeat layers with remaining batter, remaining white chocolate chunks, and remaining brown sugar-nut mixture.

5. Bake 35 to 40 minutes, or until a cake tester inserted in center comes out clean. Cut cake into squares, and serve warm or at room temperature.

100   CHOCOLATE TRUFFLE PECAN TART

Prep: 30 minutes   Cook: 20 to 21 minutes   Chill: 5 hours
Serves: 18

This fabulous dessert is smooth and rich. A little goes a long way. It's like eating a chocolate truffle. If desired, change the flavor of the tart by adding instant espresso powder or grated orange zest to the chocolate mixture. Top with caramel sauce or whipped cream.

7   tablespoons unsalted butter
2   cups finely chopped pecans
    (about 8 ounces)
⅓   cup sugar
2   cups heavy cream
1   pound bittersweet or
    semisweet chocolate, cut
    up

2   teaspoons vanilla extract
1   (12.25-ounce) jar caramel
    topping, warmed, or
    whipped cream

1. Preheat oven to 350°F. Make crust: In a small saucepan, melt 3 tablespoons butter. In a medium bowl, mix together pecans, sugar, and melted butter until well blended. Press mixture firmly into bottom and 1 inch up sides of 9- or 9½-inch springform pan. Bake 15 minutes, or until toasted and golden. Let cool.

2. Meanwhile, make truffle mixture. In a 2-quart glass bowl, combine cream and chocolate. Heat in a microwave oven on High 4 to 5 minutes, stirring once or twice, until smooth and thick. Cut up remaining 4 tablespoons butter and add to truffle mixture along with vanilla. Stir until melted, smooth, and well blended.

3. Turn truffle mixture into pecan crust. Refrigerate until firm, at least 5 hours. Cover and return to refrigerator until serving time. Serve with warm caramel topping or whipped cream.

101   CHOCOLATE PANCAKES WITH BANANAS AND WHIPPED CREAM

Prep: 20 minutes   Cook: 50 to 60 seconds per batch   Serves: 6

For a novel and tempting dessert, layer miniature chocolate pancakes with bananas, hot fudge sauce, whipped cream, and almonds. Make the pancakes in advance and reheat in a warm oven.

1   tablespoon butter, melted
1   large egg
½   cup half-and-half
¼   cup sugar
3   tablespoons unsweetened
    cocoa powder
    Dash of salt

½   cup flour
3   medium bananas, diced
    (about 3 cups)
2   teaspoons lime juice
¾   cup hot fudge sauce
½   cup heavy cream, whipped
¼   cup sliced toasted almonds

1. In a medium bowl, whisk together melted butter, egg, half-and-half, 3 tablespoons sugar, cocoa, salt, and flour until smooth.

2. Place a pancake griddle over medium-low heat; brush with oil and when hot, drop 1 generous tablespoon batter onto griddle in 4 separate places, spacing evenly. Cook only 30 seconds. With a spatula, flip pancakes over and cook 20 to 30 seconds longer. Wrap pancakes in foil to keep warm. Repeat until all batter is cooked.

3. In a small bowl, mix diced bananas with remaining 1 tablespoon sugar and lime juice. To serve, divide bananas among 6 individual dessert plates. Arrange 3 warm pancakes, overlapping, on top of bananas on each plate. Top with hot fudge sauce and whipped cream, dividing evenly. Garnish with toasted almonds. Serve immediately.

   NOTE: *If pancakes are prepared in advance, wrap slightly overlapping in foil and refrigerate. Just before serving, heat in a preheated 200°F oven 15 to 20 minutes, or until warm.*

---

102   CHOCOLATE ECSTASY
Prep: 15 minutes   Cook: 41 to 47 minutes   Chill: overnight
Serves: 12

This is a cross between a truffle and a flourless cake. But no matter what you call it, it's dense, rich, and smooth—and you'll be in ecstasy when you taste it.

1 cup sugar	2 sticks (8 ounces) unsalted
10 ounces semisweet or	butter
bittersweet chocolate, cut	5 eggs
up	1 cup heavy cream, whipped
2 (1-ounce) squares	Shaved chocolate
unsweetened chocolate,	3 cups fresh or frozen,
cut up	unsweetened raspberries

1. Preheat oven to 350°F. Grease a 9-inch springform pan. Line bottom with a round of parchment or wax paper.

2. In a 2-quart glass bowl, combine ¾ cup sugar and ⅓ cup water. Heat in microwave oven on High 1 to 1½ minutes, or until boiling. Stir in semisweet and unsweetened chocolates and butter until melted.

3. In a medium bowl, beat eggs and remaining ¼ cup sugar with an electric mixer on high speed until almost double in volume, 3 to 4 minutes. Stir egg mixture into chocolate mixture until well blended.

4. Turn into prepared springform pan. Set springform pan in a larger rectangular baking pan. Add enough water to reach 1 inch up side of springform pan.

5. Bake 40 to 45 minutes, or until cake is set. Remove springform pan from water bath. Let cake cool in pan. Refrigerate overnight. When ready to serve, run a sharp knife around inside edge of pan to loosen cake. Remove springform side. Frost top and sides with whipped cream and sprinkle with shaved chocolate, if desired. Serve raspberries alongside each slice.

103   SPECIAL S'MORES DESSERT
Prep: 10 minutes   Cook: 2 minutes   Serves: 6

This dessert has been one of the signature desserts of the Parkway Grill in Pasadena, California, for years. The Parkway makes their own marshmallows and graham crackers and uses imported European bittersweet chocolate in their sophisticated version. Here's my adaptation of a quick, easy version Parkway chef Hugo Molina developed for home cooks.

12 graham cracker squares
4   (1.55-ounce) milk chocolate
    bars

12 marshmallows, cut in half
    horizontally
    Raspberry Sauce (page 59)

1. Preheat oven to 550°F. On 6 heatproof dessert serving plates, place 2 graham crackers side by side. Cover graham crackers with chocolate, breaking up to fit and dividing evenly. Top each cracker with 2 marshmallow halves, cut sides down.

2. Place plates on baking sheets. Bake about 2 minutes (it may be necessary to bake a few plates at a time, depending on oven size), or until tops of marshmallows are golden. Watch carefully.

3. Spoon Raspberry Sauce over top and around s'mores and serve at once.

104   CHOCOLATE BAKLAVA
Prep: 30 minutes   Cook: 55 to 65 minutes   Cool: 4 hours
Makes: 50 pieces

Here's a version of the popular Middle-Eastern specialty that's filled and glazed with chocolate.

2 sticks (8 ounces) unsalted
   butter
4 cups finely chopped pecans
   (about 1 pound)
2 to 3 teaspoons ground
   cinnamon
¾ cup sugar
1 cup miniature semisweet
   chocolate chips (6 ounces)

1 (1-pound) package filo
   dough
¾ cup orange juice
1 teaspoon vanilla extract
   Thin Chocolate Glaze
   (recipe follows)

1. In a small skillet, melt butter over low heat. Let stand a few minutes. Skim off and discard white foam that rises to the top and do not use any milky residue that sinks to the bottom. The clear yellow liquid is clarified butter.

2. Preheat oven to 350°F. In a medium bowl, combine pecans, cinnamon, ¼ cup sugar, and chocolate chips; mix well. Open and stack filo sheets on a damp towel. Cover with a damp towel to prevent drying out. Brush a 12 x 18-inch sheet cake pan with clarified butter. Layer half of filo sheets (about 10 to 12) in pan, brushing each sheet with butter. Spread half of nut mixture evenly over layered filo sheets. Brush next filo sheet on both sides with butter; then place on top of nuts. Add 5 or 6 more filo sheets, brushing each with butter. Top with remaining nut mixture. Butter next filo sheet on both sides and place on top of nuts. Top with remaining filo sheets, brushing each with butter.

3. Using a sharp knife, cut pastry into 50 diamond-shape pieces. Do not remove pastry from pan. Brush top with remaining clarified butter. Bake 40 to 50 minutes, or until golden.

4. About 30 minutes before baklava is finished baking, in a small saucepan, combine remaining ½ cup sugar and orange juice. Heat to boiling over medium heat, stirring often. Reduce heat to medium-low and simmer 10 minutes. Stir in vanilla. Pour hot orange syrup over hot pastry as soon as it is removed from oven. Let stand until cool, 4 hours or overnight.

5. When baklava is cool, drizzle Thin Chocolate Glaze on top. Allow glaze to set up before serving. Baklava may be kept, covered, 4 to 5 days at room temperature. Freeze for longer storage.

THIN CHOCOLATE GLAZE

2 (1-ounce) squares semisweet   1 tablespoon butter
   chocolate

In a small glass bowl, combine chocolate, butter, and 1 tablespoon water. Heat in a microwave oven on High 30 to 45 seconds, or until melted and smooth when stirred.

---

105 CHOCOLATE PEANUT BUTTER GLAZE
Prep: 5 minutes   Cook: 1 to 1½ minutes   Chill: 10 minutes
Makes: about 1 cup

2 tablespoons butter, cut up   1 teaspoon vanilla extract
2 tablespoons creamy peanut   6 ounces semisweet chocolate
   butter   chips (1 cup)
3 tablespoons light corn syrup   ¼ cup sifted powdered sugar

In a 1-quart glass bowl, combine butter, peanut butter, corn syrup, vanilla, and 2 tablespoons water. Heat in a microwave oven on High 1 to 1½ minutes, until butter is melted and mixture is smooth when stirred. Add chocolate chips and stir until completely melted and smooth. Stir in powdered sugar until blended. Refrigerate 10 minutes, or until glaze is of spreading consistency.

106 RASPBERRY CHOCOLATE STRATA
Prep: 25 minutes   Cook: 55 minutes   Chill: 4 hours   Serves: 12

Here's a dessert you can make ahead and stash in the refrigerator well in advance of serving time.

½ pound French bread, cut into 1-inch cubes
2 (8-ounce) packages cream cheese, cut into ½-inch cubes
½ cup sliced almonds (2 ounces), toasted
12 ounces semisweet chocolate chips (2 cups)

9 eggs
2 cups milk
½ cup sugar
1 teaspoon vanilla extract
½ teaspoon salt
1 (12-ounce) package individually quick frozen unsweetened raspberries

1. Place bread cubes in a buttered 9 x 13-inch baking dish. Sprinkle cream cheese, toasted almonds, and chocolate chips evenly into dish.

2. In a large bowl, combine eggs, milk, sugar, vanilla, and salt. Beat until well blended. Pour evenly over bread mixture. Cover with plastic wrap and refrigerate 4 hours or overnight.

3. Preheat oven to 375°F. Remove strata from refrigerator and uncover. Sprinkle half of frozen raspberries over strata, pushing them down to submerge them slightly. Set aside remaining raspberries to let thaw. Cover strata with foil. Bake 30 minutes. Uncover and bake 25 minutes longer. Let stand 15 minutes. Serve hot, topped with reserved raspberries.

107 FILO CHOCOLATE-FRUIT SPECTACULAR
Prep: 45 minutes   Cook: 35 to 40 minutes   Serves: 12

Here's a showstopper to dazzle guests at dessert time. Working with filo is not difficult once you get the knack, but be aware that you must work quickly.

1½ cups peeled, chopped apples (about 3 medium)
6 ounces dried apricots, chopped
1 cup raisins
6 ounces semisweet chocolate chips (1 cup)
1½ cups chopped toasted walnuts (6 ounces)
1 cup packed brown sugar
3 sticks (12 ounces) unsalted butter, melted

1 tablespoon grated orange zest
¼ cup plus 1 tablespoon unsweetened cocoa powder
2 teaspoons cinnamon
1 (1-pound) package filo dough sheets (thaw in refrigerator if frozen)
2 tablespoons powdered sugar
1 tablespoon ground walnuts

1. In a medium bowl, mix together apples, apricots, raisins, chocolate chips, chopped walnuts, brown sugar, 1 stick melted butter, orange zest, ¼ cup cocoa, and cinnamon; set aside.

2. Preheat oven to 350°F. Brush a 14-inch round pizza pan with a ½- to ¾-inch-high rim with some of remaining melted butter. Open and stack filo sheets on a damp kitchen towel. Take 1 sheet of filo at a time and brush half of it lengthwise with some butter; fold in half lengthwise to enclose butter. Place folded filo sheet on pan with half of it extending over edge of pan and other end overlapping center of pan. Working quickly, repeat buttering and folding procedure with all remaining filo sheets, placing them overlapping in a circle around pan. Brush remaining butter all over top of filo.

3. Place fruit-nut mixture in a 6-inch-wide mound in center of filo. Starting with last filo sheet added to pan, fold up all filo sheets, one at a time, over filling, twisting the end of each filo sheet decoratively to resemble a rose. When completed, you should end up with a large package that resembles a bouquet of flowers on top.

4. Bake 35 to 40 minutes, or until dark golden brown. It may be necessary to tent the top of the filo halfway through baking with aluminum foil to prevent overbrowning.

5. Meanwhile, in a small bowl, mix together remaining 1 tablespoon cocoa, powdered sugar, and ground walnuts. When pastry is removed from oven, sprinkle mixture on top. Serve filo package warm or at room temperature, cut into wedges.

108 WON TON BEIGNETS WITH CHOCOLATE SAUCE
Prep: 15 minutes   Cook: 15 minutes   Serves: 4 to 6

A delicious idea for an informal after-dinner finale. Fry the won ton strips a day or two in advance of serving and store in an airtight container. Sprinkle with powdered sugar just before serving.

Cooking oil, for deep-frying
20 won ton wrappers
(3½ inches square)
Powdered sugar

6 ounces semisweet chocolate chips (1 cup)
¼ cup heavy cream
1 tablespoon brandy

1. In a small deep saucepan, pour oil to a depth of 2 to 2½ inches. Heat oil to 375°F, or until a 1-inch cube of bread turns brown in oil in 45 to 50 seconds. Stack won ton wrappers together in groups of 4. Cut each stack into 3 equal strips. Fry strips, a few at a time, in hot oil until golden, turning a few times to cook evenly, 15 to 30 seconds. Using a slotted spoon, transfer to a paper towel-lined plate to drain. Let cool. (Store in an airtight container if making ahead.) Before serving, sift powdered sugar over both sides of fried strips.

2. Meanwhile, in a small glass bowl, combine chocolate chips and cream. Heat in a microwave oven on High 1 to 1½ minutes, or until chocolate is melted and mixture is smooth when stirred. Stir in brandy. Let cool to lukewarm.

3. Serve won ton strips in a napkin-lined basket with a dish of the lukewarm chocolate sauce in center for dipping.

109   NANCY'S FABULOUS CHOCOLATE TERRINE

Prep: 1 hour   Cook: 15 minutes   Freeze: 3 to 4 hours   Serves: 10

This recipe was developed by pastry chef Nancy Silverton, when she was at Spago a few years ago. Nancy and her husband, Mark Peel, also a former Spago alumnus, now have their own restaurant, Campanile, in Los Angeles, California.

1   **pound plus 3 ounces bittersweet or semisweet chocolate, chopped**
2   **sticks (8 ounces) butter**
10   **egg yolks***
¼   **cup plus 1 tablespoon sugar**
1   **cup heavy cream, whipped**

2   **egg whites***
1   **to 2 pints fresh raspberries, blackberries, or strawberries**
1   **tablespoon light corn syrup**
1   **tablespoon Cognac Crème Anglaise (page 203)**

1. Butter a 10 x 4½-inch loaf pan well. Line with parchment paper or foil cut to fit, allowing a paper or foil to extend up over edges of pan. To make terrine, in top of a double boiler, over hot, not boiling, water, melt together 14 ounces chocolate and 1½ sticks butter until smooth, stirring occasionally.

2. Meanwhile, in a large bowl, beat together egg yolks and ¼ cup sugar with an electric mixer on high speed until thick and light colored, about 5 to 8 minutes. Fold egg yolks into chocolate mixture and place over simmering water. Cook, stirring constantly, until thick and shiny and mixture pulls away from sides of pan, about 1 to 2 minutes. Let mixture cool to room temperature. Whisk in whipped cream. In a medium bowl, beat together egg whites and remaining 1 tablespoon sugar with an electric mixer on high speed until stiff peaks form. Fold egg whites into chocolate mixture.

3. Turn one third of chocolate mixture into prepared loaf pan and tap on work surface to settle and evenly distribute. Top with half of raspberries, placing in an even layer to within ¼ inch of edges of pan. Repeat layers using another third of chocolate and remaining berries. Top with remaining chocolate mixture. Refrigerate until set; then freeze 2 to 3 hours.

4. Melt 2 ounces chocolate. Remove terrine from freezer but do not remove from pan. Spread with a layer of melted chocolate. Return to freezer and freeze 1 hour longer.

5. Meanwhile, in a 1-quart glass bowl, combine remaining 4 tablespoons butter and 3 ounces chocolate with corn syrup. Heat in microwave oven on High 1 to 1½ minutes, until chocolate is melted and smooth when stirred. Stir in Cognac. Let glaze cool until slightly thickened and of spreading consistency.

6. Cut a cardboard rectangle a little larger than the size of the loaf pan. Cover neatly with foil. Remove terrine from freezer; loosen sides with a knife. Invert to unmold terrine onto foil-lined cardboard rectangle. Remove all paper or foil. Spread glaze evenly over top and sides of terrine. Return to freezer. About ½ to 1 hour before serving time, transfer terrine to refrigerator.

7. To serve, cover each dessert plate with a thin layer of Crème Anglaise. Cut terrine into ⅜-inch slices with a hot knife and set in sauce on dessert plates. If terrine slices are still frozen, let soften up a few minutes before serving.

* **CAUTION:** *Because of the possible threat of salmonella—a bacteria that causes food poisoning—from raw eggs, U.S. Government officials recommend that the very young, the elderly, pregnant women, and people with serious illnesses or weakened immune systems not eat raw or lightly cooked eggs. Keep this in mind and consume raw or lightly cooked eggs at your own risk.*

---

110 CHOCOLATE-CINNAMON DESSERT NACHOS

Prep: 30 minutes   Cook: about 20 minutes   Serves: 6 to 8

End a Mexican-themed company meal with this novel creation. You can bake the chips and make the sauces ahead of serving time, but for best results, be sure to assemble the dessert just before serving.

½ cup plus 2 tablespoons
   granulated sugar
½ teaspoon cinnamon
5 tablespoons butter
6 (8-inch) flour tortillas
1 cup heavy cream
⅓ cup packed brown sugar

1 teaspoon vanilla extract
1 (1-ounce) square
   unsweetened chocolate,
   coarsely chopped
½ cup coarsely chopped
   pecans

1. Preheat oven to 350°F. In a small bowl, mix together 2 tablespoons granulated sugar and cinnamon. Melt 4 tablespoons butter. Brush melted butter on both sides of tortillas. Sprinkle cinnamon-sugar on 1 side. Stack tortillas on top of one another, sugared sides up, and cut the stack into 10 to 12 wedges. Place tortilla wedges, sugared sides up, in a single layer on buttered baking sheets.

2. Bake 12 to 14 minutes, or until tortilla wedges are crisp and golden brown.

3. Meanwhile, in a medium saucepan, combine cream, remaining ½ cup granulated sugar, and brown sugar. Heat to boiling over medium heat, stirring often. Boil 5 minutes, stirring occasionally, until slightly thickened. Remove from heat; stir in vanilla. Transfer half of mixture to a bowl. Add chocolate and stir until melted. To remaining mixture, stir in remaining 1 tablespoon butter. Let both sauces cool to lukewarm.

4. To assemble nachos, scatter tortilla pieces in a single layer over a large serving platter. Drizzle some chocolate sauce and caramel sauce over tortillas and sprinkle about 3 tablespoons nuts on top. Repeat layers until all ingredients are used. Serve immediately.

111   CHOCOLATE CAKE GERMAN STYLE

Prep: 25 minutes   Cook: 25 to 30 minutes   Serves: 10 to 12

This is not the German chocolate cake you'll find on the German's brand sweet chocolate bar box. Rather this cake is dark chocolate with a fabulously rich Coconut-Pecan Frosting, which may remind you of the original version.

½ cup vegetable oil	2 teaspoons vanilla extract
2 large eggs	1¾ cups flour
1 cup buttermilk	1¼ teaspoons baking soda
2 cups sugar	½ teaspoon baking powder
¾ cup unsweetened cocoa powder	Coconut-Pecan Frosting (recipe follows)

1. Preheat oven to 350°F. Grease two 9-inch round cake pans; line with wax paper and grease again.

2. In a large bowl, combine oil, eggs, buttermilk, sugar, and cocoa. Beat with an electric mixer on medium-low speed until well blended, 2 to 3 minutes. With mixer on low speed, gradually add 1 cup hot water, beating until well incorporated.

3. Combine flour with baking soda and baking powder: Add to egg mixture and beat thoroughly until well blended. Turn batter into prepared cake pans.

4. Bake 25 to 30 minutes, or until tops of cakes spring back when lightly touched. Let cakes cool in pan 15 to 20 minutes, then remove to racks to let cool completely. When cool, fill cake layers with Coconut-Pecan Frosting in between and frost top and sides of cake. Refrigerate cake at least 1 hour, or until serving time.

COCONUT-PECAN FROSTING

1 cup powdered sugar	1½ to 2 cups coarsely chopped pecans
2 tablespoons cornstarch	
2 cups heavy cream	
2½ cups shredded or flaked coconut	

1. In a large saucepan, mix together powdered sugar and cornstarch. Whisk in cream until smooth. Cook over medium heat, whisking constantly, until mixture boils and thickens. Cook, whisking, 1 minute.

2. Remove from heat and stir in coconut and pecans. Let cool before using to frost cake.

112 PECAN CARAMEL TART

Prep: 45 minutes   Cook: 28 to 32 minutes   Chill: 3 hours
Serves: 10

Topped with chocolate, this wonderful mixture of caramel with pecans in a cookie pastry crust will remind you of a candy bar. Serve thin wedges, accompanied with ice cream.

1 **cup sugar**	**Sweet Pastry Tart Crust**
2 **tablespoons light corn syrup**	**(recipe follows)**
7 **tablespoons butter**	6 **ounces semisweet chocolate**
1½ **cups heavy cream, heated**	**chips (1 cup)**
2 **cups coarsely chopped**	½ **teaspoon vanilla extract**
pecans	

1. To make filling, in a deep, heavy 10-inch skillet, combine sugar, corn syrup, and ⅓ cup water. Cook over medium heat, stirring occasionally with a wooden spoon, until sugar dissolves, about 3 minutes.

2. Increase heat to medium-high and boil syrup without stirring, shaking pan back and forth occasionally, until pale golden in color, 4 to 5 minutes.

3. Remove from heat and add 6 tablespoons butter. Return to medium-high heat and stir to combine most of butter. Before completely melted, gradually stir in 1 cup warm cream; be careful as it will bubble up. Whisk vigorously (mixture will be hard in places) until smooth. Continue to boil, stirring often, until golden tan colored and thickened, 5 to 7 minutes. Remove from heat and stir in pecans. Set aside ½ hour to cool.

4. After filling has been cooling 15 minutes, preheat oven to 425°F. Carefully pour caramel-nut mixture over chilled Sweet Pastry Tart Crust. Bake 15 minutes, or until crust is light golden. Cool tart thoroughly.

5. Meanwhile, in a 2-cup glass measure, combine chocolate chips and remaining ⅓ cup cream. Heat in a microwave oven on High 1 to 1½ minutes, until melted and smooth when stirred. Stir in remaining 1 tablespoon butter and vanilla. Let chocolate topping cool to room temperature.

6. Spread chocolate topping evenly over tart. Refrigerate at least 3 hours, until chocolate is set, before serving.

SWEET PASTRY TART CRUST

1 **cup flour**	2 **tablespoons solid vegetable**
1 **tablespoon sugar**	**shortening, chilled**
4 **tablespoons butter, cold and**	
cut up	

1. In a food processor, process flour with sugar to combine. Add butter and shortening. Turn processor on and off in short spurts 6 times. With machine on, add 2 to 2½ tablespoons cold water through feed tube, just until dough forms a ball.

2. Press dough into bottom and up sides of 9½ x 1-inch fluted metal tart pan with removable bottom. Refrigerate until ready to use.

113   CHOCOLATE DECADENCE
Prep: 20 minutes   Cook: 14 to 17 minutes   Serves: 8 to 10

This cake is dense and rich and tastes like a chocolate truffle. Served topped with whipped cream zipped up with a sprinkling of your favorite liqueur or in a pool of raspberry sauce or crème anglaise. Or simply top with fresh raspberries and a dollop of whipped cream.

1 **pound semisweet or bittersweet chocolate, cut up**	**Whipped cream and fresh raspberries or Raspberry Sauce (page 59) and/or Crème Anglaise (page 203)**
1 **stick (4 ounces) butter**	
4 **eggs**	
1 **tablespoon flour**	

1. Preheat oven to 425°F. In a 1-quart glass bowl, combine chocolate, butter, and 1 tablespoon hot water. Heat in microwave oven on High 2 minutes, or until chocolate is melted and smooth when stirred. Set aside.

2. In a large bowl, beat eggs 3 to 4 minutes with an electric mixer on high speed until thickened and increased in volume. Beat in flour and chocolate mixture until well blended.

3. Spread evenly in an 8-inch springform pan buttered and lined with a round of parchment or wax paper.

4. Bake 12 to 15 minutes. Cake will be soft in center, but will firm up when cold. Let stand until cool, then refrigerate until serving time. Run sharp knife around edge of cake and remove springform side. Serve slices topped with whipped cream and fresh raspberries or Raspberry Sauce and/or Crème Anglaise.

114   CHOCOLATE INDULGENCE
Prep: 1 hour   Cook: none   Serves: 12 to 16

When you want something special to serve at a party, consider this sensational dessert. Although it has several components, it's really not difficult to prepare. Make the cake base and the chocolate mousse mixture a day or two ahead of time, so the dessert is all ready to assemble.

6 **ounces semisweet chocolate chips (1 cup)**	1½ **cups heavy cream**
⅓ **cup very hot brewed coffee or water**	1 **(8-inch) baked Chocolate Truffle Cake (page 107)**
4 **egg yolks***	7 **ounces almond paste**
1½ **teaspoons vanilla extract**	**Powdered sugar**
1 **stick (4 ounces) butter, cut into pieces and softened**	**Chocolate Glaze (recipe follows)**

1. In a food processor, combine chocolate chips and hot coffee. Process until mixture is smooth. With machine on, add egg yolks and vanilla through feed tube. Then add butter, piece by piece, through feed tube, processing until well blended. Transfer mixture to a large bowl.

2. In a medium bowl, beat cream until stiff. Blend a large spoonful of whipped cream into chocolate mixture. Then fold in remaining cream.

3. Line a 1½-quart heatproof glass bowl with plastic wrap, leaving about 5 inches extending over each side. Spoon chocolate mixture into bowl. Bring overhanging plastic wrap up over top to cover. Freeze several hours or overnight, until firm.

4. To assemble dessert, carefully remove Chocolate Truffle Cake from springform pan and invert onto a serving plate; remove foil from cake. Remove bowl of frozen chocolate mousse mixture from freezer. Invert mousse to unmold on top of truffle cake, rounded-side up. Refrigerate.

5. Flatten almond paste and place between 2 sheets of wax paper sprinkled with powdered sugar. Using a rolling pin, roll from center out in all directions to ¹⁄₁₆-inch thickness, or until large enough to fit completely over domed surface and cake. Refrigerate almond paste for 10 minutes. Remove top sheet of wax paper and invert almond paste onto mousse-topped cake. Remove paper from almond paste and press gently all over dome-shaped surface of mousse and cake. Trim any edges of almond paste, if necessary. Refrigerate ½ hour.

6. Pour Chocolate Glaze evenly over entire cake. Spread with a knife or spatula to cover. Refrigerate cake until chocolate is set. Cut into wedges to serve.

NOTE: *For those not fond of almond paste, cake can be prepared without almond paste layer. Proceed as directed above, frosting mousse-topped cake with Chocolate Glaze.*

CHOCOLATE GLAZE

4 tablespoons butter	**¾ cup semisweet chocolate**
3 tablespoons light corn syrup	**chips**
Dash of salt	

In a 1-quart glass bowl, combine butter, corn syrup, salt, and 2 tablespoons water. Heat in a microwave oven on high 1 to 1½ minutes, or until boiling, stirring once. Stir in chocolate chips until glaze is melted and smooth. Set aside to cool to room temperature and thicken slightly to spreading consistency. Glaze should not be thick.

* CAUTION: *Because of the possible threat of salmonella—a bacteria that causes food poisoning—from raw eggs, U.S. Government officials recommend that the very young, the elderly, pregnant women, and people with serious illnesses or weakened immune systems not eat raw or lightly cooked eggs. Keep this in mind and consume raw or lightly cooked eggs at your own risk.*

115   FLOURLESS BITTERSWEET APRICOT-WALNUT TORTE

Prep: 35 minutes   Cook: 38 to 39 minutes   Serves: 10

If you love the combination of apricots and chocolate, this dense rich cake flavored with Grand Marnier is for you. A chocolate glaze is the glorious finishing touch.

1 cup finely chopped dried apricots	14 ounces bittersweet or semisweet chocolate, chopped
¼ cup Grand Marnier or other orange-flavored liqueur	3 eggs
1½ cups walnut pieces (about 6 ounces)	¾ cup sugar
	1 tablespoon light corn syrup
1½ sticks (6 ounces) butter	6 dried apricot halves and 6 walnut halves

1. In a small dish, mix together chopped apricots and Grand Marnier; set aside 15 minutes.

2. Preheat oven to 350°F. Spread walnuts on a baking sheet and bake 5 to 7 minutes, until lightly toasted. Finely chop walnuts. Leave oven on. Grease an 8-inch springform pan. Line bottom with parchment paper round; butter parchment. Dust with flour; tap out excess.

3. In a 1-quart glass bowl, combine 1 stick butter and 8 ounces chocolate. Heat in a microwave oven on High 1½ to 2 minutes, stirring once or twice, until melted and smooth when stirred; set aside.

4. In a medium bowl, beat eggs and sugar with an electric mixer on medium speed, until light and thickened, about 5 minutes. Add melted chocolate mixture and beat until well blended, about 2 minutes. Mix in 1 cup chopped walnuts and reserved apricot mixture. Turn batter into prepared pan.

5. Bake 35 minutes, or until a cake tester inserted 1½ inches from center comes out clean. Let cake cool thoroughly in pan.

6. To make glaze, in a 1-quart glass bowl, combine remaining ½ stick butter and 6 ounces chocolate. Heat in microwave oven on High 1 to 1½ minutes, until melted and smooth when stirred. Stir in corn syrup. Let cool 15 minutes, or until glaze is thick enough to spread.

7. Run a sharp knife around edge of pan to loosen cake and remove springform side of pan. Invert to unmold cake onto a serving plate. Peel off parchment. Spread glaze over top and sides of cake. Decorate top edge of cake with apricot halves and walnut halves. Sprinkle remaining chopped walnuts over center. Refrigerate until glaze is set. Cover and refrigerate until 1 hour before serving.

116   FRENCH SILK CHOCOLATE TART

Prep: 25 minutes   Cook: about 5 minutes   Chill: 2 to 3 hours
Serves: 12 to 16

Reminiscent of a classic silk pie, this version with walnut crust, is exceptional. Be sure the eggs are fresh and uncracked prior to using in this creation.

6   ounces semisweet or
    bittersweet chocolate,
    cut up
1   stick (4 ounces) butter
½   cup powdered sugar
2   tablespoons coffee liqueur
    or dark rum

2   eggs*
    Chocolate Walnut Pie Crust
    (recipe follows), baked in
    11-inch tart pan
    Whipped cream and shaved
    chocolate

1. In a microwave oven or over low heat, melt chocolate until smooth and shiny when stirred. Set aside to cool.

2. In a medium bowl, beat butter and powdered sugar with an electric mixer on medium speed until light and fluffy, about 2 minutes. Beat in coffee liqueur and cooled chocolate until well blended. Beat in eggs, one at a time, beating 2 to 3 minutes after each addition.

3. Spread filling evenly in baked Chocolate Walnut Pie Crust. Refrigerate 2 to 3 hours, or until set. Serve slices, garnished with whipped cream and shaved chocolate.

    * **CAUTION:** *Because of the possible threat of salmonella—a bacteria that causes food poisoning—from raw eggs, U.S. Government officials recommend that the very young, the elderly, pregnant women, and people with serious illnesses or weakened immune systems not eat raw or lightly cooked eggs. Keep this in mind and consume raw or lightly cooked eggs at your own risk.*

---

117   CHOCOLATE WALNUT PIE CRUST

Prep: 5 minutes   Cook: 12 to 15 minutes   Makes: a single 11-inch tart crust or 9-inch pie crust

1   cup walnut pieces (4 ounces)
1   cup flour
½   cup sugar
4   tablespoons butter, cut into
    pieces

1   (1-ounce) square semisweet
    chocolate, cut up

1. Preheat oven to 350°F. In a food processor, combine walnuts, flour, sugar, butter, chocolate, and 1 tablespoon water. Process until consistency of fine crumbs.

2. Press into bottom and up sides of an ungreased 11-inch fluted metal tart pan with removable bottom or a 9-inch pie pan. Bake 12 to 15 minutes, or until golden and set. Let cool before filling.

118   CHOCOLATE MOUSSE BOMBE SUPREME

Prep: 30 minutes   Cook: 7 to 10 minutes   Chill: 6 hours
Serves: 12 to 14

Spoon chocolate mousse into a pound cake-lined bowl for an attractive presentation. An hour prior to serving, coat completely with a chocolate glaze for an attractive and unusual presentation. Present slices of this specialty on individual serving plates lined with melted vanilla ice cream or Crème Anglaise.

2¾ cups semisweet chocolate
    chips (16½ ounces)
3 (1-ounce) squares
    unsweetened chocolate
1 stick (4 ounces) plus 2
    tablespoons butter
4 egg yolks*
¾ cup sugar
2 cups heavy cream

2 tablespoons orange-flavored
    liqueur
1 (10¾-ounce) frozen all-
    butter pound cake,
    thawed
1 tablespoon corn syrup
    Crème Anglaise (page 203)
    or melted vanilla ice
    cream

1. In a 1-quart glass bowl, combine 2 cups chocolate chips, unsweetened chocolate, and 1 stick butter. Heat in a microwave oven on High 1 to 2 minutes, or until melted and smooth when stirred. Let cool slightly.

2. In a large bowl, beat egg yolks with an electric mixer on high speed 5 to 7 minutes, or until thick, light lemon colored, and increased in volume.

3. Meanwhile, in a small heavy saucepan, combine sugar and ⅓ cup water. Cook over medium-low heat, swirling pan occasionally, until sugar dissolves. Increase heat to medium-high and cook, uncovered, until syrup reaches 236°F on a candy thermometer (soft ball stage). With mixer on high speed, gradually beat sugar syrup into yolks in a slow, steady stream. Add melted chocolate mixture and continue beating until well mixed, 2 to 3 minutes; set aside to let cool.

4. In a medium bowl, whip cream and orange liqueur with an electric mixer on high speed until stiff peaks form. Fold into cooled chocolate mixture.

5. Line a 2- or 2½-quart glass or stainless steel bowl completely with plastic wrap, allowing wrap to overhang edges of bowl 3 to 4 inches. Cut pound cake lengthwise into ¼- to ⅜-inch-thick slices and use to line bowl completely. Spoon chocolate mixture into cake-lined bowl; smooth top. Lay remaining pound cake slices on top of mousse. Bring overhanging plastic wrap up over pound cake to cover. Cover with foil. Refrigerate at least 6 hours or overnight.

6. About 1¼ hours before serving, in a small glass bowl, combine remaining ¾ cup chocolate chips and 2 tablespoons butter with corn syrup and 1 tablespoon water. Heat in a microwave oven on High 50 to 60 seconds, or until melted and smooth when stirred. Let cool about 15 minutes, until glaze is spreading consistency.

7. About 1 hour before serving, unmold mousse by inverting onto a serving plate, rounded side up. Remove plastic wrap. Spread glaze over bombe. Return to refrigerator until set and time to serve. To serve, cut into slices. Place each slice on an individual serving plate covered with several spoonfuls of Crème Anglaise or melted vanilla ice cream.

> *** CAUTION:** *Because of the possible threat of salmonella—a bacteria that causes food poisoning—from raw eggs, U.S. Government officials recommend that the very young, the elderly, pregnant women, and people with serious illnesses or weakened immune systems not eat raw or lightly cooked eggs. Keep this in mind and consume raw or lightly cooked eggs at your own risk.*

---

119   CHOCOLATE ALMOND TORTE
Prep: 35 minutes   Cook: 66 minutes   Chill: 2 to 3 hours   Serves: 12

1 cup sliced natural almonds	2 tablespoons milk
2 cups flour	1 egg
1½ cups sugar	½ cup lightly packed almond
⅓ cup unsweetened cocoa	paste
powder	6 ounces semisweet chocolate
2½ sticks (10 ounces) butter—	chips (1 cup)
1½ sticks cut up, 1 stick	3 tablespoons heavy cream
softened	1 tablespoon light corn syrup

1. Preheat oven to 325°F. Spread out almonds on a large baking sheet and bake, shaking pan once or twice, until toasted and light brown, 5 to 7 minutes. Transfer to a plate to let cool. Increase oven temperature to 350°.

2. In a food processor, combine 1 cup flour, ¼ cup sugar, and cocoa; process a few seconds to mix. Add 1 stick cut-up butter and process until particles are the size of peas. Blend in milk and process until dough forms a ball. Press dough evenly into bottom and 1 inch up sides of a 9-inch springform pan.

3. Bake 15 minutes. Remove from oven and let cool 5 minutes. Leave oven on.

4. Meanwhile, in a medium bowl, beat together 1 cup sugar and 1 stick softened butter with an electric mixer on medium speed until light and fluffy, 1 to 2 minutes. Add egg and almond paste; beat until very smooth and creamy, about 5 minutes. Gradually beat in remaining 1 cup flour.

5. In a 2-cup glass bowl, combine chocolate chips and cream. Heat in a microwave oven on High 1 to 1¼ minutes, until chocolate is melted and smooth when stirred. Spread evenly over baked crust. Spoon reserved almond paste mixture over chocolate.

6. Bake torte 50 minutes, or until golden brown.

7. Meanwhile, prepare topping. In a small saucepan, melt remaining ½ stick (4 tablespoons) butter. Stir in remaining ¼ cup sugar. Heat until sugar dissolves. Blend in corn syrup. Add toasted almonds and toss to coat lightly. Spoon over baked torte. Refrigerate torte 2 to 3 hours before serving.

120   TRIPLE CHOCOLATE NAPOLEONS WITH RASPBERRY SAUCE

Prep: 1 hour   Cook: 5 to 10 minutes   Chill: 3¼ hours   Serves: 6

Although time-consuming to prepare, this beautiful intricate dessert, designed by Pierre Pollin, chef of the excellent Le Titi de Paris restaurant in Arlington Heights, Illinois, is well worth the effort for a special occasion.

8 ounces imported bittersweet or semisweet chocolate
4 ounces milk chocolate
4 ounces imported white chocolate
2 egg yolks *

¼ cup plus 3 tablespoons sugar
1 cup heavy cream
3 cups fresh raspberries
1 tablespoon orange-flavored liqueur

1. To prepare chocolate rectangles to use in place of pastry layers, which are traditionally used in napoleons: Melt 4 ounces bittersweet chocolate in a small bowl set over a saucepan of simmering water. Pour onto a baking sheet lined with plastic wrap. Using a spatula, spread chocolate into a 6 x 4-inch rectangle about ⅜ inch thick.

2. Repeat this melting and spreading process with milk and white chocolates to make 3 different chocolate rectangles.

3. Refrigerate chocolate rectangles just until firm, 7 to 8 minutes. (If refrigerated much longer, chocolate will become brittle, causing it to break when cut.) Cut each rectangle into 6 (2-inch) squares, cutting right through the plastic wrap. Refrigerate with plastic wrap attached, until completely firm, at least 15 minutes, or overnight.

4. To prepare mousse, melt remaining 4 ounces bittersweet chocolate in a small bowl set over a saucepan of simmering water; set bowl aside. In a medium bowl set over another saucepan of simmering water, beat egg yolks, 3 tablespoons sugar, and 2 tablespoons water until thickened, about 4 minutes. Stir in melted chocolate; let cool to room temperature.

5. Beat cream until soft peaks form. Fold whipped cream into chocolate mixture. Cover and refrigerate 3 hours or overnight.

6. For the raspberry sauce, in a food processor, combine 1½ cups raspberries, remaining ¼ cup sugar, and orange liqueur. Process until pureed. Strain puree through a fine sieve into a bowl; discard seeds. Cover and refrigerate strained sauce.

7. To assemble dessert, carefully remove and discard plastic wrap from chocolate squares. Spoon chocolate mousse into a pastry bag fitted with a ½-inch plain or star tip. Assembling one napoleon at a time, place a bitter-sweet chocolate square on a chilled dessert plate. Pipe a thick layer of chocolate mousse (about 2 tablespoons) over surface of chocolate square. From the remaining 1½ cups raspberries, arrange 6 raspberries on top of chocolate mousse. Place a milk chocolate square on top of raspberries. Repeat layering with a portion of chocolate mousse and 6 more raspberries. Top with a white chocolate square. Pipe a dollop of chocolate mousse in center of white chocolate square; top with a raspberry.

8. Repeat procedure to make a total of 6 mousse-filled napoleons. Spoon a portion of the chilled raspberry sauce around each napoleon and garnish with remaining raspberries. Serve at once.

   * CAUTION: *Because of the possible threat of salmonella—a bacteria that causes food poisoning—from raw eggs, U.S. Government officials recommend that the very young, the elderly, pregnant women, and people with serious illnesses or weakened immune systems not eat raw or lightly cooked eggs. Keep this in mind and consume raw or lightly cooked eggs at your own risk.*

---

121 DESSERT SPRING ROLLS
Prep: 40 minutes   Cook: 10 minutes   Serves: 6 to 12

   The combination of apricots, milk chocolate, and crisp eggroll skins is dynamite. Although this recipe is a bit time-consuming, the results are worth the trouble.

12 ounces dried apricots	½ cup heavy cream
1 cup orange-flavored liqueur	12 (6-inch) square eggroll skins
½ cup orange juice	Peanut oil, for frying
1 (11.5-ounce) package milk chocolate chips (2 cups)	½ cup sliced almonds (2 ounces), toasted

1. To make apricot filling, in a small saucepan, bring 9 ounces dried apricots and ½ cup orange liqueur to a boil over high heat and cook 3 minutes. Remove from heat and let cool.

2. Meanwhile, prepare apricot sauce. In a small saucepan, combine remaining dried apricots, remaining ½ cup orange liqueur, and orange juice. Heat to boiling. Remove from heat and let cool. Puree in a blender until smooth; set aside.

3. To prepare chocolate sauce, in a small glass bowl, combine 1 cup milk chocolate chips and cream. Heat in a microwave oven on High 1 to 1½ minutes, or until chocolate is melted and mixture is smooth when stirred; set aside.

4. Chop cooled apricot filling and toss with remaining milk chocolate chips. Place 1 tablespoon of mixture in a strip along a side of 1 eggroll skin about 1 inch from edge. Moisten edges of eggroll skin and, starting from end closest to filling, fold up over filling. Fold in sides about ¾ inch, pressing to seal. Fold remaining open edge of eggroll skin over to completely enclose, pressing gently to seal. Repeat with remaining eggroll skins and filling. Place filled rolls on wax paper.

5. In a large skillet, heat ½ inch peanut oil to 350° F. Fry 2 to 3 rolls at a time in hot oil for 20 seconds; turn over and fry 15 seconds longer, or until golden brown. Transfer to paper towels to drain.

6. To serve, place 1 or 2 rolls on each dessert plate and drizzle reserved apricot sauce over half of each roll and reserved chocolate sauce over the other half. Garnish with a sprinkling of almonds.

122   BLACK BOTTOM TIRAMISU
Prep: 35 minutes   Cook: none   Serves: 10 to 12

There are probably as many variations on the Italian dessert tiramisu (which means "pick me up"), as there are Italian restaurants and cooks. Instead of being prepared in a square or rectangular dish, this version is made in a springform pan for attractive presentation.

1½ cups heavy cream
1 (17½-ounce) container mascarpone (available at Italian markets and in some supermarkets)
½ cup powdered sugar
1 cup plus 3 tablespoons hot, freshly brewed espresso or coffee
¼ cup plus 2 tablespoons coffee-flavored liqueur

6 ounces semisweet chocolate chips (1 cup), melted and cooled slightly
1½ (7-ounce) packages crisp, dry imported Italian ladyfingers (Un Fagotto di Savoiardi)
1½ tablespoons unsweetened cocoa powder

1. In a chilled bowl with chilled beaters, whip cream until stiff. In a large bowl, combine mascarpone, powdered sugar, 3 tablespoons cool coffee, and 2 tablespoons coffee liqueur. Beat with an electric mixer on medium speed 1 to 2 minutes, just until well blended; do not overbeat. Fold whipped cream into mascarpone mixture. Divide mixture in half. Fold melted chocolate into one half until no white streaks remain.

2. Combine remaining 1 cup hot coffee and remaining ¼ cup coffee-flavored liqueur in a pie plate. Quickly dip *one* side of enough ladyfingers to line bottom of a 9-inch springform pan in coffee mixture. (It is important to dip ladyfingers quickly in coffee mixture so they don't get too wet and soggy.) Place ladyfingers dry side down in bottom of springform pan.

3. Trim enough remaining ladyfingers to go around inside edge of pan so they are even with top of pan when standing up. Stand cut undipped ladyfingers rounded side up around inside edge of pan. Brush inside of ladyfingers with coffee mixture to moisten.

4. Spread chocolate mascarpone mixture over ladyfingers in bottom of pan. Cover with another layer of ladyfingers that have been quickly dipped on one side in coffee mixture, setting them dipped side up. Spread remaining white mascarpone mixture over ladyfingers. Set pan on a double thickness of aluminum foil and bring foil up around edges of pan to catch any leaks.

5. Cover with plastic wrap and refrigerate 6 hours or overnight. Just before serving, run knife around edge of cake to loosen from pan. Remove springform side. Sift cocoa over top of cake.

123   CHOCOLATE MERINGUE MOUSSE TORTE
Prep: 1¼ hours   Cook: 60 to 65 minutes   Chill: 8 hours   Serves: 10

This is an adaptation of the famous French pastry maker Gaston Lenotre's Concorde, which has been served in various renditions at numerous restaurants around the country over the years. It sounds more difficult to make than it really is. Lenotre presents his version in an oval; this one is round.

⅓ cup unsweetened cocoa
    powder
1¼ cups powdered sugar
  6 egg whites
½ teaspoon cream of tartar
⅛ teaspoon salt

¾ cup granulated sugar
    Chocolate Mousse Filling
    and Frosting (recipe
    follows)
    Powdered sugar

1. Preheat oven to 300°F. In a medium bowl, sift together cocoa and powdered sugar; set aside.

2. Line 2 baking sheets with parchment or wax paper. Using a 9-inch cake pan as a pattern, trace two 9-inch circles on one baking sheet and one 9-inch circle at one end of the other baking sheet.

3. In a large bowl, beat together egg whites, cream of tartar, and salt with an electric mixer on medium speed, until soft peaks form. Turn mixer to high and gradually beat in granulated sugar until glossy, stiff peaks form. Reduce mixer speed to low and gradually beat in reserved cocoa mixture, scraping down sides of bowl often, until well incorporated.

4. Fill a pastry bag fitted with a ½- or ⅝-inch round tip three quarters full with chocolate meringue. Starting at the center of each of the 3 circles, pipe meringue in a spiral until circle is completely covered. Refill pastry bag as needed; use about three quarters of meringue to make circles.

5. Place remaining meringue in a pastry bag fitted with an ⅛-inch round tip. On baking pan with 1 circle, pipe out long thin strips of meringue, about ½ inch apart. These will be used to decorate top and sides of cake.

6. Bake meringues 15 minutes. Reduce oven temperature to 275°F. Bake 45 to 50 minutes longer, until dry and crisp. Let cool on pans, then carefully remove from parchment. (If desired, meringues can be made a day ahead of assembling.)

7. To assemble torte, place 1 meringue layer on a large serving plate. Spread about one quarter of Chocolate Mousse Filling and Frosting evenly over meringue. Add second meringue layer and cover with another layer of mousse. Top with remaining meringue layer. Spread remaining mousse over top and sides of torte. Cut thin meringue strips into ½-inch sticks and press gently into top and sides of cake. Refrigerate at least 8 hours or overnight. Sift powdered sugar lightly over before serving.

124 CHOCOLATE MOUSSE FILLING AND FROSTING

Prep: 15 minutes   Cook: 5 minutes   Makes: enough to fill and frost a 2-layer 9-inch cake

1 pound bittersweet or semisweet chocolate, cut up
6 eggs, separated*
1 stick (4 ounces) unsalted butter, softened and cut up

2 tablespoons Grand Marnier
⅓ cup sugar
Dash of salt

1. In a 2-quart glass bowl, melt chocolate in a microwave oven on Medium 3 minutes; stir. Heat on Medium 2 minutes longer, or until melted and smooth when stirred.

2. Whisk in egg yolks (the heat of the chocolate will thicken the yolks), then butter and Grand Marnier; whisk until butter is melted. Let cool to room temperature.

3. In a large bowl, beat egg whites with an electric mixer on medium speed until foamy. Turn mixer speed to high and gradually beat in sugar and salt. Beat until stiff, glossy peaks form.

4. Mix a dollop of egg whites into chocolate until well blended. Fold in remaining whites until no streaks remain.

* **CAUTION:** *Because of the possible threat of salmonella—a bacteria that causes food poisoning—from raw eggs, U.S. Government officials recommend that the very young, the elderly, pregnant women, and people with serious illnesses or weakened immune systems not eat raw or lightly cooked eggs. Keep this in mind and consume raw or lightly cooked eggs at your own risk.*

125 BUTTER ALMOND CHOCOLATE TORTE

Prep: 30 minutes   Cook: 31 minutes   Chill: 2 to 3 hours   Serves: 10

1 cup sliced blanched almonds (about 4 ounces)
⅔ cup plus ½ cup semisweet chocolate chips
1 stick (4 ounces) plus 2 tablespoons butter, softened

¼ cup sugar
1½ teaspoons vanilla extract
2 tablespoons flour
3 eggs
Butter Cookie Crust (recipe follows)
1½ tablespoons light corn syrup

1. Preheat oven to 350°F. In a food processor, grind together almonds and ⅔ cup chocolate until grated; remove and set aside.

2. In same processor bowl, combine 1 stick butter and sugar and process until well blended. Add 1 teaspoon vanilla, flour, and eggs. Process until well blended. Mix in ground almonds and chocolate.

3. Spread filling evenly over prebaked Butter Cookie Crust. Bake 30 minutes, or until golden and let cool.

4. In a 2-cup glass measure, combine remaining 2 tablespoons butter and ½ cup chocolate chips with corn syrup and 1 tablespoon water. Microwave on High 45 to 60 seconds, stirring until smooth. Stir in remaining ½ teaspoon vanilla. Let cool.

5. When cool, spread glaze evenly over top of cooled torte. Refrigerate at least 2 to 3 hours or overnight before serving.

BUTTER COOKIE CRUST

1 **stick (4 ounces) butter**	1 **egg**
⅓ **cup sugar**	1 **teaspoon vanilla extract**
1¼ **cups flour**	

1. Preheat oven to 350°F. Slice butter in pieces into a food processor bowl. Add sugar and process until blended, about 1 minute. Add flour and process until well mixed. With machine on, add egg and vanilla through feed tube. Process just until dough clings together and leaves sides of bowl.

2. Press dough over bottom and up sides of 9½-inch fluted metal tart pan with removable bottom. Line with foil and pie weights or dried beans and bake 10 minutes. Remove weights and foil and continue baking 10 minutes longer, or until golden. Let cool before filling.

---

126   CHOCOLATE SHEET CAKE, TEXAS STYLE
Prep: 15 minutes   Cook: 20 to 25 minutes   Makes: 48 pieces

This recipe has been making the rounds for several years. It's a good dessert choice for a potluck offering or when you'll be serving a large crowd because the recipe makes plenty with little effort.

2 **cups flour**	2 **eggs**
2 **cups sugar**	1 **teaspoon baking soda**
2 **sticks (8 ounces) margarine,** cut up	2 **teaspoons vanilla extract**
⅓ **cup unsweetened cocoa** powder	**Chocolate Pecan Icing** (recipe follows)
½ **cup buttermilk or sour** cream	

1. Preheat oven to 375°F. Grease a 10 x 15-inch jelly-roll pan.

2. In a medium bowl, combine flour and sugar; set aside. In a medium saucepan, mix together margarine, cocoa, and 1 cup water. Heat to boiling over medium heat, stirring often. Pour over flour and sugar mixture. Add buttermilk, eggs, baking soda, and vanilla, and mix to blend well. Turn batter into prepared pan.

3. Bake 20 to 25 minutes, or until a cake tester inserted in center comes out clean. Immediately frost top of hot cake with Chocolate Pecan Icing. Let cool, then cut into 48 squares.

127   CHOCOLATE PECAN ICING

Prep: 5 minutes   Cook: none   Makes: about 3 cups

1   stick (4 ounces) margarine, softened
¼   cup unsweetened cocoa powder
⅓   cup milk

1   (1-pound) box powdered sugar
1   teaspoon vanilla extract
1   cup chopped pecans

In a medium bowl, beat together margarine, cocoa, and milk with an electric mixer on medium speed until light and fluffy, about 2 minutes. Add powdered sugar and vanilla and beat on high speed until well blended. Stir in pecans.

128   CHOCOLATE ZUCCOTTO

Prep: 40 minutes   Cook: none   Freeze: 8 hours   Serves: 10 to 12

This fabulous-looking, Italian-inspired, dome-shaped cake filled with chocolate and orange ricotta mixtures is the creation of pastry chef Jackie Ravel-Knezevich at DC3, a trendy restaurant located at the airport in Santa Monica, California. Although preparation is lengthy, it's not difficult. An added advantage: the dessert can be prepared and frozen well in advance of serving.

Chocolate Chiffon Cake (recipe follows)
1   pound ricotta cheese
½   cup sugar
2¾   cups heavy cream
1   tablespoon vanilla extract
1   tablespoon amaretto (almond-flavored liqueur)
6   ounces semisweet chocolate chips (1 cup), melted

2   tablespoons orange-flavored liqueur
1   tablespoon grated orange zest
½   cup chopped roasted almonds or chocolate-covered almonds
Shaved chocolate

1. Lightly oil a 2½-quart heatproof glass mixing bowl. Line with plastic wrap, allowing 4 to 5 inches to extend beyond edge of bowl. Cut an 8-inch-round cake layer from Chocolate Chiffon Cake in jelly-roll pan as close to one end of the pan as possible, cutting right through wax paper. Cut another cake round as large as possible from remaining chiffon cake; reserve all trimmings. Invert larger round into prepared bowl. Press cake gently against bottom and sides of bowl; peel off and discard paper.

2. Cut remaining chiffon cake scraps (*not* reserved 8-inch round) into pieces or strips and use to line sides of bowl above cake round already in bowl.

3. In a large bowl, beat together ricotta cheese, sugar, 2 cups cream, vanilla, and amaretto with an electric mixer on high speed until thick and smooth like whipped cream, about 3 minutes. Transfer half of mixture to another bowl and set aside. To remaining mixture, add melted chocolate. Beat until no streaks of white remain.

4. To reserved ricotta mixture, add orange liqueur, orange zest, and almonds; mix well. Spoon orange-flavored ricotta mixture into cake-lined bowl. Smooth evenly to flatten surface. Spoon chocolate ricotta mixture on top and smooth evenly to flatten surface. Invert reserved 8-inch round of chiffon cake on top; peel off wax paper. Bring plastic wrap up over cake. Cover top with foil and freeze until firm, 8 hours or overnight.

5. A couple of hours before serving, invert zuccotto onto a serving platter. (Use plastic wrap overhang to help ease cake out of bowl.) In a medium bowl, beat remaining ¾ cup cream with an electric mixer on high speed until almost stiff. Spread over entire surface of cake. Sprinkle shaved chocolate over all. Return cake to freezer until 30 to 45 minutes before serving. Using a sharp knife, cut into 10 to 12 wedges.

129   CHOCOLATE CHIFFON CAKE
Prep: 20 minutes   Cook: 25 to 30 minutes   Serves: 10 to 12

6 egg whites	1 cup flour
1½ cups sugar	¾ cup unsweetened cocoa
4 egg yolks	powder
1 teaspoon vanilla extract	2 teaspoons baking powder
¾ cup cooking oil	1 teaspoon baking soda

1. Preheat oven to 350°F. Line a 10 x 15-inch jelly-roll pan with wax paper. Grease paper and sides of pan. Dust with flour; tap out excess.

2. In a medium bowl, beat egg whites with an electric mixer on medium speed until soft peaks form. Gradually beat in ½ cup sugar. Increase speed to high and beat until whites are stiff and glossy.

3. In a large bowl, whisk together egg yolks, ½ cup water, vanilla, and oil until well blended. In a medium bowl, mix together remaining 1 cup sugar, flour, cocoa, baking powder, and baking soda. Whisk dry ingredients into egg yolk mixture until smooth and blended. Fold in reserved egg whites.

4. Turn batter into prepared pan. Bake 25 to 30 minutes, or until a cake tester inserted in center comes out clean. Let cool in pan.

130   CHOCOLATE ALMOND STEAMED PUDDING

Prep: 30 minutes   Cook: 3 hours   Serves: 12 to 14

Friend, recipe tester, and hostess extraordinaire Patti Gray developed this recipe, which she serves during the Christmas holidays, as the finale to an English dinner, for her husband, who is fond of chocolate, but doesn't care for traditional steamed puddings. This outstanding pudding can be prepared in advance, kept refrigerated, and reheated in simmering water an hour before serving.

½ cup coarsely chopped blanched almonds
½ cup sliced blanched almonds
1 cup plus 2 tablespoons sugar
1 stick (4 ounces) unsalted butter
½ teaspoon almond extract
3 tablespoons chocolate-flavored liqueur or brandy
3 tablespoons amaretto or other almond-flavored liqueur
½ teaspoon salt
1 teaspoon instant espresso powder
½ cup firmly packed unsweetened cocoa powder (preferably Dutch-processed)
3 (1-ounce) squares semisweet chocolate, melted
4 eggs
1¾ cups cake flour
1 tablespoon baking powder
1 cup half-and-half
All-Purpose Chocolate Sauce (recipe follows)

1. Preheat oven to 325°F. Spread out chopped and sliced almonds on a large baking sheet, keeping them separate. Bake 5 minutes, or until lightly toasted. Butter two 1-quart pudding molds and dust each with 1 tablespoon sugar. Set a rack on the bottom of a large pot, fill pot with water, and bring to a simmer.

2. Meanwhile, in a large bowl, beat butter and remaining 1 cup sugar with an electric mixer on medium speed until light and fluffy, 1 to 2 minutes. Add almond extract, chocolate liqueur, amaretto, salt, espresso powder, cocoa, and melted chocolate. Beat until well blended. Add eggs, one at a time, beating well after each addition. Sift together cake flour and baking powder and add to chocolate mixture alternately with half-and-half, beating only enough to combine. Stir in chopped almonds.

3. Divide mixture evenly between 2 prepared molds; each should be about ¾ full. Place a round of buttered wax paper on top of each mold. Place lids on molds and lower onto rack in pot of simmering water. Water should reach two thirds of the way up sides of molds. Cover pot and steam over low heat 3 hours, adding more water to pot if necessary.

4. Remove molds from pot and let stand 10 minutes before unmolding. Cut into slices to serve. Serve hot, topped with All-Purpose Chocolate Sauce and sprinkled with sliced almonds.

131   ALL-PURPOSE CHOCOLATE SAUCE
Prep: 5 minutes   Cook: 3 to 5 minutes   Makes: about 2 cups

Vary the liqueurs in this recipe to suit your taste and the dessert you are serving. If you prefer to keep the sauce nonalcoholic, omit both liqueurs and add ¼ cup strong coffee.

1 cup powdered sugar
1 cup heavy cream
1 stick (4 ounces) butter, cut
      into pieces
½ cup firmly packed
      unsweetened cocoa
      powder
3 ounces bittersweet or
      semisweet chocolate, cut
      up

2 tablespoons amaretto or
      other almond-flavored
      liqueur
2 tablespoons chocolate-
      flavored liqueur

In a small saucepan, combine powdered sugar, cream, butter, cocoa, and chocolate. Place over low heat and cook, stirring constantly, until chocolate melts and sauce is smooth and glossy, 3 to 5 minutes. Remove from heat and stir in amaretto and chocolate liqueur. Let cool to room temperature.

132   CHOCOLATE ORANGE QUICHE
Prep: 15 minutes   Cook: 40 to 45 minutes   Serves: 10 to 12

If you've never thought of serving a dessert quiche, there's always a first time. This version is spectacular and rich.

4 eggs
1½ cups half-and half
½ cup sugar
1 tablespoon grated orange
      zest
4 ounces bittersweet
      chocolate, cut into chunks

4 ounces imported white
      chocolate, cut into chunks
1 cup chopped pecans
      Chocolate Pecan Pastry
      (recipe follows)

1. Preheat oven to 375°F. Make filling: In a medium bowl, whisk together eggs, half-and-half, and sugar. Stir in orange zest, bittersweet chocolate, white chocolate, and pecans.

2. Press Chocolate Pecan Pastry into bottom and up sides of a fluted 11 x 1-inch metal tart pan with removable bottom. Turn filling into crust and spread evenly. Bake 40 to 45 minutes, or until filling is set and top is golden brown. Let cool.

133   CHOCOLATE PECAN PASTRY

Prep: 10 minutes   Cook: none   Makes: enough for a single-crust 9-inch pie or an 11-inch tart

1   stick (4 ounces) butter, cut into tablespoons
1   tablespoon solid butter-flavored shortening
1   cup flour
¼   cup unsweetened cocoa powder
1   tablespoon sugar
1   teaspoon salt
¼   cup ground pecans

In a food processor, combine butter, shortening, flour, cocoa, sugar, salt, and pecans. Process with on and off turns until mixture resembles coarse meal, about 30 seconds. With machine on, add 2 to 3 tablespoons cold water through feed tube. Process until dough forms a ball. Refrigerate until ready to use.

134   WHITE CHOCOLATE RASPBERRY TART

Prep: 50 minutes   Cook: 19 to 21 minutes   Chill: 2 hours Serves: 12

A little of this rich sophisticated tart—a recipe shared by Jennifer Powers, pastry chef at I Cugini restaurant in Santa Monica, California—goes a long way. A white chocolate and cream mixture covers raspberries and pistachio nuts in a butter cookie crust. Try this idea for a special dessert for your next dinner party.

1   stick (4 ounces) plus 3 tablespoons unsalted butter, softened
¼   cup sugar
1   teaspoon vanilla extract
1   cup flour
12   ounces imported white chocolate, chopped
⅓   cup heavy cream
1¾   cups fresh raspberries, rinsed and well drained (do not substitute frozen)
¾   cup coarsely chopped pistachio nuts

1. Make crust: In a food processor, combine 1 stick butter, sugar, and vanilla. Process until well blended. Add flour and process just until dough forms a ball.

2. Press into bottom and up sides of a 9½- or 10-inch fluted metal tart pan with removable bottom. Refrigerate 15 to 20 minutes.

3. Preheat oven to 350°F. Bake crust 18 to 20 minutes, or until golden. Let cool.

4. Meanwhile, prepare filling and topping. In a 1-quart glass bowl, combine white chocolate and remaining 3 tablespoons butter, cut up. In a small glass bowl, heat cream in a microwave oven on High 60 to 70 seconds, or until boiling. Pour hot cream over white chocolate and butter, stirring until melted and smooth. If necessary, heat mixture in microwave on Medium 1 minute to melt white chocolate completely. Let cool 15 minutes.

5. Place raspberries in cooled crust. Sprinkle ½ cup pistachios over berries. Carefully pour white chocolate mixture on top, spreading evenly. Sprinkle remaining ¼ cup pistachios in 1-inch-wide ring around outer edge of tart. Refrigerate until set, at least 2 hours. Before serving, remove side of pan and, using a sharp knife, cut tart into thin slices.

135 CHOCOLATE TRUFFLE CAKE
Prep: 10 minutes   Cook: 52 to 57 minutes   Serves: 10 to 12

This dense, rich cake is one of my favorite and most versatile chocolate recipes. As a dessert, it can stand alone. It can be sliced thinly and topped with whipped cream and fresh raspberries. Slices can be set in a pool of raspberry sauce, blackberry sauce, strawberry sauce, crème anglaise, or melted vanilla ice cream. It is the base of my recipe for Chocolate Indulgence (page 90).

2 sticks (8 ounces) butter	2 (1-ounce) squares
½ cup sugar	unsweetened chocolate,
½ cup strong brewed coffee	cut up
6 ounces semisweet or	4 eggs
bittersweet chocolate, cut up	

1. Preheat oven to 350°F. Line an 8-inch springform pan with foil. Butter foil generously. Dust with flour; tap out excess.

2. In a 2-quart glass bowl, combine butter, sugar, coffee, semisweet chocolate, and unsweetened chocolate. Heat in a microwave oven on High 1½ to 2 minutes, or until chocolate and butter are melted and mixture is smooth when stirred. Remove from heat. Whisk in eggs until smooth and well blended.

3. Pour batter into prepared pan. Bake 50 to 55 minutes, or until top has a crust and is dry to the touch. Let cool in pan. Run a sharp knife around edge of pan to loosen cake and remove springform side of pan. Invert cake to unmold, peel off foil, then place cake right side up on a serving plate. Store cake, covered, in refrigerator or freezer.

Chapter 5

Quick Fixes with Mixes

Who in this day and age isn't looking for something quick to fix with a mix that tastes fabulous, as if you spent hours in the kitchen when you don't have a minute to spare? These shortcut recipes all start with mixes of some sort —cake mixes, brownie mixes, refrigerated crescent rolls, pudding and pie filling mixes, buttermilk baking mix, and the like. Some of these creations are down to earth, others more sophisticated, but all are chocolatey, good, and a cinch to make.

Although some of the recipes require longer baking times than others, all have been designed to be whipped up in short order with minimum preparation time. Some of my favorites are Chocolate Café au Lait Cake, Black Forest Coffeecake, Chocolate Brandy Cake, Quick Crème de Menthe Pie, Quick Chocolate Zucchini Picnic Cake, Streusel Chocolate Chip Bundt Cake, Rocky Road Refrigerator Cake, Speedy Chocolate Cherry-Pineapple Bake, and Banana Split Cake. They are all sure to please the most discriminating guests. Keep these easy chocolate desserts in mind for office parties and potlucks, to tote to meetings, and when you need a chocolate fix *fast*!

---

136 BANANA SPLIT CAKE
Prep: 15 minutes   Cook: 45 minutes   Serves: 12

¼ teaspoon baking soda
1 cup buttermilk
1 (18.25-ounce) package
    yellow cake mix with
    pudding included
3 medium very ripe bananas,
    mashed

4 tablespoons butter, melted
    and cooled slightly
3 eggs
1½ cups chopped walnuts
½ cup hot fudge sauce

1. Preheat oven to 325°F. In a large bowl, dissolve baking soda in buttermilk. Add cake mix, mashed bananas, melted butter, and eggs. Beat with an electric mixer on medium speed 2 minutes.

2. Spoon half of batter into a greased 9 x 13-inch baking pan. Sprinkle 1 cup nuts evenly over batter and drizzle fudge sauce over nuts. Top with remaining cake batter, spreading evenly. Sprinkle remaining ½ cup nuts over top.

3. Bake about 45 minutes, or until a cake tester inserted in center comes out clean. Let cool in pan.

137   CHOCOLATE BRANDY CAKE
Prep: 10 minutes   Cook: 45 to 55 minutes   Serves: 12 to 14

This scrumptious cake is so moist and delicious, your friends will never guess it's made with a mix.

1 (18.25-ounce) package devil's food cake mix with pudding included	1½ cups semisweet chocolate chips
1 cup brandy	4 tablespoons butter
½ cup vegetable oil	1 tablespoon light corn syrup
3 eggs	1 teaspoon brandy extract
	1 cup powdered sugar, sifted

1. Preheat oven to 350°F. In a large bowl, combine cake mix, ⅔ cup brandy, ½ cup water, oil, and eggs. Beat with an electric mixer on high speed 2 minutes, scraping down bowl a few times. Stir in 1 cup chocolate chips. Turn into a well-greased 12-cup bundt pan.

2. Bake 35 to 45 minutes, or until a cake tester inserted in center comes out clean.

3. During last 7 minutes of cake baking time, prepare glaze. In a small saucepan, combine butter, remaining ⅓ cup brandy, corn syrup, brandy extract, and 2 tablespoons water. Cook over low heat, stirring occasionally, until butter melts. Stir in remaining ½ cup chocolate chips and powdered sugar. Simmer, stirring, over low heat 5 minutes.

4. Immediately upon removal from oven, spoon two thirds of hot glaze over cake. Let cake cool in pan 25 minutes, then invert onto a cake plate. Reheat remaining glaze and spoon evenly over top of cake. Let cool completely. Cake is best if made a day in advance of serving time to allow flavors to mellow.

138   CHOCOLATE CAFE AU LAIT CAKE
Prep: 20 minutes   Cook: 31 to 37 minutes   Serves: 12

This cake is an old family favorite I've been baking since childhood. It's still delicious, easy, and good for today's fast-paced cook's recipe repertoire.

1 stick (4 ounces) margarine	1½ cups heavy cream
1½ cups graham cracker crumbs	1½ tablespoons instant coffee powder
6 ounces semisweet chocolate chips (1 cup)	⅓ cup sifted powdered sugar
½ cup chopped walnuts	
1 (18.25-ounce) package devil's food or chocolate fudge cake mix	

1. Melt margarine in a medium saucepan over low heat, or in a 1-quart glass bowl in a microwave oven on High 1 to 1¼ minutes. Stir in graham cracker crumbs and let cool. When cool, stir in chocolate chips and walnuts; set aside.

2. Preheat oven to 350°F. Grease and flour two 9-inch round cake pans. Prepare cake mix according to package directions. Turn batter into prepared pans. Sprinkle crumb-walnut-chocolate chip mixture over cake batter, dividing evenly between pans. Using fingertips or back of a spoon, lightly press mixture into batter (crumb mixture should not sink all the way into batter).

3. Bake cake as package directs (30 to 35 minutes), or until a cake tester inserted in center comes out clean. Remove cakes from oven; let cool completely in pans before unmolding. Keep layers crumb side up.

4. In a medium bowl, beat cream, coffee powder, and powdered sugar with an electric mixer on high speed until stiff. Place one cooled cake layer, crumb side up, on a serving plate. Spread three quarters of whipped cream mixture over cake. Top with remaining cake layer, crumb side up. Frost sides of cake with remaining whipped cream; do not frost top of cake. Refrigerate until serving time.

139 QUICK MOCHA NAPOLEONS
Prep: 45 minutes   Cook: 23 to 25 minutes   Chill: 6 hours
Serves: 36

Here's a great idea to whip up when you're having a crowd or a dessert buffet. It's easy on the cook as it utilizes frozen puff pastry and instant pudding mix. For fewer guests, the recipe can be halved easily.

1 **(17¼-ounce) package frozen puff pastry, thawed**
2 **cups milk**
½ **cup strong brewed coffee, cooled**
¼ **cup coffee-flavored liqueur**
2 **(6-ounce) packages instant chocolate fudge flavor pudding and pie filling mix**

1 **cup heavy cream, whipped**
½ **cup chocolate sauce**
½ **cup sliced almonds, lightly toasted**

1. Preheat oven to 350°F. Unwrap thawed puff pastry sheets and cut each sheet into thirds at the fold marks. Place on 2 ungreased baking sheets; prick all over with a fork. Bake 15 minutes. Prick with a fork again and bake 8 to 10 minutes longer, or until pastry is golden brown. Let cool completely on baking sheets. When cool, cut each piece of pastry crosswise into 6 equal pieces. Split each piece in half horizontally, keeping tops and bottoms together.

2. In a large mixing bowl, combine milk, cold coffee, coffee liqueur, and pudding mix. Beat with an electric mixer on low speed until well combined, 1 minute. Fold in whipped cream. Cover and refrigerate 1½ hours.

3. To assemble, place a generous tablespoonful of pudding mixture on bottom half of each puff pastry piece, then replace top piece of puff pastry. Drizzle chocolate sauce lightly over each napoleon, then sprinkle toasted almonds on top. Refrigerate 6 hours before serving.

140   CALIFORNIA RICOTTA CAKE
Prep: 30 minutes   Cook: 30 to 35 minutes   Serves: 12

A handsome cake you make with a mix.

1   (18.25-ounce) devil's food
     cake mix
1   (15- or 16-ounce) container
     ricotta cheese
⅓   cup powdered sugar
⅓   cup heavy cream
2   teaspoons vanilla extract

2   teaspoons grated orange zest
⅓   cup miniature semisweet
     chocolate chips
⅔   cup diced roasted almonds
2   tablespoons orange-flavored
     liqueur

1. Preheat oven to 350°F. Grease and flour two 9-inch round cake pans. Prepare cake mix according to package directions. Turn batter into prepared pans. Bake according to package directions (30 to 35 minutes). Let cake cool in pans 15 minutes, then unmold and let cool completely on wire racks.

2. In a medium bowl, combine ricotta cheese, powdered sugar, cream, vanilla, and orange zest. Beat with an electric mixer on medium speed until light and fluffy, about 2 minutes. Stir in chocolate chips and ⅓ cup almonds.

3. Sprinkle 1 tablespoon orange liqueur over top of each cake layer. Stack cake layers together with cheese filling in between and on top and sides. Sprinkle remaining ⅓ cup almonds around top edge of cake in a 1-inch-wide ring. Refrigerate until serving time.

141   CHOCOLATE ALMOND-RASPBERRY CAKE
Prep: 30 minutes   Cook: 46 to 48 minutes   Serves: 12

If you love almond paste and want to rustle up a cake quick, try this one with a mix.

7   ounces almond paste
1   (18.25-ounce) package
     devil's food cake mix
     (without pudding
     included)
½   teaspoon cinnamon
¼   teaspoon grated nutmeg
¾   cup sherry
½   teaspoon almond extract
3   eggs

½   cup vegetable oil
3   tablespoons seedless
     raspberry jam
6   ounces semisweet chocolate
     chips (1 cup)
2   tablespoons butter
1   tablespoon light corn syrup
¼   cup slivered blanched
     almonds, toasted

1. Preheat oven to 350°F. To prepare cake, in a food processor, process almond paste until finely chopped. Add cake mix, cinnamon, and nutmeg; process until thoroughly mixed. Add sherry, almond extract, eggs, ½ cup water, and oil. Process until smooth.

2. Turn cake batter into a well-greased 12-cup bundt pan. Bake about 45 minutes, or until cake springs back when touched lightly. Let cool in pan 15 to 20 minutes, then invert onto a serving plate or rack to cool completely.

3. Meanwhile, prepare glaze: In a 1-quart glass bowl, combine raspberry jam, chocolate chips, butter, and corn syrup. Heat in a microwave oven on High 1 to 1½ minutes, or until chocolate is melted and mixture is smooth when stirred. Drizzle glaze over top of cake. Sprinkle almonds over glaze. Allow glaze to set up before serving.

142   FAVORITE CHOCOLATE BUNDT CAKE

Prep: 15 minutes   Cook: 50 to 60 minutes   Serves: 12 to 16

1 (18.25-ounce) package devil's food or other chocolate cake mix (without pudding included)
1 (4-ounce) package instant chocolate fudge or chocolate flavor pudding and pie filling mix

4 eggs
½ cup vegetable oil
1 cup sour cream
12 ounces semisweet chocolate chips (2 cups)
Powdered sugar

1. Preheat oven to 350°F. In a large bowl, combine cake mix, pudding mix, eggs, oil, sour cream, and ½ cup water. Beat with an electric mixer on low speed just until blended. Beat on medium speed 4 minutes, scraping down sides of bowl often. Stir in chocolate chips.

2. Turn into a well-greased 12-cup bundt pan. Bake 50 to 60 minutes, or until a cake tester inserted in center comes out clean. Let cool 10 to 15 minutes in pan, then invert to unmold onto a rack or serving plate and let cool completely. Sift powdered sugar over top.

Variation: **MOCHA ORANGE CHOCOLATE CAKE**

Before beating, add ¼ cup coffee-flavored liqueur and 2 tablespoons grated orange zest to cake mix along with other ingredients. Proceed as directed in recipe above.

Variation: **RASPBERRY FUDGE CAKE**

Before beating, add ¼ cup raspberry-flavored liqueur to cake mix along with other ingredients. After adding chips to batter, gently mix in ½ cup raspberry jam. Proceed as directed in recipe above.

Variation: **PEANUT BUTTER PUDDING CAKE**

Substitute 1 (4⅛-ounce) package instant chocolate peanut butter chip pudding and pie filling mix for chocolate fudge or chocolate pudding mix. Use 1½ or 2 cups peanut butter-flavored chips instead of chocolate chips. Proceed as directed in recipe above.

143   STREUSEL CHOCOLATE CHIP BUNDT CAKE

Prep: 15 minutes   Cook: 50 to 60 minutes   Serves: 12

1 (18.25-ounce) package
    yellow cake mix (without
    pudding included)
1 (3½-ounce) instant vanilla or
    French vanilla flavor
    pudding and pie filling
    mix
⅓ cup vegetable oil

4 eggs
1 teaspoon vanilla extract
12 ounces semisweet chocolate
    chips (2 cups)
¾ cup chopped walnuts
⅔ cup packed brown sugar
2 tablespoons cinnamon
    Powdered sugar

1. Preheat oven to 350°F. To prepare batter, in a large bowl, beat cake mix, pudding mix, oil, eggs, vanilla, and 1 cup water with an electric mixer on medium speed, 2 minutes.

2. To prepare streusel, in a medium bowl, mix together chocolate chips, walnuts, brown sugar, and cinnamon.

3. Turn half of batter into a greased and floured 12-cup bundt pan. Top evenly with half of streusel mixture. Add remaining batter, then remaining streusel. Swirl streusel gently through batter with a knife.

4. Bake 50 to 60 minutes, or until a cake tester inserted in center comes out clean. Let cake cool in pan on rack 15 to 20 minutes, then invert onto a serving plate to cool completely. Before serving, sprinkle with powdered sugar.

144   CHOCOLATE EGGNOG PUDDING CAKE

Prep: 25 minutes   Cook: 70 to 75 minutes   Serves: 12 to 14

Moist and rich, this is a timely offering during the holiday season. The good eggnog flavor in the frosting is a result of reducing eggnog over medium-low heat to concentrate its flavor.

1 (18.25-ounce) package Swiss
    chocolate or milk
    chocolate cake mix
    (without pudding
    included)
4 eggs
2 cups canned eggnog

½ cup corn oil
2 (3½-ounce) packages instant
    vanilla pudding and pie
    filling mix
1 teaspoon grated nutmeg
    Eggnog Butter Cream
    Frosting (recipe follows)

1. Preheat oven to 350°F. In a large bowl, combine cake mix, eggs, eggnog, oil, pudding mix, and nutmeg. Beat with an electric mixer on medium speed 2 minutes. Turn batter into a well-greased 12-cup bundt pan.

2. Bake 60 to 65 minutes, or until a cake tester inserted in center comes out clean. Let cake cool in pan 20 minutes, then invert onto a wire rack to let cool completely. When cool, frost with Eggnog Butter Cream Frosting.

EGGNOG BUTTER CREAM FROSTING

2 cups canned eggnog	4 tablespoons butter, softened
1 teaspoon grated nutmeg	2 cups powdered sugar

1. In a medium saucepan, bring eggnog and nutmeg to a boil over medium-high heat. Reduce heat to medium-low and simmer, stirring occasionally, until eggnog is reduced to ½ cup, about ½ hour. Remove from heat and let cool completely.

2. In a medium bowl, combine cooled reduced eggnog, butter, and powdered sugar. Beat with an electric mixer on high speed until light and fluffy. Use immediately to frost cooled cake.

---

145 MILE-HIGH CELEBRATION CAKE FOR A CROWD

Prep: 1½ hours   Cook: 35 to 40 minutes per cake   Serves: 36 to 40

This is great for birthdays, kids' parties, or any event when you need a large cake for a crowd. Its sheer size is impressive, and what makes it best is that it is made quickly and easily with mixes. To avoid last-minute hassle, directions call for baking the cakes in advance and freezing them.

3 (18.25-ounce) packages your favorite flavor chocolate cake mixes	2 tablespoons instant espresso powder or instant coffee
1 (8-ounce) package cream cheese, softened	2 (1-pound) boxes powdered sugar
2 sticks (8 ounces) butter, softened	1½ cups seedless raspberry jam
½ cup firmly packed unsweetened cocoa powder	1½ cups orange marmalade

1. Prepare each cake mix according to package directions, baking each in a greased and floured 9 x 13-inch baking pan. When cool, remove cakes from pans, wrap well in foil, and freeze.

2. When ready to assemble, prepare mocha butter cream frosting as follows: In a large mixing bowl, beat cream cheese and butter with an electric mixer on high speed until smooth and well blended, 2 to 3 minutes. Add cocoa and coffee powder; beat well. With mixer on medium, gradually add powdered sugar and when incorporated, turn mixer to high and beat until light and fluffy.

3. To assemble cake, place one frozen cake on a large rectangular platter or tray. Cover with raspberry jam. Top with a second cake layer and cover with orange marmalade. Place remaining cake on top. Frost top and sides with mocha butter cream. Refrigerate until ready to serve.

4. Decorate top with fresh (nontoxic) flowers, chocolate-dipped strawberries, colored sprinkles, or piping.

146 QUICK CHOCOLATE BANANA BUNDT CAKE

Prep: 15 minutes   Cook: 50 to 60 minutes   Serves: 12

Here's an easy way to use a couple of stray ripe bananas. Made with a packaged mix, this cake goes together in a jiffy.

2 **very ripe bananas, mashed (about 1 cup)**
1 **(18.25-ounce) package devil's food cake mix (without pudding included)**
1 **(3½-ounce) package vanilla or chocolate flavor pudding and pie filling mix**

4 **eggs**
1 **cup sour cream**
¼ **cup vegetable oil**
½ **cup chopped walnuts**

1. Preheat oven to 350°F. In a large bowl combine bananas, cake mix, pudding mix, eggs, sour cream, oil, and ¼ cup water. Beat with electric mixer on low speed until combined. Increase speed to medium and beat 2 minutes. By hand, mix in nuts.

2. Turn batter into a well-greased and floured 12-cup bundt or tube pan. Bake 50 to 60 minutes, or until a cake tester inserted in center comes out clean. Let cool in pan 10 to 15 minutes before removing from pan to cool completely.

147 QUICK CHOCOLATE ZUCCHINI PICNIC CAKE

Prep: 10 minutes   Cook: 40 to 45 minutes   Serves: 10 to 12

This is an ideal choice to tote to a picnic.

1 **(18.25-ounce) package devil's food cake mix (without pudding included)**
1 **(4-ounce) package instant chocolate or chocolate fudge flavor pudding and pie filling mix**
4 **eggs**
¼ **cup vegetable oil**

3 **cups packed shredded zucchini (3 medium)**
1 **tablespoon cinnamon**
1 **tablespoon grated orange zest**
½ **cup flaked or shredded coconut**
½ **cup chopped walnuts**
   Powdered sugar

1. Preheat oven to 350°F. In a large bowl, beat cake mix, pudding mix, eggs, oil, zucchini, cinnamon, and orange zest with an electric mixer on medium speed, 3 to 4 minutes, until fluffy and thoroughly blended. Stir in coconut and walnuts. Turn into a greased and floured 9 x 13-inch baking pan.

2. Bake 40 to 45 minutes, or until a cake tester inserted in center comes out clean. Let cake cool in pan. Sprinkle powdered sugar over top before serving.

148   ROCKY ROAD REFRIGERATOR CAKE

Prep: 25 minutes   Cook: 25 to 28 minutes   Chill: 4 to 5 hours
Serves: 10

1 **(21.5-ounce) package fudge
   brownie mix**
1½ **teaspoons instant coffee
   powder**
1½ **teaspoons rum extract**
⅔ **cup chopped walnuts**
1 **cup heavy cream**

2 **tablespoons unsweetened
   cocoa powder**
3 **tablespoons powdered
   sugar**
   Dash of salt
1 **cup miniature
   marshmallows**

1. Preheat oven to 350°F. Line a 9-inch square baking pan with foil. Grease foil. Prepare brownie mix according to package directions. Stir in coffee powder, 1 teaspoon rum extract, and ⅓ cup nuts. Turn batter into prepared baking pan. Bake according to package directions, 25 to 28 minutes, being careful not to overbake. Let cool completely.

2. To prepare rocky road filling and topping: In a medium bowl, with an electric mixer on medium speed beat cream to soft peaks. Beat in cocoa, powdered sugar, and salt until well mixed. Fold in remaining ⅓ cup nuts, remaining ½ teaspoon rum extract, and marshmallows.

3. To assemble cake, cut brownie square into 3 equal strips. Stack strips together with rocky road filling in between and on top. Refrigerate 4 to 5 hours or overnight to allow flavors to meld. To serve, cut into ¾- to 1-inch slices.

149   QUICK KAHLUA CHOCOLATE CREAM PIE

Prep: 10 minutes   Cook: none   Chill: 1 hour   Serves: 6 to 8

1 **cup milk**
¼ **cup Kahlua or other coffee-
   flavored liqueur**
1 **(4-ounce) package instant
   chocolate fudge pudding
   and pie filling mix**
1½ **teaspoons grated orange zest**

1 **cup heavy cream, whipped**
1 **(8-inch) baked chocolate
   crumb crust (store-bought
   or see page 135)**
½ **cup diced roasted almonds**

1. In a medium bowl, combine milk, Kahlua, and pudding mix. Beat with an electric mixer on low speed 1 minute. Fold in orange zest and whipped cream.

2. Turn mixture into crumb crust, spreading evenly. Sprinkle almonds over top. Refrigerate 1 hour or longer, until set.

150   BLACK FOREST COFFEECAKE
Prep: 15 minutes   Cook: 25 to 30 minutes   Serves: 8

½ cup unsweetened cocoa
    powder
3 cups buttermilk baking mix
    (such as Bisquick)
½ cup sugar
4 tablespoons butter or
    margarine, melted

½ teaspoon almond extract
3 eggs
1 (21-ounce) can dark sweet
    cherry filling or topping,
    undrained
6 ounces semisweet chocolate
    chips (1 cup)

1. Preheat oven to 350°F. In a large bowl, combine cocoa, baking mix, sugar, butter, almond extract, eggs, and ⅔ cup water. Beat with an electric mixer on medium speed 15 to 20 seconds.

2. Spread half of batter in a well-greased 7½ x 11¾-inch baking dish. Pour undrained cherry filling over batter and sprinkle chocolate chips over filling. Spoon remaining batter on top, allowing some of filling to show through. Bake 25 to 30 minutes. Cut into squares and serve warm or at room temperature.

151   BANANA CHOCOLATE CHANTILLY PIE
Prep: 15 minutes   Cook: none   Chill: 1 hour   Serves: 6 to 8

Whip this up on a moment's notice. It looks terrific and rates raves.

1 (3-ounce) package cream
    cheese, softened
1¼ cups milk
1 (3¾-ounce) package French
    vanilla pudding and pie
    filling mix
1 cup heavy cream, whipped
1 (8-inch) chocolate crumb
    crust or graham cracker
    crust (prepared or
    homemade)

1 large banana, sliced
½ cup thick chocolate fudge
    sauce (bottled) or Dark
    Chocolate Fudge Sauce
    (page 206)
½ cup diced roasted almonds

1. In a medium bowl, combine cream cheese, milk, and pudding mix. Beat with an electric mixer on low speed 2 minutes. Fold whipped cream into pudding mixture.

2. Turn half of pudding mixture into crust. Top with banana slices, then drizzle ¼ cup fudge sauce over bananas. Cover with remaining pudding mixture and drizzle remaining ¼ cup fudge sauce on top. With a knife, swirl fudge sauce into pudding slightly. Sprinkle almonds over pie.

3. Refrigerate 1 hour or longer, until set. Cut into slices to serve.

152   QUICK CREME DE MENTHE PIE
Prep: 15 minutes   Cook: none   Chill: 1 hour   Serves: 6 to 8

This pie is quick to fix and tastes great! So when time is at a premium, keep this recipe in mind.

1 cup heavy cream	1 (8-inch) baked chocolate
1 cup milk	crumb crust
¼ cup crème de menthe	Whipped cream and shaved
1 (4-ounce) package instant	semisweet chocolate
chocolate fudge pudding	
and pie filling mix	

1. In a medium bowl, beat cream with an electric mixer on high speed until stiff, 2 or 3 minutes.

2. In a medium bowl, combine milk, crème de menthe, and pudding mix. Beat with electric mixer on low speed 1 minute. Fold in whipped cream until well blended.

3. Turn mixture into crumb crust, spreading evenly. Refrigerate 1 hour or longer, until set. Top with whipped cream and shaved chocolate. Refrigerate any leftovers.

153   CHOCOLATE APPLE CRUMBLE
Prep: 10 minutes   Cook: 40 to 45 minutes   Serves: 9

This is fast to fix with convenience foods: a Swiss chocolate cake mix and a can of spiced apple pie filling. It's best served warm, the same day it's baked, with plenty of whipped cream or ice cream.

1 (21-ounce) can cinnamon 'n'	1 stick (4 ounces) unsalted
spice apple filling or	butter or margarine,
topping	melted
2 teaspoons lemon juice	¾ cup chopped walnuts
1 (18.25-ounce) package Swiss	1 teaspoon cinnamon
chocolate cake mix	¼ teaspoon grated nutmeg
(without pudding	Whipped cream or vanilla
included)	ice cream

1. Preheat oven to 350°F. Spread undrained pie filling evenly over bottom of a 9-inch square baking pan. Drizzle lemon juice on top.

2. In a medium bowl, combine dry cake mix, butter, walnuts, cinnamon, and nutmeg. Mix until crumbly. Sprinkle over pie filling. Press in lightly.

3. Bake 40 to 45 minutes, until set. Serve warm or cold topped with whipped cream or ice cream.

154   NO-TOIL DEVILISH PINEAPPLE DESSERT
Prep: 10 minutes   Cook: 25 to 30 minutes   Serves: 12 to 16

This goes together in short order and is best served the day baked with plenty of whipped cream or ice cream.

1 (20-ounce) can crushed
   pineapple packed in
   unsweetened pineapple
   juice
1 (18.25-ounce) package
   devil's food cake mix
   (without pudding
   included)

1½ sticks (6 ounces) butter,
   melted
1 cup slivered blanched
   almonds
Whipped cream or vanilla
   ice cream

1. Preheat oven to 350°F. Spread undrained pineapple evenly in a 9 x 13-inch baking dish. Sprinkle dry cake mix on top. Drizzle melted butter evenly over cake. Sprinkle almonds on surface.

2. Bake 25 to 30 minutes. Cut into squares. Serve warm or cold topped with whipped cream or ice cream.

155   CHOCOLATE CARAMEL BARS
Prep: 20 minutes   Cook: 30 to 33 minutes   Chill: 1 hour   Makes: 48

1 (18.25-ounce) package
   devil's food cake mix
1 cup chopped walnuts
1 (5-ounce) can evaporated
   milk

4 tablespoons butter or
   margarine, melted
6 ounces semisweet chocolate
   chips (1 cup)
¾ cup caramel topping

1. Preheat oven to 350°F. Line a 9 x 13-inch baking pan with aluminum foil. Grease foil generously.

2. In a medium mixing bowl, combine dry cake mix, walnuts, evaporated milk, and melted butter. Mix with a fork or wooden spoon until well blended. Spread half of cake mixture (batter will be stiff) into prepared pan. Bake 10 minutes. Remove from oven; leave oven on.

3. Sprinkle chocolate chips evenly over hot crust. Let stand 5 minutes until melted, then spread evenly over crust with a knife. Drizzle caramel topping over chocolate. Then drop remaining cake mixture by small spoonfuls over all and carefully spread with knife. Bake 20 to 23 minutes. Let cool slightly in pan. Refrigerate 1 hour or longer, until caramel is set. Cut into 1½-inch squares. Remove foil from bottoms of cookies prior to serving.

156 PRONTO CHOCOLATE CREAM CHEESE PINWHEELS

Prep: 15 minutes   Cook: 20 minutes   Serves: 6 to 8

These are ideal to serve as a coffee snack or for brunch or dessert for a not-too-sweet but easy offering.

1 (8-ounce) package refrigerated crescent dinner rolls
4 ounces cream cheese, softened

2 tablespoons apricot jam
½ cup miniature semisweet chocolate chips
⅓ cup chopped walnuts

1. Preheat oven to 375°F. On a lightly floured sheet of wax paper, unroll crescent rolls, but do not separate. Pat rolls to form a rectangle; pinch seams together. Lightly flour dough rectangle; top with another sheet of wax paper and roll with a rolling pin to a 10 x 15-inch rectangle.

2. Mix cream cheese with jam until smooth. Spread over dough to within 1 inch of edges. Sprinkle chocolate chips and then nuts evenly over dough. Roll up from a long side, jelly-roll fashion, pressing together any loose seams as you go. Cut roll into 9 equal slices. Place slices cut sides down in a greased 9-inch pie pan; flatten slightly to fill pan. Bake 20 minutes, or until golden brown. Serve warm.

157 SPEEDY CHOCOLATE CHERRY-PINEAPPLE BAKE

Prep: 15 minutes   Cook: 55 to 60 minutes   Serves: 12 to 16

This is the ultimate dump cake—dessert can't get much easier to make—and it is a great potluck offering. Best served within a day of making.

1 (20-ounce) can crushed pineapple packed in juice
1 (21-ounce) can dark sweet cherry filling or topping
1 (18.25-ounce) package devil's food cake mix (without pudding included)

1 cup chopped pecans
1 cup flaked or shredded coconut
2 sticks (8 ounces) butter, melted
Whipped cream

1. Preheat oven to 325°F. Spread undrained pineapple over bottom of a 9 x 13-inch baking dish. Add undrained cherry filling, distributing evenly. Sprinkle dry cake mix over fruit; smooth top. Sprinkle pecans and then coconut over cake mix. Drizzle melted butter evenly over all.

2. Bake 55 to 60 minutes, or until edges are bubbly and top is golden brown. Serve warm or cold topped with whipped cream.

Chapter 6

Chocolate in the Freezer

Frozen chocolate desserts in this chapter run the gamut from homemade ice creams to more elaborate ice cream-based creations to those made with whipped cream or cream cheese and chocolate frozen solid in one form or another. In this collection you'll find yummy treats, such as Mud Pie, Coffee Ice Cream Cookie Loaf, Peanutty Chocolate Ice Cream Torte, Frozen Chocolate Banana Squares, Cream Puffs with Peppermint Ice Cream and Hot Fudge, Mandarin Chocolate Sherbet, Mocha Chip Frozen Yogurt, Chocolate Baked Alaska, and much more.

Not only are frozen desserts dazzling and delicious, but they are easy on the cook because they can be stashed in the freezer well in advance of serving time, freeing the hostess or cook for other last-minute details. Most freezer desserts can be prepared with a minimum of time and effort, particularly if you rely on store-bought ice cream in combination with purchased or homemade components, such as crumb crusts, cakes, brownies, and the like, for the base of such finales.

Frozen ice cream desserts can be molded decoratively in metal or glass bowls, springform pans, loaf pans, round layer cake pans, bundt cake pans, angel food cake pans, and gelatin molds. If you are uncertain about the size of a mold you want to use, measure it by filling it with water.

When preparing this collection of frozen desserts, use the best-quality ingredients, particularly if they are purchased prepared. Premium ice cream will make a big difference. Keep in mind that ice cream will lose some of its volume with softening and repeated handling, so work quickly and soften only very slightly, just enough to mix or shape.

While the amount of time required to freeze or solidify assembled frozen desserts varies, generally figure that six to eight hours will be necessary to produce a firmly molded loaf, bombe, pie, or cake. Overnight freezing is preferable if time allows. Once a frozen dessert has firmed up, be sure to wrap it tightly with a couple thicknesses of foil so freezer odors won't penetrate.

For ease in cutting, frozen desserts often require 10 to 20 minutes' thawing time in the refrigerator or at room temperature. Let the recipe be your guide. However, be sure to watch closely to avoid ending up with mush.

If you want to try your hand at making homemade ice cream and plan to make it often, invest in an electric ice cream maker for best results. They're not only fun and easy to use, but you control what goes into the ice cream and thus can avoid the stabilizers and emulsifiers found in commercial ice cream products. To tempt you into making your own ice cream, I've included a number of fabulous flavors like Chocolate Pralines-and-Cream Ice Cream, Orange Chocolate Flake Ice Cream, Chocolate Cheesecake Ice Cream, and Chocolate Chocolate Chunk Ice Cream in the pages that follow.

You can eat these ice creams soft, immediately after making them or wait until they have "ripened" (and hardened) in the freezer for three to four hours. Most will keep well for up to two weeks.

Although it's feasible to make homemade ice creams without an ice cream machine by freezing it in metal pans in the freezer, it's necessary to stir often and beat with an electric mixer or food processor to break up the ice crystals and aerate the mixture and then refreeze, which is a big nuisance. Therefore this procedure has not been addressed in the recipes here.

You'll never have time to get bored with these tempting frosty dessert creations in your repertoire. They are ready when you are. They make great eating anytime of year, but don't forget to pull them out especially during the summer months when you want to stay cool.

158 FROZEN CHOCOLATE CHEESECAKE TORTE

Prep: 20 minutes   Cook: 10 minutes   Freeze: 8 hours   Serves: 10

Whipped cream in combination with cream cheese and chocolate makes this easy torte filling rich and creamy. Make in advance of serving, pop into the freezer, and there's no more fuss.

1 cup chocolate wafer cookie crumbs
4 tablespoons butter, melted
1 (8-ounce) package cream cheese, softened
1 cup sugar
1 teaspoon vanilla extract

⅛ teaspoon salt
3 (1-ounce) squares unsweetened chocolate, melted and cooled
1½ cups heavy cream, whipped
¾ cup chopped pecans

1. Preheat oven to 350°F. In a small bowl, combine crumbs and butter; mix well. Press firmly into bottom of a 9-inch springform pan. Bake 10 minutes. Let cool.

2. In a medium bowl, combine cream cheese, sugar, vanilla, and salt. Beat with an electric mixer on medium speed until smooth. Add chocolate and beat 2 minutes. Fold whipped cream into chocolate mixture. Stir in pecans. Turn into baked crust, spreading evenly. Freeze 8 hours or longer, until firm. Cover tightly and store in freezer. Remove from freezer ½ hour before serving for ease in cutting.

159 FROZEN CHOCOLATE CHIP MINT TORTE

Prep: 35 minutes   Cook: 11 to 12 minutes   Freeze: 3 hours
Serves: 8 or more

This is a cinch to make any time of year and keep handy in the freezer. Keep it in mind when you're looking for a St. Pat's Day dessert.

- 1 cup chocolate wafer cookie crumbs
- 2 tablespoons butter, melted
- 3 cups miniature marshmallows (½ of a 10½-ounce package)
- ⅔ cup plus 3 tablespoons half-and-half or milk
- ⅓ cup crème de menthe
- ½ teaspoon peppermint extract
- 4 drops green food coloring (optional)
- 2 egg whites*
- 2 tablespoons sugar
- 2 cups heavy cream, whipped
- ¾ cup plus ⅓ cup miniature semisweet chocolate chips
- 1 tablespoon corn syrup

1. To prepare crust, in a small bowl, mix together cookie crumbs and butter. Press onto bottom of an 8½-inch springform pan. Refrigerate.

2. To make filling, in medium saucepan, combine marshmallows and ⅔ cup half-and-half. Heat over medium heat, stirring constantly, just until marshmallows melt. Let cool. Add crème de menthe, peppermint extract, and food coloring and blend well. Cover and refrigerate until mixture begins to thicken.

3. In a medium bowl, beat egg whites and sugar with an electric mixer on high speed until stiff. In a separate medium bowl, beat cream with mixer on high speed until stiff. Mix large dollops of egg whites and whipped cream into marshmallow mixture to lighten. Fold in remaining egg whites and whipped cream until thoroughly blended. Fold in ⅓ cup chocolate chips. Turn mixture into crust. Freeze at least 3 hours or overnight, until set.

4. In a 2-cup glass measure, combine remaining ¾ cup chocolate chips and 3 tablespoons half-and-half. Heat in a microwave oven on High 1 to 1½ minutes, or until melted and smooth when mixed. Stir in corn syrup until smooth. Let chocolate topping cool.

5. Spread cooled chocolate topping evenly over top of frozen torte. Return to freezer until topping is set.

6. At serving time, remove springform side. Serve immediately from freezer or let stand 15 minutes to soften slightly.

* **CAUTION:** *Because of the possible threat of salmonella—a bacteria that causes food poisoning—from raw eggs, U.S. Government officials recommend that the very young, the elderly, pregnant women, and people with serious illnesses or weakened immune systems not eat raw or lightly cooked eggs. Keep this in mind and consume raw or lightly cooked eggs at your own risk.*

160 COFFEE ICE CREAM COOKIE LOAF

Prep: 20 minutes   Cook: none   Freeze: 1 day   Serves: 12 or more

This goes together in no time flat with purchased cookies and ice cream. Vary the ice cream flavors to suit individual tastes. Keep the loaf stashed in the freezer for an emergency dessert.

1 (12½-ounce) package chocolate chocolate chip walnut cookies
½ gallon coffee or mocha almond fudge ice cream, softened slightly
½ cup miniature semisweet chocolate chips

1 cup heavy cream
¼ cup powdered sugar
2 tablespoons unsweetened cocoa powder
1 tablespoon instant coffee powder

1. Line a 9 x 5 x 3-inch loaf pan with foil and then with plastic wrap. Cover bottom of pan with a single layer of cookies, placing flat sides down and fitting together closely. Cover with half of ice cream, pressing firmly into pan. Sprinkle chocolate chips over ice cream. Top with half of remaining cookies, crumbling slightly. Cover with remaining ice cream, pressing in firmly. Top with remaining cookies, arranging in a single layer, flat sides up. Cover and freeze 1 day or longer.

2. Just before serving, in a medium bowl, whip cream with powdered sugar, cocoa, and coffee powder with an electric mixer on high speed, until stiff peaks form. Invert loaf onto a serving plate. Remove foil and plastic wrap. Spread whipped cream mixture over top and sides of cake or pipe on using a pastry bag fitted with an open star tube.

161 RASPBERRY MOUSSE TORTE

Prep: 1 hour 15 minutes   Cook: none   Freeze: 8 hours   Serves: 10

1½ cups chocolate wafer cookie crumbs
¾ cup plus 2 tablespoons granulated sugar
4 tablespoons butter, melted
2 (12-ounce) bags frozen unsweetened red raspberries, partially thawed

1 envelope unflavored gelatin
1½ cups heavy cream
½ pint fresh raspberries
2 tablespoons powdered sugar
Chocolate Leaves (page 221) or chocolate shavings

1. To prepare crust, in medium bowl, combine crumbs, 2 tablespoons granulated sugar, and melted butter; mix well. Press into bottom and about 1 inch up sides of a 9-inch springform pan. Refrigerate.

2. To make mousse mixture, in a food processor, combine partially thawed frozen raspberries and remaining ¾ cup granulated sugar. Process until pureed. Transfer to a medium bowl.

3. Scoop ⅓ cup raspberry puree into a small saucepan. Sprinkle gelatin on top and let stand 5 minutes to soften. Place over low heat and cook, stirring constantly, until gelatin dissolves. Stir into remaining raspberry puree in a medium bowl and refrigerate until syrupy and thick, about 30 minutes or longer.

4. In a medium bowl, beat 1 cup cream with an electric mixer on high speed until stiff. Blend a big spoonful of whipped cream into chilled raspberry mixture. Then fold in remaining whipped cream.

5. Fold in fresh raspberries. Spoon filling into prepared crust. Cover pan and freeze 8 hours or overnight. About 1 hour before serving time, whip remaining ½ cup cream with powdered sugar with an electric mixer on high speed until stiff. Fill a pastry bag fitted with an open star tube with whipped cream and pipe border around torte; or spoon dollops around edge. Garnish with chocolate leaves or shaved chocolate. Refrigerate and serve within 1 hour (torte is best served partially frozen).

---

162 BITTERSWEET CHOCOLATE-WHITE CHOCOLATE CHUNK ICE CREAM
Prep: 15 minutes   Cook: 5 minutes   Chill: 6 hours
Makes: about 2 quarts

This deep dark chocolate ice cream is dotted throughout with chunks of white chocolate. It's fantastic—rich and creamy! Since the mixture is cooked, cooled, and refrigerated before freezing in an ice cream machine, preparation is easiest started a day in advance of when you plan to eat the ice cream.

3 cups half-and-half	1½ cups sugar
1 cup heavy cream	4 ounces imported white
1 cup firmly packed	chocolate, cut into ½-inch
unsweetened cocoa	chunks
powder (preferably	
Dutch-processed)	
2 (1-ounce) squares	
unsweetened chocolate,	
melted	

1. In a medium saucepan, combine half-and-half, cream, cocoa, melted unsweetened chocolate, and sugar. Bring to a simmer over medium-high heat, stirring constantly. Cook 2 minutes, stirring constantly. Remove from heat and let cool. Cover and refrigerate 6 hours or overnight.

2. Transfer mixture to a container of an ice cream machine and freeze according to manufacturer's directions. When ice cream is at soft serve stage, add white chocolate chunks and let machine run a few minutes longer. Place ice cream in freezer to ripen at least 3 hours, or until firm. Ice cream can be stored in a tightly covered plastic container in freezer for up to 3 weeks.

163   FROZEN CHOCOLATE BANANA SQUARES

Prep: 30 minutes   Cook: none   Freeze: 6 hours   Serves: 9

If well wrapped, this yummy layered creation will keep in the freezer for up to 2 weeks.

1 stick (4 ounces) plus 3 tablespoons butter or margarine, softened
1 cup finely crushed chocolate wafer cookie crumbs
1 (8-ounce) package cream cheese, softened
1¼ cups powdered sugar

¼ cup unsweetened cocoa powder
3 tablespoons milk
2 medium bananas, sliced
2½ cups thawed frozen whipped topping (about ¾ of an 8-ounce container)
½ cup chopped pecans

1. To make crust, melt 3 tablespoons butter. In a small bowl, mix together cookie crumbs and melted butter. Press mixture evenly over bottom of an 8-inch square baking pan.

2. In a medium bowl, combine remaining 1 stick butter and cream cheese. Beat with an electric mixer on medium speed until smooth. Add powdered sugar, cocoa, and milk. Beat until smooth and blended.

3. Spread cream cheese mixture evenly over prepared crust. Top with banana slices. Spread whipped topping over dessert and sprinkle nuts on top. Cover and freeze at least 6 hours before serving. To serve, cut into 9 squares.

164   PEANUTTY CHOCOLATE ICE CREAM TORTE

Prep: 25 minutes   Cook: 32 to 38 minutes   Freeze: 7 to 8 hours Serves: 10

Peanut butter and chocolate aficionados will cheer when they taste this.

12 ounces semisweet chocolate chips (2 cups)
1½ sticks (6 ounces) butter or margarine
½ cup sugar
2 eggs
2 teaspoons vanilla extract
¾ cup flour
¼ teaspoon baking soda

Dash of salt
½ cup chopped peanuts (optional)
1 quart chocolate or vanilla ice cream, softened slightly
½ cup heavy cream
½ cup crunchy peanut butter
2 tablespoons light corn syrup

1. Preheat oven to 350°F. In a 2-quart glass bowl, combine 1 cup chocolate chips and 4 tablespoons (½ stick) butter. Heat in a microwave oven on High 1 to 1½ minutes, or until melted and smooth when stirred. Using a fork, stir in sugar, eggs, 1 teaspoon vanilla, and 2 tablespoons hot water until thoroughly mixed. Add flour, baking soda, and salt; blend well. Stir in peanuts.

2. Turn into a greased 9-inch springform pan; spread evenly. Bake 30 to 35 minutes, or until set but still moist in center. Do not overbake. Let cool in pan.

3. Working quickly, in a medium bowl, mix together ice cream, cream, and peanut butter with a heavy spoon until well blended. Spoon evenly over top of cooled brownie cake. Freeze until firm, 6 hours or overnight.

4. A few hours before serving time, prepare glaze. In a 1-quart microwave glass bowl, combine remaining 1 stick butter, remaining 1 cup chocolate chips, and corn syrup. Heat in microwave oven on High 1 to 1½ minutes, or until melted and smooth when stirred. Stir in remaining 1 teaspoon vanilla. Let cool to room temperature or until slightly thickened and of spreading consistency.

5. Run sharp knife around edge of torte to loosen. Remove side of spring-form pan. Spread cooled glaze over top and sides of torte. Return to freezer until frozen, 1 to 2 hours.

---

165   JIFFY RASPBERRY CHOCOLATE ICE CREAM CAKE

Prep: 2 to 3 hours   Cook: 22 to 28 minutes   Freeze: 5 to 6 hours
Serves: 10

This couldn't be easier, and it's always a hit.

1 (12-ounce) bag slightly sweetened or unsweetened frozen red raspberries, thawed
1 tablespoon cornstarch
2 tablespoons light corn syrup
2 tablespoons orange-flavored liqueur

2 cups flaked or shredded coconut
4 tablespoons butter, melted
½ gallon raspberry chocolate truffle ice cream or your favorite chocolate ice cream flavor

1. Drain syrup from raspberries into a medium saucepan; set berries aside. Whisk cornstarch into syrup until mixture is free of lumps. Cook over medium-high heat, stirring constantly, until mixture boils, clears, and thickens, 2 to 3 minutes. Stir in corn syrup, orange liqueur, and raspberries. Sieve to remove seeds, if desired. Cover and refrigerate sauce until chilled, 2 to 3 hours.

2. Preheat oven to 325°F. To prepare crust, in a medium bowl, mix together coconut and butter. Spread evenly over bottom and partway up sides of 9-inch springform pan that has been lined on the outside with a double thickness of foil (to catch any butter that may leak through). Bake 20 to 25 minutes, or until golden. Let cool.

3. When sauce and crust are both cold, assemble cake. Spread half of ice cream evenly over cooled crust. Spoon half of cold raspberry sauce over ice cream. Top with remaining ice cream, spreading evenly. Freeze cake until set, 1 to 2 hours; refrigerate remaining sauce.

4. Spread remaining raspberry sauce over top of cake. Cover and freeze until firm, 4 hours or overnight. Cut into wedges to serve.

166   FROZEN CHOCOLATE ICE CREAM PIE

Prep: 10 minutes   Cook: 1 to 1½ minutes   Freeze: 2 to 3 hours
Serves: 8

This pie sports a chocolate cornflake and marshmallow crust. Use your favorite ice cream flavor.

6 ounces semisweet chocolate chips (1 cup)	1½ quarts chocolate or chocolate chocolate chip ice cream
2 tablespoons butter	Whipped cream and
1½ cups coarsely crumbled cornflakes	maraschino cherries
½ cup miniature marshmallows	

1. In a 2-quart glass bowl, combine chocolate chips and butter. Heat in microwave oven on High 1 to 1½ minutes, or until chocolate is melted and smooth when stirred. Add cornflakes and marshmallows and stir to coat well.

2. Press evenly into bottom and up sides of a 9-inch metal pie pan. Spread ice cream evenly in shell. Freeze 2 to 3 hours, or until firm. Wrap well and store in freezer.

3. Remove pie from freezer 5 to 10 minutes before serving. Serve slices topped with whipped cream and a maraschino cherry.

167   FROZEN CHOCOLATE CHIP PEACH ICE CREAM LOAF

Prep: 35 minutes   Cook: 5 minutes   Freeze: 7 hours
Serves: 10 to 12

This summertime dessert is good to keep stashed in the freezer to serve on short notice when you have unexpected company.

1 (1-pound) loaf pound cake	2 tablespoons Grand Marnier or other orange-flavored liqueur
1 quart toasted almond ice cream, softened slightly	
2 cups chopped peeled firm, ripe fresh peaches (about 2 large)	¾ cup plus 2 tablespoons sugar
	¾ cup unsweetened cocoa powder
1 cup miniature semisweet chocolate chips	½ cup heavy cream
	4 tablespoons butter

1. Cut pound cake lengthwise into 6 even slices or layers. Line bottom of a 9 x 5-inch glass loaf dish with a strip of plastic wrap so ends extend 2 inches over ends of pan. Using 4 cake slices, line dish completely with cake as follows: Place 1 cake slice in bottom of dish to cover. Place 1 cake slice along each long side of dish to cover. Cut 1 cake slice crosswise in half and place each half on short sides of dish.

2. Working quickly, in a medium bowl, combine ice cream, peaches, chocolate chips, and Grand Marnier; mix well. Spoon half of ice cream mixture evenly into cake-lined dish. Top with 1 of remaining cake slices, then spread evenly with remaining ice cream mixture. Top with remaining cake slice. If any cake extends over top of dish, trim off so cake is even with top of dish. Cover and freeze until firm, 6 hours or overnight.

3. When cake is firm, prepare glaze. In a small saucepan, combine sugar, cocoa, and cream. Whisk until blended; mixture will be stiff. Place over medium heat and whisk constantly until mixture boils. Boil 1 to 2 minutes. Remove from heat; whisk in butter. Cool to room temperature, until mixture thickens but is still spreadable.

4. Cut a rectangle of sturdy cardboard ½ to 1 inch larger all around than bottom of cake. Cover tightly with foil. To unmold, invert firm cake onto foil-lined cardboard. Return cake to freezer 10 to 15 minutes. Remove from freezer and peel off plastic wrap. Spread cool glaze evenly over top and sides of cake. Return to freezer; freeze until glaze is set, about 45 minutes. Then cover with plastic wrap and freeze until serving time. Use within 1 month. With sharp knife, cut into slices to serve.

---

168 SOFI'S FROZEN CHOCOLATE DESSERT

Prep: 20 minutes   Cook: 1½ to 2 minutes   Freeze: 4 hours
Serves: 8 to 10

Los Angeles chef-owner Sofi Konstantinidas brought this chocolate recipe from her native Greece. You won't believe how easily it's made.

12 ounces semisweet chocolate, cut up	4 eggs,* separated
2 cups heavy cream	1 teaspoon vanilla extract
¼ cup powdered sugar	Dash of salt
	½ cup diced roasted almonds

1. Melt chocolate in a double boiler or microwave oven until melted and smooth when stirred, 1½ to 2 minutes. Set aside until cooled to room temperature.

2. Meanwhile, in a medium bowl, beat cream with an electric mixer on high speed until almost stiff. Add powdered sugar and beat until stiff peaks form. With mixer on low speed, beat in egg yolks and vanilla just until well blended. Turn into a 9-inch springform pan; spread evenly. Place in freezer.

3. In a medium bowl, beat together egg whites and salt with an electric mixer on high speed until stiff peaks form. Fold egg whites into melted and cooled chocolate and spread evenly over top of cream mixture in springform pan. Sprinkle almonds over top. Return to freezer and freeze until firm, about 4 hours or overnight. Cover tightly. To serve, cut into slices.

* **CAUTION:** *Because of the possible threat of salmonella—a bacteria that causes food poisoning—from raw eggs, U.S. Government officials recommend that the very young, the elderly, pregnant women, and people with serious illnesses or weakened immune systems not eat raw or lightly cooked eggs. Keep this in mind and consume raw or lightly cooked eggs at your own risk.*

169   LAYERED ICE CREAM FUDGE CANDY TORTE

Prep: 20 minutes   Cook: none   Freeze: 6½ hours   Serves: 12

Use the store-bought ice cream flavors that you favor and layer with fudge sauce in this terrific but easy dessert, great for company.

1   (10-ounce) package bakery-style coconut macaroons (soft type)
½   gallon almond praline, mocha chip, or chocolate chocolate chip ice cream, softened slightly
   Dark Chocolate Fudge Sauce (page 206), at room temperature

1   (5-ounce) package chocolate-covered English toffee candy bars (such as Heath Bars), chopped (about ¾ cup chopped)
   Whipped cream

1. With fingers, crumble cookies into small pieces. Press two thirds of pieces over bottom of a 9-inch springform pan.

2. Spread half of ice cream in even layer over cookie pieces. Quickly spread evenly with half of Dark Chocolate Fudge Sauce. Sprinkle remaining cookie pieces on top. Freeze 30 minutes.

3. Spread remaining ice cream evenly over cookie pieces. Top with remaining Dark Chocolate Fudge Sauce, spreading evenly. Sprinkle with candy pieces. Freeze until firm, 6 hours or overnight. When firm, cover with foil, wrap well, and keep frozen until ready to serve.

4. At serving time, run knife around rim to loosen. Remove side of springform and cut torte into slices. Top each with a spoonful of whipped cream, if desired.

170   MUD PIE

Prep: 35 minutes   Cook: 1 to 1½ minutes   Freeze: 4½ hours Serves: 6 to 8

This is a favorite with all age groups. Keep one of these stashed in the freezer to serve on a moment's notice.

2   cups chocolate wafer cookie crumbs
4   tablespoons butter, melted
1½   quarts your favorite chocolate or coffee-flavor ice cream, softened slightly

6   ounces semisweet chocolate chips (1 cup)
3   tablespoons milk
1   tablespoon corn syrup
1   teaspoon vanilla extract
¼   cup diced roasted almonds

1. In a medium bowl, mix together chocolate cookie crumbs and butter. Press into bottom and up sides of a 9-inch pie pan. Freeze ½ hour. Spread softened ice cream evenly over crust, rounding off top slightly. Freeze until ice cream is firm, at least 2 hours.

2. Meanwhile, in a 1-quart glass bowl, combine chocolate chips and milk. Heat in a microwave oven on High 1 to 1½ minutes, or until melted and smooth when stirred. Stir in corn syrup and vanilla. Refrigerate until chilled but not set, stirring a couple of times.

3. Spread cool chocolate mixture over top of frozen pie. Sprinkle almonds on top and return to freezer until firm, about 2 hours.

171 FROZEN CHOCOLATE-PEANUT BUTTER PIE

Prep: 40 minutes   Cook: 1 to 1½ minutes   Freeze: 6½ hours Serves: 8 to 10

Make this ahead and keep handy in the freezer to serve on a moment's notice. Chocolate and peanut butter fans gave it high marks.

1½ cups heavy cream
4 (1-ounce) squares semisweet chocolate, cut up
   Cocoa Graham Crust (recipe follows)

1 (8-ounce) package cream cheese, softened
1 cup powdered sugar
¾ cup peanut butter
¼ cup chopped peanuts

1. In a small glass bowl, combine ½ cup cream and chocolate. Heat in microwave oven on High 1 to 1½ minutes, until melted and smooth when stirred. Let cool slightly.

2. Spread half of chocolate mixture over bottom of Cocoa Graham Crust. Freeze ½ hour, or until set.

3. Meanwhile prepare filling. In a medium bowl, beat cream cheese, powdered sugar, and peanut butter with an electric mixer on medium speed until well blended and fluffy, 1 to 2 minutes. Whip remaining 1 cup cream until stiff; beat half of whipped cream into peanut butter mixture until well mixed, then fold in remaining whipped cream.

4. Spread filling evenly over chocolate mixture in crust. Freeze ½ hour. Then carefully spread remaining chocolate mixture over top and sprinkle peanuts over surface. Freeze 6 hours or overnight. Wrap tightly and store in freezer. Transfer pie to refrigerator 1 hour before serving. Cut into wedges to serve.

172 COCOA GRAHAM CRUST

Prep: 5 minutes   Cook: none   Makes: 1 (9-inch) crust

1½ cups graham cracker crumbs
4 tablespoons butter, melted
¼ cup sugar

½ cup unsweetened cocoa powder

In a medium bowl, mix together graham cracker crumbs, butter, sugar, and cocoa until well blended. Press firmly into bottom and up sides of 9-inch pie pan. Freeze while preparing pie filling and topping.

173 CHOCOLATE BAKED ALASKA

Prep: 25 minutes   Cook: 4 to 5 minutes   Freeze: 8 hours
Serves: 8 to 10

2 (1.4-ounce) butter toffee
   candy bars (such as Skor
   bars), chopped
½ gallon rocky road ice cream
4 egg whites
½ cup sugar

3 tablespoons unsweetened
   cocoa powder
1 teaspoon vanilla extract
1 (7- or 8-inch) single sponge
   cake layer, flavor of your
   choice

1. Line a 1½-quart heatproof glass bowl with plastic wrap, extending 5 to 6 inches over edges. Sprinkle chopped candy over bottom of bowl. Spoon ice cream into bowl over candy, packing in with back of large spoon; smooth top. Fold plastic wrap up over ice cream to cover. Freeze 8 hours or overnight until hard.

2. When ready to serve, preheat oven to 450°F. Prepare meringue. In a medium bowl, beat egg whites with an electric mixer on medium speed until foamy. On high speed, gradually beat in sugar and cocoa; beat until stiff peaks form. Beat in vanilla.

3. Place sponge cake layer on a jelly-roll pan. Invert bowl to unmold ice cream on top of cake layer; remove plastic wrap. Working quickly, spread meringue completely over cake right down to pan to seal in ice cream.

4. Immediately bake 4 to 5 minutes, or until meringue browns lightly. Do not let burn. Serve immediately. Return any leftovers to freezer and serve frozen.

174 WHITE CHOCOLATE RASPBERRY ICE CREAM

Prep: 15 minutes   Cook: 5½ to 6 minutes   Chill and freeze: about 5 hours   Makes: about 1¼ quarts

This ice cream, which uses no eggs, is soft and creamy when it comes out of an ice cream machine, but hardens when placed in the freezer.

2 cups heavy cream
1 cup milk
⅓ cup sugar
8 ounces imported white
   chocolate, cut up

1 teaspoon vanilla extract
½ pint raspberries

1. In a 2-quart glass bowl, combine cream, milk, and sugar; mix well. Heat in a microwave oven on High 5½ to 6 minutes, stirring twice, until mixture is boiling and sugar is dissolved. Stir in white chocolate until melted and mixture is smooth. Stir in vanilla. Let cool to room temperature. Cover and refrigerate until mixture is completely chilled, 3 to 4 hours or overnight.

2. Transfer mixture to a container of an ice cream machine and freeze according to manufacturer's directions. About 10 to 15 minutes before ice cream is done, add raspberries and continue freezing. Serve immediately or place in freezer to ripen 3 to 4 hours. Ice cream can be stored in a plastic container, covered tightly, in freezer 2 to 3 weeks.

NOTE: *Ice cream will take approximately 35 to 45 minutes to freeze in an ice cream machine. Exact time depends on the brand of the machine used.*

175 CHOCOLATE MINT FREEZER PIE
Prep: 20 minutes   Cook: none   Freeze: 3 to 4 hours   Serves: 6

1½ sticks (6 ounces) butter	1½ teaspoons vanilla extract
1½ cups powdered sugar	½ teaspoon peppermint extract
3 (1-ounce) squares unsweetened chocolate, melted	1 (9-inch) baked Chocolate Wafer Crust (recipe follows)
3 eggs*	Whipped cream

1. In a medium bowl, beat together butter and powdered sugar with an electric mixer on medium speed until light and fluffy, 2 to 3 minutes. Add melted chocolate and continue beating 2 minutes. Add eggs, one at a time, beating well after each addition. Add vanilla and peppermint extract and beat well. Turn into cooled Chocolate Wafer Crust. Freeze 3 to 4 hours, or until firm.

2. Remove pie from freezer 15 to 20 minutes before serving. Serve partially frozen slices, garnished with a dollop of whipped cream.

* CAUTION: *Because of the possible threat of salmonella—a bacteria that causes food poisoning—from raw eggs, U.S. Government officials recommend that the very young, the elderly, pregnant women, and people with serious illnesses or weakened immune systems not eat raw or lightly cooked eggs. Keep this in mind and consume raw or lightly cooked eggs at your own risk.*

176 CHOCOLATE WAFER CRUST
Prep: 10 minutes   Cook: 8 minutes   Makes: a single 8- or 9-inch crust

This is a good basic chocolate cookie crust. Use it baked or unbaked, depending on what the recipe specifies.

1½ cups chocolate wafer cookie crumbs	1 tablespoon sugar
	4 tablespoons butter, melted

Preheat oven to 350°F. Mix together cookie crumbs, sugar, and butter. Press into bottom and up sides of a 9-inch pie pan. Bake 8 minutes. Let cool before filling.

NOTE: *Crust can also be used unbaked when recipes specify an unbaked 9-inch chocolate wafer crust. Prepare as directed above but do not bake crust.*

177   ORANGE CHOCOLATE FLAKE ICE CREAM

Prep: 10 minutes   Cook: none   Chill: 2 hours
Makes: about 2 quarts

1¼ cups sugar
 ⅓ cup unsweetened cocoa
      powder
  3 cups heavy cream

1 cup half-and-half
1 teaspoon orange extract
6 ounces bittersweet
      chocolate, melted

1. In a medium bowl, whisk together sugar, cocoa, cream, half-and-half, and orange extract just until combined and smooth. Stir in half of melted chocolate. Refrigerate 2 hours.

2. Transfer mixture to a container of an ice cream machine and freeze according to manufacturer's directions. When ice cream is at the soft serve stage, carefully add remaining melted chocolate while machine is running if possible; the chocolate will flake. Continue to process 3 to 4 minutes longer, or until ice cream firms up. Serve immediately or place in freezer to ripen 3 to 4 hours, or until firm. Ice cream can be stored in a tightly covered plastic container in freezer 2 to 3 weeks.

178   CHOCOLATE CHOCOLATE CHUNK ICE CREAM

Prep: 15 minutes   Cook: 3 to 4 minutes   Chill: 4 hours
Makes: about 1¼ quarts

 2 cups heavy cream
12 ounces bittersweet
      chocolate, cut into ¾-inch
      chunks
 ½ cup sugar

2 cups milk
1 teaspoon vanilla extract
    Dash of salt
½ cup chopped pecans

1. In a 2-quart glass bowl, combine cream, 8 ounces cut-up chocolate, and sugar. Heat in a microwave oven on High 3 to 4 minutes, or until chocolate is melted and mixture is very smooth, stirring twice.

2. Whisk in milk, vanilla, and salt. Cover and refrigerate 4 hours or longer, until mixture is completely chilled. Combine remaining 4 ounces chocolate with pecans and refrigerate until needed.

3. Transfer chocolate cream mixture to a container of an ice cream machine and freeze according to manufacturer's directions. Remove dasher and quickly stir in cold chocolate chunks and nuts. Serve immediately or place in freezer to ripen 3 to 4 hours, or until firm. Ice cream can be stored in a tightly covered plastic container in freezer 2 to 3 weeks.

179 CHOCOLATE CHEESECAKE ICE CREAM
Prep: 20 minutes   Cook: 5 minutes   Chill: 6 hours
Makes: about 2 quarts

When you prefer eating your cheesecake as ice cream, try this terrific chocolate version.

1½ cups sugar
2 cups half-and-half
1 cup heavy cream
1 egg
½ cup unsweetened cocoa powder (preferably Dutch-processed)

2 (1-ounce) squares unsweetened chocolate, melted
1 (8-ounce) package cream cheese, softened
1 teaspoon chocolate extract

1. In a medium saucepan, whisk together sugar, half-and-half, cream, egg, and cocoa. Place over medium heat and whisk until mixture comes to a simmer. Do not boil, or egg will curdle. Stir in melted chocolate and simmer 3 minutes, stirring constantly with a wooden spoon. Do not let boil.

2. Remove from heat and stir in cream cheese, mixing thoroughly until smooth. Refrigerate mixture 6 hours or overnight. Stir in chocolate extract.

3. Transfer mixture to a container of an ice cream machine and freeze according to manufacturer's directions. Serve immediately or place in freezer to ripen 3 to 4 hours, or until firm. Ice cream may be stored in a tightly covered plastic container in freezer 2 to 3 weeks.

180 MANDARIN CHOCOLATE SHERBET
Prep: 15 minutes   Cook: none   Chill: 4 hours   Makes: 1½ quarts

This sherbet is loaded with chocolate and orange. It's dark colored and unbelievably great! No cooking is required.

2 cups milk
¾ cup frozen orange juice concentrate, thawed
1⅓ cups sugar
¾ cup unsweetened cocoa powder

4 ounces bittersweet chocolate, melted
1 teaspoon orange extract

1. In a medium bowl, whisk together milk, orange juice concentrate, sugar, cocoa, melted chocolate, and orange extract. Cover and refrigerate mixture 4 hours to chill well.

2. Transfer mixture to a container of an ice cream machine and freeze according to manufacturer's directions. Serve immediately or place in freezer to ripen 3 to 4 hours, until firm. Sherbet may be stored in a tightly covered plastic container in freezer 2 to 3 weeks.

181   CHOCOLATE PRALINES-AND-CREAM ICE CREAM

Prep: 15 minutes   Cook: 5 minutes   Makes: about 2 quarts

¾ cup packed dark brown
    sugar
½ cup buttermilk
1 tablespoon butter
1 cup chopped pecans
2 cups half-and-half

2 cups heavy cream
1¼ cups granulated sugar
1 cup unsweetened cocoa
    powder
1½ teaspoons vanilla extract

1. In a small saucepan, combine brown sugar, buttermilk, and butter. Bring to a boil over high heat and cook, stirring constantly, 3 minutes. Remove from heat and stir in pecans. Spread praline mixture out on an oiled baking sheet. Let cool until hard, then break into small pieces.

2. In a medium bowl, whisk together half-and-half, cream, granulated sugar, cocoa, and vanilla until smooth and well blended.

3. Transfer mixture to a container of an ice cream machine and freeze according to manufacturer's directions. When mixture is at soft serve stage, add praline pieces and process 1 minute longer. Serve immediately or place in freezer to ripen 3 to 4 hours, or until firm. Ice cream can be stored in a tightly covered plastic container in freezer 2 to 3 weeks.

182   DOUBLE CHOCOLATE-ORANGE ICE CREAM BALLS

Prep: 20 minutes   Cook: none   Freeze: 6 hours   Serves: 6

These are similar to a terrific ice cream dessert known as tartufo. It's hard to believe that anything so tasty can be so simple.

1 quart premium dark
    chocolate or French
    vanilla ice cream
¼ cup finely chopped candied
    orange peel

2 tablespoons Grand Marnier
8 to 10 ounces bittersweet
    chocolate, chopped into
    ¼-inch chunks

1. Let ice cream stand until slightly softened but not melted, 5 to 10 minutes. In a medium bowl, mix together ice cream, candied orange peel, and Grand Marnier. Using an ice cream scoop, quickly shape mixture into 6 balls. Place in a covered freezer container and freeze until hard, 6 hours or overnight.

2. Place chopped chocolate on a sheet of wax paper or in a shallow dish. One at a time, remove balls from freezer and quickly roll in chocolate to coat completely. Press chocolate into ice cream. Return to freezer immediately and keep frozen for up to 10 days before serving.

183 CREAM PUFFS WITH PEPPERMINT ICE CREAM AND HOT FUDGE

Prep: 25 minutes   Cook: 30 to 40 minutes   Serves: 8 to 10

The combination of peppermint and chocolate is old-fashioned but still delicious.

1 stick (4 ounces) margarine	1½ quarts peppermint stick ice
1 cup flour	cream
⅛ teaspoon salt	Hot Fudge Sauce (page 205)
4 eggs	

1. Preheat oven to 400°F. To make cream puffs, in a medium saucepan, bring margarine and 1 cup water to a boil over medium heat, stirring occasionally. Add flour and salt, reduce heat to low, and cook, stirring vigorously with a wooden spoon until mixture forms a ball, about 1 minute.

2. Remove from heat. Beat in eggs, one at a time, beating until smooth after each addition.

3. Drop dough from a tablespoon into 8 to 10 mounds 3 inches apart on greased baking sheet. Bake 25 to 35 minutes, or until puffed, golden brown, and dry. Cool slowly away from drafts.

4. At serving time, with a sharp knife, split each puff in half or cut off top. Scoop out any soft dough inside. Fill with a scoop or two of peppermint ice cream. Replace tops. Drizzle Hot Fudge Sauce over top of puffs. Serve immediately.

184 MOCHA CHIP FROZEN YOGURT

Prep: 10 minutes   Cook: none   Makes: about 2 quarts

Make your own frozen yogurt in an ice cream maker with this delicious recipe.

1 quart plain lowfat yogurt	1 tablespoon instant espresso
1½ cups sugar	powder
½ cup firmly packed	6 ounces miniature semisweet
unsweetened cocoa	chocolate chips (1 cup)
powder	

1. In a medium bowl, stir together yogurt, sugar, cocoa, and espresso powder until sugar and espresso powder are dissolved, 2 to 3 minutes.

2. Transfer mixture to a container of an ice cream machine and freeze according to manufacturer's directions. Add chocolate chips and process 2 minutes longer. Serve immediately or place in a freezer to ripen 3 to 4 hours or until firm. Yogurt can be stored in a tightly covered plastic container in freezer for up to 3 weeks.

185   O'GRAYDIE'S IRISH CHOCOLATE ICE CREAM

Prep: 20 minutes   Cook: 5 to 8 minutes   Chill: 6 hours
Makes: 1½ quarts

Great tasting with cocoa, coffee powder, vanilla, coconut extract, and Irish whiskey, this recipe was developed by my Irish friend Patti Gray. Be sure to allow time for cooking and chilling the mixture prior to freezing in an ice cream maker.

2   cups heavy cream
1   cup half-and-half
1   cup sugar
2   egg yolks
½   cup unsweetened cocoa
        powder

1   tablespoon instant coffee
        powder
1   tablespoon vanilla extract
1   tablespoon coconut extract
1   tablespoon Irish whiskey

1. In a medium saucepan, combine cream, half-and-half, sugar, egg yolks, cocoa, and coffee powder. Bring to a simmer over medium heat, stirring constantly with a wooden spoon. Do not boil, or egg yolks will curdle. Simmer, stirring constantly, 3 minutes. Remove from heat and let cool at room temperature 1 hour.

2. Stir in vanilla and coconut extract. Refrigerate 6 hours or overnight.

3. Transfer mixture to a container of an ice cream machine and freeze according to manufacturer's directions. Just before ice cream is finished, stir in whiskey. Serve immediately or place in freezer to ripen 3 to 4 hours, until firm. Ice cream may be stored in a tightly covered plastic container in freezer 2 to 3 weeks.

Chapter 7

Melting in the Microwave

Want to zap out a chocolate dessert really fast? Rely on the microwave oven. It's great for fuss-free candies, puddings, some cakes, brownies, pies, sauces, and poached fruits, and for melting chocolate for dipping dried and fresh fruits and more.

Some favorite casual recipe possibilities include Microwave Chocolate Crazy Cake, Microwave Rocky Road, Old-Fashioned Microwave Chocolate Pudding, Easy No-Fail Fudge, Microwave Chocolate Crazy Cake, and Easy as 1-2-3 Microwave Brownies. For sophisticated offerings elegant enough to serve the most discriminating guests, whip up Pears with Port and Chocolate, Chocolate Fondue Supreme, or a sensational Microwave Candy Bar Pie. All of the recipes included here can be fixed in no time flat with a minimum of muss and fuss.

For best results when microwaving, remember to open the oven and check the dessert often to avoid overcooking. Set the oven for the minimum time (or a tad less) recommended in a recipe and check for doneness, adding more time as needed.

Always be sure to use microwave-safe dishes in the microwave. If you're unsure about a dish (china, ceramic, pottery, porcelain, glass) and want to find out if it is microwave-safe, place one cup of water in a glass measure in one corner of the microwave and place the utensil to be tested in the center of the oven. Cook on High power 1 minute. At the end of the time, the water should be warm and the dish should be cold. If the dish is cold, it is safe to use. If the dish is warm, don't use it. It means it either contains metallic flakes or hasn't been fired long and high enough to prevent moisture absorption. Pyrex is microwave-safe, as is any ovenproof glass.

Not only does the microwave oven offer a time-saving way to prepare chocolate desserts, but it's a timesaver as well when it comes to melting chocolate to use in other recipes.

As noted in the introduction, the microwave is the method I prefer for melting chocolate in the majority of cases. Simply melt the chocolate, uncovered, in a glass measuring cup or custard cup (or a glass plate), checking progress carefully. Keep in mind that the chocolate will retain its shape and may not look melted. When the appearance changes from dull to shiny, that is the signal to stir the chocolate until smooth. I generally figure that 1 cup of semisweet chocolate chips will take around 1 to 2 minutes on High, but stir after 1 and 1½ minutes. When chocolate is melted and smooth when stirred, it is ready to use "as is" or in making other desserts.

Because the microwave is so good at melting chocolate, I use it to make my chocolate truffles. Truffles are one of my favorite homemade candies because they look and taste so professional. And I've found that the microwave speeds up the truffle-making process considerably. In short order you can have the truffle mixture chilling in the refrigerator. Be sure to allow enough time for the truffle mixture to firm up (but not get totally hard and too difficult to scoop) before shaping the candy. To avoid a mess when shaping the balls, use a small ice cream scoop with an automatic release lever. You'll keep your hands mess- and chocolate-free and can speed along on the task at hand.

While many candy experts recommend dipping candies in tempered chocolate, I've found it's not practical or necessary. Although some of these truffles are dipped in melted chocolate, they are topped with nuts, cocoa, or powdered sugar, so if the chocolate isn't shiny, no one will know. Also if you melt the chocolate slowly and carefully in the microwave oven, stirring often and avoiding overheating, you shouldn't have any problem when using it for dipping. Select the chocolate flavor for coating truffles according to personal preference. Semisweet, bittersweet, white chocolate, or combinations of chocolates can be used. If you want to avoid the tempering or melted chocolate dipping issue completely, simply roll truffles in sifted unsweetened cocoa powder for a professional look.

All of the recipes that follow have been developed and tested using a 600- to 700-watt microwave oven. If you have a lower wattage microwave unit, a little additional cooking time will be required.

And don't forget the microwave oven for reheating all kinds of chocolate sauces or toppings for serving warm over desserts.

186   CHOCOLATE FONDUE SUPREME
Prep: 15 minutes   Cooks: 3 to 4 minutes   Serves: 8 (2½ cups fondue)

This is the easiest way to make fondue, and it tastes great. Use your favorite fruits and even cake cubes for dipping. Note that bananas and apples are tossed with a touch of lemon juice just to prevent discoloration while they stand.

1   **pound bittersweet or semisweet chocolate**
1   **cup heavy cream**
2   **tablespoons rum**
1   **bunch seedless green grapes**
1   **pint fresh strawberries**
1   **(20-ounce) can pineapple chunks, well drained**

2   **bananas, sliced and tossed with a little lemon juice**
1   **apple, thinly sliced and tossed with a little lemon juice**
2   **oranges, peeled and segmented**
8   **marshmallows**

1. In a 2-quart glass bowl, combine chocolate and cream. Heat in a microwave oven on High 2 to 2½ minutes or longer, until mixture is smooth and melted when stirred. Heat 1 to 1½ minutes longer, or until warm throughout. Stir in rum. Transfer to a fondue pot and keep warm.

2. Arrange fruit and marshmallows attractively on serving platter. To serve, have guests, using fondue forks, dip fruit and marshmallows as desired into warm chocolate.

> **NOTE:** *Other fresh fruits in season can be used for dipping instead of those mentioned above. Try melon, papaya, tangerines, pears, cherries, peaches, nectarines, etc. Bite-size pieces of angel food cake, pound cake, or sponge cake also make good dippers. For a smaller gathering, this recipe can be halved.*

187   WHITE CHOCOLATE FONDUE
Prep: 15 minutes   Cook: 3 minutes   Serves: 6 to 8 (1¾ cups fondue)

⅔   **cup heavy cream**
12   **ounces imported white chocolate, chopped**
1   **tablespoon Chambord, Grand Marnier, apricot brandy, or other fruit-flavored liqueur**

For dipping: strawberries, seedless green grapes, seedless red grapes, cantaloupe cubes, orange segments, bite-size pieces of chocolate cake or brownies

1. In a 1-quart glass bowl, heat cream in a microwave oven on High 1 minute, or until very hot. Add white chocolate and mix well.

2. Return to microwave and heat on Medium 1 minute. Stir until most or all chocolate is melted. Heat 1 minute longer, or until mixture is warm throughout. Stir in liqueur. Transfer to a fondue pot and keep warm.

3. Arrange fruit and cake attractively on a serving platter. To serve, have guests, using fondue forks, dip fruit and cake as desired into white chocolate.

188   OLD-FASHIONED MICROWAVE CHOCOLATE PUDDING
Prep: 10 minutes   Cook: 7 to 9 minutes   Serves: 4

There's no need to buy a pudding mix when you have this recipe handy. By cooking puddings in the microwave, you avoid long cooking, constant stirring, and scorched pans.

½ **cup sugar**
3 **tablespoons cornstarch**
⅛ **teaspoon salt**
2½ **cups milk**

2 **(1-ounce) squares unsweetened chocolate, cut up**
1 **teaspoon vanilla extract**

1. In a 2-quart glass bowl, mix together sugar, cornstarch, and salt until well blended. Gradually whisk in milk until cornstarch is completely dissolved. Add chocolate.

2. Cook in a microwave oven on High 7 to 9 minutes, whisking every 2 minutes, until mixture is cooked through, smooth, and thickened. Whisk in vanilla. Pour into 4 individual serving dishes. Cover with plastic wrap to prevent a skin from forming on top. Refrigerate until cold.

---

189   MICROWAVE CHOCOLATE CRAZY CAKE
Prep: 20 minutes   Cook: 7 to 8 minutes   Serves: 8

Over the years, this recipe has gone by many names, including wacky cake and crazy cake. It's so simple a child can make it. This version can be baked in either the microwave or a conventional oven. Some say it was a World War II recipe. It's a jiffy sort of cake that contains no eggs. The cake is prepared and baked in the same dish, so there is no mess to clean up.

1½ **cups flour**
1 **cup granulated sugar**
3 **tablespoons unsweetened cocoa powder**
1 **teaspoon baking soda**
½ **teaspoon salt**
⅓ **cup vegetable oil**
2 **teaspoons cider vinegar**

2½ **teaspoons vanilla extract**
½ **cup semisweet chocolate chips**
2 **tablespoons butter**
1 **tablespoon light corn syrup**
2 **tablespoons powdered sugar**

1. In an ungreased 6 x 10-inch microwave-safe glass baking dish, mix together flour, granulated sugar, cocoa, baking soda, and salt. Make 3 holes (one large, one medium, and one small) in mixture. Add oil to large hole, vinegar to medium hole, and 2 teaspoons vanilla to small hole. Pour 1 cup cold water over all. Stir well with fork or whisk to blend. Scrape down sides of dish with a rubber spatula.

2. Cook in a microwave oven on Medium 4 minutes, turning dish twice during cooking time. Then cook on High 2 to 2½ minutes, or until done. Do not overcook. Let cool.

3. In a small glass bowl, combine chocolate chips, butter, and corn syrup. Heat in microwave on High 45 to 60 seconds, or until melted and smooth when stirred. Add 1 tablespoon hot water, powdered sugar, and remaining ½ teaspoon vanilla; mix until smooth. Spread frosting over cooled cake and let stand until set.

NOTE: *To bake cake in a conventional oven, preheat oven to 350°F. Prepare cake as directed above. Bake cake 25 to 30 minutes, or until a cake tester inserted in center comes out clean. Prepare frosting in a small saucepan over low heat and spread on cool cake.*

190 MICROWAVE CANDY BAR PIE
Prep: 25 minutes   Cook: 4½ to 5 minutes   Chill: 3 to 4 hours
Serves: 8

4 tablespoons butter
2 cups crushed chocolate chip cookie crumbs
1 (8-ounce) milk chocolate bar, broken into pieces
2 (1-ounce) squares unsweetened chocolate, cut up

¾ cup milk
3 cups miniature marshmallows
2 cups heavy cream
⅓ to ½ cup chopped Heath Bar candy or other chocolate-covered English toffee

1. To make crust, in a 9-inch deep glass pie dish, melt butter in microwave oven on High 1 minute. Using a fork, stir in cookie crumbs until well mixed. Press mixture evenly and firmly over bottom and up sides of pie dish. Cook on High 30 seconds to set. Set aside to let cool.

2. To prepare filling, in a 2-quart glass bowl, combine milk chocolate and unsweetened chocolate, milk, and marshmallows. Cook on High 2 minutes; stir well. Cook 1 to 1½ minutes longer, or until chocolate is melted and marshmallows are completely dissolved when stirred. Let cool completely. Use an ice water bath or refrigerator to hasten process, if desired, but do not allow mixture to harden.

3. In a medium bowl, whip cream with an electric mixer on high speed until stiff. Remove 1 cup and set aside. Fold cold chocolate mixture into remaining whipped cream.

4. Turn chocolate filling into crust, spreading evenly. Spread reserved 1 cup whipped cream over top. Sprinkle chopped candy over whipped cream.

5. Refrigerate until firm, 3 to 4 hours or overnight. To serve, cut into slices with a sharp knife.

NOTE: *Pie can be frozen before adding candy. Remove from freezer to refrigerator at least 1 hour prior to serving. Sprinkle with candy shortly before serving.*

191   EASY AS 1-2-3 MICROWAVE BROWNIES
Prep: 10 minutes   Cook: 5½ to 6 minutes   Makes: 16 or 25

When you need brownies in a jiffy, try these. They're easy enough for kids to make.

1   stick (4 ounces) butter or margarine
1   cup granulated sugar
2   eggs
1   teaspoon vanilla extract

½   cup unsweetened cocoa powder
⅔   cup flour
1   cup chopped pecans
    Powdered sugar

1. In a medium bowl, beat together butter, sugar, eggs, and vanilla with an electric mixer on medium speed until light and fluffy, 1 to 2 minutes. Beat in cocoa. Add flour and beat until well blended. By hand stir in pecans. Spread evenly in a wax paper-lined 8-inch square glass dish.

2. Cook in a microwave oven on High 3 minutes. Turn dish a quarter turn and cook 2½ to 3 minutes longer. Let cool. Sift powdered sugar over top. Cut into 16 or 25 squares.

192   MICROWAVE ROCKY ROAD
Prep: 15 minutes   Cook: 6 minutes   Chill: 2 hours
Makes: about 3½ to 4 pounds

Friend and microwave cooking expert, Thelma Pressman, shared this "to die for" fattening favorite she has been making for years.

3   (12-ounce) packages semisweet chocolate chips
3   (1-ounce) squares unsweetened chocolate cut up

½   cup plus 1 tablespoon solid vegetable shortening
40   large marshmallows
2   cups whole toasted almonds

1. In a 1-quart glass bowl, combine 1 package (12 ounces) chocolate chips, 1 square unsweetened chocolate, and 3 tablespoons shortening. Heat in a microwave oven on High 2 minutes, or until melted and smooth when stirred. Turn into a deep 2-quart casserole or soufflé dish, spreading evenly. Sprinkle half of marshmallows and half of almonds evenly over chocolate.

2. Repeat process, melting another package chocolate chips, square unsweetened chocolate, and 3 tablespoons shortening and layering with remaining marshmallows and almonds. Then top with a final layer of chocolate mixture (of remaining chocolate and shortening). Refrigerate until firm, about 2 hours. Cut or break into large pieces. Store in airtight container.

193   WHITE CHOCOLATE RIBBON FUDGE
Prep: 20 minutes   Cook: 3 to 4 minutes   Chill: 2 hours
Makes: 25 pieces

When you want to turn out a fast food gift or sweet offering, turn to this creation. Semisweet chocolate is nestled between white chocolate layers for fabulous fudge.

1¼ pounds white chocolate, cut up	Dash of salt
1 (14-ounce) can sweetened condensed milk	1½ cups chopped walnuts
1½ to 2 teaspoons rum extract	6 ounces semisweet chocolate chips (1 cup), melted
1½ teaspoons white vinegar or lemon juice	

1. In a 2-quart glass bowl, melt white chocolate with sweetened condensed milk in microwave oven on Medium 3 to 4 minutes, or until melted and smooth when stirred. Stir in rum extract, vinegar, and salt; mix well. Stir in walnuts.

2. Spread half of white chocolate mixture into a buttered 8- or 9-inch square baking pan. Refrigerate about 10 minutes, or until almost set. Spread melted semisweet chocolate over white chocolate. Carefully top with remaining white chocolate mixture, spreading evenly over all. Refrigerate until firm, about 2 hours or longer. Cut into 25 squares. Store in refrigerator in tightly covered container.

194   EASY NO-FAIL FUDGE
Prep: 10 minutes   Cook: 2½ to 3 minutes   Chill: 2 hours
Makes: 16 pieces

When you need some fudge fast, reach for this recipe. It's smooth and great tasting!

12 ounces semisweet chocolate chips (2 cups)	Dash of salt
2 (1-ounce) squares unsweetened chocolate, cut up	1½ teaspoons vanilla extract
1 (14-ounce) can sweetened condensed milk	1½ to 2 teaspoons grated orange zest
	1 cup chopped walnuts or pecans

1. In a 1-quart glass bowl, combine chocolate chips, unsweetened chocolate, and sweetened condensed milk. Heat in microwave oven on High 2½ to 3 minutes, or until chocolate melts and mixture is smooth when stirred. Stir in salt, vanilla, orange zest, and nuts.

2. Spread evenly in a wax paper-lined 8-inch square baking pan. Refrigerate 2 hours, or until firm. Cut into 16 squares. Store, covered, in refrigerator.

195   RASPBERRY TRUFFLES

Prep: 35 minutes   Cook: 4 to 5 minutes   Chill and freeze: 5½ hours
Makes: about 2 dozen

22 ounces bittersweet
    chocolate, cut into small
    pieces
6 tablespoons unsalted butter

⅓ cup seedless raspberry jam
2 tablespoons Chambord or
    raspberry brandy

1. In a 1-quart glass measure, combine 10 ounces chocolate and butter. Heat in a microwave oven on High 1 to 1½ minutes, until melted and smooth when stirred. Stir in jam and liqueur until well blended. Cover and refrigerate until firm, about 4 hours or overnight.

2. Using a melon baller or small ice cream scoop, scrape mixture into 1-inch balls. (If mixture is too hard, let stand at room temperature ½ hour before shaping.) Place truffles on wax paper-lined baking pan and freeze firm, 1 hour or longer.

3. In a small glass dish, place remaining 12 ounces chocolate. Heat in microwave oven on Medium 3 to 3½ minutes, stirring often, until melted, smooth, and warm. Using a fork, dip truffles quickly, one at a time, into chocolate, tapping fork on edge of dish to shake off excess. Place on wax paper-lined baking pan. Repeat dipping process, stirring chocolate often and scraping down sides of dish, if necessary, to prevent chocolate from hardening. Refrigerate until chocolate is set, about ½ hour. Wrap in an airtight container and store in refrigerator 2 weeks or in freezer 1 month. Serve in paper candy cups.

NOTE: *Truffles can also be rolled in finely chopped nuts and sifted unsweetened cocoa powder instead of dipped in chocolate. Roll in nuts or cocoa immediately after shaping into balls. Store in refrigerator or freezer as directed above.*

196   FABULOUS CHOCOLATE TRUFFLES

Prep: 35 minutes   Cook: 4½ to 6 minutes   Chill and freeze: about 5½ hours   Makes: 20 large

These are so easy and so professional-looking. And if you're careful when you heat the chocolate for dipping and refrigerate the truffles, there's no need to temper the chocolate.

22 to 24 ounces imported
    bittersweet chocolate, cut
    into small pieces

¾ cup heavy cream
4 tablespoons unsalted butter,
    cut into small pieces

1. In a 1-quart glass bowl, combine 10 ounces chocolate and cream. Heat in microwave oven on High 1½ to 2 minutes, or until mixture is melted and smooth when stirred. Stir in butter until smooth and melted. Cover and refrigerate until firm, about 4 hours or overnight.

2. Using a 1¼-inch ice cream scoop or a tablespoon, scrape up moisture into 20 balls, about 1½ inches each. Place truffles on wax paper-lined baking pans and freeze until firm, 1 hour or longer.

3. In a small glass dish, place remaining 12 to 14 ounces cut-up chocolate. Heat in microwave oven on medium 3 to 4 minutes, stirring often, until chocolate is melted, smooth, and warm. Using a fork, dip truffles quickly, one at a time, into chocolate, tapping fork on edge of dish to shake off excess. Place on wax paper-lined baking sheet. Repeat dipping process, stirring chocolate often and scraping down sides of dish, if necessary, to prevent chocolate from hardening. Refrigerate truffles until chocolate is set, 30 to 40 minutes. Wrap in an airtight container and store in refrigerator 2 weeks or in freezer 1 month. Serve in paper candy cups.

   NOTE: *Truffles can also be rolled in finely chopped nuts or sifted unsweetened cocoa powder instead of dipped in chocolate. Roll in nuts or cocoa immediately after shaping into balls. Store in refrigerator or freezer as directed above.*

197 ESPRESSO TRUFFLES
Prep: 30 minutes   Cook: 3 to 4 minutes   Chill: 7 to 8 hours
Makes: about 44

   These creamy truffles explode with the intense flavor of chocolate and espresso. They make wonderful gifts or a great ending to a meal.

1 **cup milk**	2 **tablespoons instant espresso**
½ **cup heavy cream**	**powder**
1½ **pounds good-quality**	⅔ **cup unsweetened cocoa**
semisweet or bittersweet	**powder, sifted**
chocolate, finely chopped	
1 **stick (4 ounces) butter, cut**	
up and softened	

1. In a 2-quart glass bowl, combine milk and cream. Heat in a microwave oven on High 3 to 4 minutes, or until boiling. Whisk in chopped chocolate and butter until melted and smooth. (If necessary, return to microwave oven on High about 1 minute to melt chocolate and butter completely.) Whisk in espresso powder. Refrigerate 5 to 6 hours, or until mixture is firm enough to hold its shape.

2. With a small ice cream scoop or melon baller, scoop chilled mixture into 1¼-inch balls. Roll in cocoa to coat completely. Place on wax paper-lined jelly-roll pans. Refrigerate until firm, about 2 hours. Store in an airtight container in refrigerator 2 weeks or in freezer 1 month. Serve at room temperature.

198   QUICK PEANUT BUTTER-CHOCOLATE CANDY

Prep: 10 minutes   *Cook: 2½ to 3½ minutes*   *Chill: 1½ hours*
Makes: 25

If you love peanut butter candy cups, you'll love this creation which is easy enough for kids to make.

1 cup plus 2 tablespoons crunchy peanut butter	⅓ cup plus 2 tablespoons chopped peanuts
1¼ cups powdered sugar	6 ounces semisweet chocolate
¼ cup milk	chips (1 cup)

1. In a 1-quart glass bowl, combine 1 cup peanut butter, powdered sugar, and milk. Heat in microwave oven, uncovered, on High 1 to 1½ minutes, or until mixture is smooth and well blended when stirred. Stir in ⅓ cup peanuts.

2. Turn mixture into a foil-lined 8-inch square pan. Spread evenly.

3. In a clean 1-quart glass bowl, combine chocolate chips and remaining 2 tablespoons peanut butter. Heat, uncovered, on High 1½ to 2 minutes, or until mixture is melted and blended when stirred. Carefully spread chocolate mixture evenly over peanut butter mixture in pan. Sprinkle remaining 2 tablespoons peanuts on top; press lightly into chocolate. Cool at room temperature, then refrigerate 1½ hours, or until firm. Cut into 25 squares. Store, covered, in refrigerator.

---

199   SWIRLED CHOCOLATE-PEANUT BUTTER CANDY

Prep: 10 minutes   *Cook: 4 to 5½ minutes*   *Chill: 2 hours*
Makes: about 9½ dozen squares

1⅓ cups chunky peanut butter	10 ounces semisweet or bittersweet chocolate, cut up
14 ounces imported white chocolate, cut up	

1. In a 1-quart glass bowl, combine peanut butter and white chocolate. Heat in a microwave oven on Medium 3 to 3½ minutes, stirring twice, until white chocolate is melted and mixture is well blended. Turn into a foil-lined 9 x 13-inch pan; spread evenly.

2. In a small glass dish, melt semisweet chocolate in microwave oven on High 1 to 2 minutes, stirring once or twice until melted and smooth.

3. Drizzle spoonfuls of semisweet chocolate over white chocolate mixture in pan. With a knife, swirl dark chocolate into white chocolate mixture. Refrigerate 2 hours, or until firm. Cut into 1-inch squares. Keep refrigerated, covered, until serving time.

200 PEANUT BUTTER WHITE CHOCOLATE CANDY DREAMS

Prep: 20 minutes   Cook: about 2 to 3 minutes   Makes: 18 candies

Come holiday time, these sweets make great gifts or a wonderful addition to a candy or cookie tray. If you prefer, you can substitute bittersweet or semisweet chocolate for the white chocolate, or use a little of each, sandwiching the peanut butter mixture between a layer each of dark and white chocolate. To make these, you'll need 18 paper candy cups 2 inches in diameter and ¾ to 1 inch high.

½ cup crunchy or creamy
    peanut butter
½ cup powdered sugar
1 to 2 tablespoons heavy
    cream

12 ounces imported white
    chocolate
½ cup finely chopped toasted
    almonds
18 whole natural almonds

1. In a small glass bowl or dish, heat peanut butter in a microwave oven on High 30 to 40 seconds to soften. Mix in powdered sugar and cream; mixture should be stiff, not runny.

2. In a medium glass bowl, melt white chocolate in microwave oven on Medium 1½ to 2½ minutes, stirring once halfway through cooking time, or until melted and smooth. Stir in chopped almonds.

3. Spoon a little white chocolate mixture into bottom of each of 18 paper candy cups 2 inches in diameter, swirling with back of a teaspoon to make an even layer. Drop a little peanut butter mixture on top of white chocolate in each cup and spread around with back of spoon to make an even layer. Spoon remaining white chocolate over peanut butter, using back of spoon to swirl evenly. Top each cup with a whole almond. Refrigerate until firm. Store candies in refrigerator for up to a week.

201 PRONTO PEANUT CLUSTERS

Prep: 10 minutes   Cook: 1½ minutes   Chill: 30 to 60 minutes
Makes: 25

These are speedy, delicious, and easy enough for children to make.

6 ounces semisweet chocolate
    chips (1 cup)

¼ cup chunky peanut butter
1 cup dry-roasted peanuts

1. In a 1-quart glass bowl, combine chocolate chips and peanut butter. Heat in a microwave oven on High about 1½ minutes, until melted and smooth when stirred. Stir in peanuts.

2. Drop by teaspoonfuls onto a wax paper-lined baking pan to make 25 clusters. Refrigerate until set, 30 to 60 minutes. Cover and keep refrigerated until serving time.

202   PEANUT BUTTER 'N' WHITE CHOCOLATE RITZ

Prep: 20 minutes   Cook: 2 to 3 minutes   Chill: 1 hour   Makes: 28

These novel goodies nestle peanut butter between Ritz crackers and are then dipped into white chocolate. I received them as a holiday gift, and they vanished within a day.

56 Ritz crackers	**12 ounces imported white**
½ to ⅔ cup smooth peanut	**chocolate**
butter	

1. Sandwich together 2 Ritz crackers with about 1 teaspoon peanut butter in between. Set aside.

2. Place white chocolate in a medium glass dish. Heat in a microwave oven on Medium 2 to 3 minutes, stirring twice, until melted and smooth.

3. Using a fork, dip filled crackers into melted white chocolate; allow excess to drip off. Place on a wax paper-lined 10 x 15-inch jelly-roll pan. Refrigerate until set, at least 1 hour. Store, covered, in refrigerator.

203   CHOCOLATE-DIPPED STRAWBERRIES

Prep: 10 minutes   Cook: 3 to 3½ minutes   Chill: 1 hour   Makes: 20

These are elegant, great tasting, and belie the simplicity involved in making them. Be sure to melt the chocolate with care for best results.

20 fresh medium-large	**1 tablespoon solid vegetable**
strawberries	**shortening or vegetable**
6 ounces semisweet or	**oil**
bittersweet chocolate,	
cut up	

1. Rinse strawberries with cold water and dry well on several thicknesses of paper towels. In a 1- or 2-cup glass measure, combine chocolate and shortening. Heat in a microwave oven on Medium 2 minutes; stir well. Heat in microwave on Medium 1 to 1½ minutes longer, or just until chocolate is melted and smooth when stirred. Do not overcook.

2. Holding onto stem or green hull of dry strawberries, dip one at a time into chocolate, coating about ¾ of berry (it looks most attractive to leave some of the red as well as the green hull showing). Place berries ¾ inch apart on a wax paper-lined jelly-roll pan. Refrigerate berries until firm, about 1 hour. Do not plan to keep chilled berries more than 8 hours, as they will begin to soften.

204   CHOCOLATE-DIPPED APRICOTS

Prep: 10 minutes   Cook: 1 to 1½ minutes   Chill: 45 minutes
Makes: 35

These are a delicious addition to a snack or goodie tray anytime. Serve in paper candy cups, if desired.

½ cup semisweet chocolate
    chips
1½ teaspoons solid vegetable
    shortening

35 dried apricot halves

1. In a 1-cup glass measure, heat together chocolate chips and shortening in a microwave oven on High 1 to 1½ minutes, stirring twice, until chocolate is melted and smooth when stirred. Watch carefully as chocolate should not become too hot.

2. Dip each apricot half halfway into melted chocolate. Place ½ to 1 inch apart on wax paper-lined baking pan. Refrigerate until firm, about 45 minutes. Store, tightly covered, in refrigerator.

205   TRIPLE CHOCOLATE NUT BARK

Prep: 15 minutes   Cook: 3½ to 4 minutes   Makes: about 3 dozen

These are easy to make and delicious with three different chocolates and three kinds of nuts.

6 ounces semisweet chocolate,
    cut up
6 ounces milk chocolate,
    cut up
6 ounces white chocolate,
    cut up
½ cup chopped pecans

½ cup diced roasted almonds
1 cup roasted unsalted
    cashews
2 (1.4-ounce) milk chocolate
    crisp butter toffee candy
    bars (such as Skor bars),
    chopped

1. In a 2-quart glass bowl, combine semisweet, milk, and white chocolates. Heat in a microwave oven on Medium 2 minutes; stir. Heat 1½ to 2 minutes longer, just until melted and smooth when stirred.

2. Stir in nuts and candy pieces. Drop by teaspoonfuls ¾ inch apart onto 2 wax paper-lined jelly-roll pans. Let stand at room temperature or refrigerate until set.

206 NUTTY NOODLES
Prep: 15 minutes   Cook: 2 to 2½ minutes   Makes: 60

6 ounces semisweet chocolate chips (1 cup)

6 ounces butterscotch-flavored chips or white chocolate, chopped

1 (5-ounce) can chow mein noodles

1 cup unsalted dry-roasted peanuts

1. In a 2-quart glass bowl, melt together chocolate and butterscotch chips in a microwave oven on High 2 to 2½ minutes, stirring twice.

2. Meanwhile, place noodles in a food processor and chop with an on and off motion until broken up into smaller pieces. Do not process into crumbs. Or crush noodles in paper bag using rolling pin.

3. Add noodles and peanuts to chocolate mixture. Stir to coat well. Drop by teaspoonfuls 1-inch apart on wax paper-lined baking pans to make 60 clusters. Refrigerate until firm.

207 PEARS WITH PORT AND CHOCOLATE
Prep: 20 minutes   Cook: 10 minutes   Serves: 4

You won't believe how sophisticated this dessert cooked entirely in the microwave looks and tastes. For best results, prepare it 4 to 8 hours in advance to allow the pears to marinate in the port-flavored cooking liquid.

2 cups port wine

½ cup sugar
Strips of zest from ½ orange

4 fresh pears, peeled, with stems intact

6 ounces semisweet chocolate chips (1 cup)

½ cup heavy cream
Whipping cream

1. In a 2-quart glass bowl, combine 1½ cups port, sugar, orange zest, and ½ cup water. Heat in a microwave oven on High 4 minutes, stirring once halfway through cooking time.

2. Trim bottoms of pears, if necessary, so they will stand upright on a plate for serving. Place pears in hot port-flavored liquid. Spoon some of liquid over pears to moisten completely. Cover bowl with a sheet of wax paper. Cook in microwave oven on High 4 minutes, or until pears are tender but not mushy when pierced with a fork. Spoon liquid over pears. Let pears cool in liquid, at least 4 hours and up to 8 hours at room temperature, turning and basting with liquid occasionally.

3. Meanwhile, prepare chocolate sauce. In a 1-quart glass bowl, combine chocolate chips, cream, and remaining ½ cup port. Heat in microwave on High 2 minutes, or until chocolate is melted and sauce is smooth when stirred. Refrigerate until serving time; reheat slightly, if necessary, to liquify.

4. To serve, place 3 tablespoons chocolate sauce in center of each of 4 individual dessert plates; tilt plate so sauce covers completely. Stand 1 well-drained pear upright in center. Drizzle 1 tablespoon chocolate sauce over each pear. Garnish side of pear with a spoonful of whipped cream. Serve immediately.

NOTE: *If you plan to keep pears longer than 8 hours, refrigerate in enough cooking liquid to cover until serving time.*

208   QUICK CHOCOLATE MINTS
Prep: 10 minutes   Cook: 2½ to 3 minutes   Chill: 2 to 3 hours   Makes: 25

These are a wonderful after-dinner offering any time of year. Keep them in mind for a holiday sweet buffet, too. You won't believe something so simple to make tastes so good.

> 2 (10-ounce) packages mint
>   semisweet chocolate
>   chips
>
> 1 (14-ounce) can sweetened
>   condensed milk
> 1 teaspoon vanilla extract

1. In a 1-quart glass bowl, combine mint chocolate chips and sweetened condensed milk. Heat in a microwave oven on High 1½ minutes; stir well. Heat 1 to 1½ minutes longer, or until mixture is smooth and chocolate is melted when stirred. Stir in vanilla.

2. Turn into a buttered 8-inch square baking pan. Refrigerate 2 to 3 hours, or until firm. Cut into 25 squares. Store, tightly covered, in refrigerator.

209   HAWAIIAN BON BONS
Prep: 10 minutes   Cook: 3½ to 4 minutes   Chill: 1 hour   Makes: 25

> 8 ounces imported white
>   chocolate, cut up
> 1 cup unsalted macadamia
>   nuts
>
> ½ cup flaked coconut
> 1 teaspoon grated orange zest
>   (optional)

1. In a 1-quart glass bowl, heat white chocolate in a microwave oven on Medium 2 minutes; stir. Return to microwave and heat on Medium 1½ to 2 minutes longer, or until melted and smooth when stirred.

2. Stir in nuts, coconut, and orange zest. Carefully spoon into 25 (1½-inch) paper bon bon cups, filling to top. Let stand at room temperature, or refrigerate 1 hour or longer, until firm. Store, well wrapped, in refrigerator.

Chapter 8

Chocolate's Fun for Kids

Big kids, little kids, kids of all ages love chocolate. And it's no wonder. From the time we are small, chocolate in some form—be it chocolate cookies, chocolate candy, chocolate ice cream, or some other chocolate goodie—was more often than not offered as a reward for good behavior or as tender consolation.

I remember fondly the chocolate-covered raisins that my grandfather always gave us when we went to visit him, the candy jar filled with Hershey's kisses at our neighbor's house, and the chocolate-covered M&M's we simply adored whenever we could get them. And of course who could forget the pink and white covered-chocolate snowballs (cupcakes) that we traded away in our lunch boxes. As we grew older there were those unforgettable Frango Mints from Marshall Field's in Chicago (that still remain a favorite), the assorted See's chocolate candies and truffles we can't live without to this day. The list of chocolate memories goes on and on, even as our chocolate tastes change and we become more sophisticated.

This chapter is devoted to chocolate goodies that are fun for children to make and to eat. They're easy, and depending on the age of the child, many can probably be managed without adult assistance.

The recipes here have been designed to combine chocolate with other favorite foods of the younger set, such as potato chips, pretzels, bananas, peanut butter, peanuts, marshmallows, and ice cream sandwiches. For starters, teenagers will enjoy offering Chocolate-Coated Potato Chips or White Chocolate-Dipped Pretzels to their friends. Don't turn up your nose until you try them. Another dessert that's fun to make and to eat is the Brownie Pizza, topped with chocolate chips and nuts.

Frozen Chocolate Banana Pops are a cinch to whip together with chocolate chips and peanut butter. Keep these in mind when you have ripe bananas on hand, and you don't know what to do with them.

The Ice Cream Cookie Sandwiches, which go together in a jiffy with store-bought ice cream, store-bought cookies, and a homemade chocolate mixture, were an overwhelming hit at our house. Let the children select their favorite ice cream and cookie flavors, and they're bound to ask for more.

210   FROZEN CHOCOLATE FUN PIE

Prep: 10 minutes   Cook: none   Freeze: 6 hours   Serves: 8

Let kids customize this pie by adding their own mix-ins, such as crushed English toffee, favorite cut-up candy bars, coconut, miniature marshmallows, and the like.

1⅓ cups cold milk (lowfat or
    nonfat if desired)
1 (4-ounce) package chocolate
    fudge flavor instant
    pudding and pie filling
    mix
1 (8-ounce) container frozen
    whipped topping,
    thawed
½ cup semisweet chocolate
    chips or cut-up candy
    pieces, such as chocolate-
    covered English toffee,
    peanut butter cups, or
    cut-up cookies

½ cup chopped nuts
½ cup miniature
    marshmallows or flaked
    coconut
1 (9-inch) unbaked Chocolate
    Wafer Crust (page 135)

1. In a large bowl, combine milk and pie filling mix. Whisk until well blended, about 1 minute. Let stand 5 minutes.

2. Fold in whipped topping until no white streaks remain. Fold in chocolate chips, nuts, and marshmallows. Spoon into Chocolate Wafer Crust.

3. Freeze until firm, about 6 hours or overnight. Remove from freezer and let stand 10 minutes to soften before serving.

211   MICROWAVE S'MORES

Prep: 1 minute   Cook: 20 to 25 seconds   Serves: 1

When a campfire isn't close by, but you have a hankering for s'mores, try the microwave oven. Children will devour this home version.

2 (2½-inch) graham cracker
    squares
½ of a 1.55-ounce milk
    chocolate candy bar

1 large marshmallow

1. Place 1 graham cracker on a paper plate. Top with chocolate bar piece, then marshmallow. Heat in a microwave oven on High 20 to 25 seconds, or until marshmallow puffs up.

2. Remove from microwave and top with remaining graham cracker, pressing down on top of marshmallow. Let stand 30 seconds. Then eat immediately.

212   PEANUT BUTTER ROCKY ROAD

Prep: 10 minutes   Cook: 2 to 2½ minutes   Chill: 1 to 2 hours
Makes: 35

This is the fastest and simplest way to make rocky road. The chocolate never streaks and no tempering is required. To give as a gift, put each candy piece in a paper candy cup.

3 cups semisweet chocolate
    chips or 18 ounces
    semisweet chocolate, cut
    up
¾ cup crunchy or smooth
    peanut butter

¾ cup chopped peanuts or
    walnuts
3 cups miniature
    marshmallows

1. In a large 2-quart glass bowl, combine chocolate and peanut butter. Heat in microwave oven on High 2 to 2½ minutes, stirring once halfway through cooking time. Stir until chocolate is melted and smooth. Stir in peanuts and marshmallows.

2. Immediately spread in foil-lined 11 x 7-inch baking pan. Refrigerate 1 to 2 hours, or until firm. Cut into 35 pieces. Keep refrigerated.

213   ICE CREAM COOKIE SANDWICHES

Prep: 25 minutes   Cook: 2 to 2½ minutes   Freeze: 2 hours
Serves: 12

These are versatile and a snap to make. Children love them. Use your favorite cookie and chocolate ice cream flavors.

24 (2½- or 3-inch) oatmeal
    chocolate chip cookies
    (12-ounce package)
1 quart chocolate ice cream,
    softened slightly

12 ounces semisweet chocolate
    chips (2 cups)
¼ cup milk
4 tablespoons butter

1. Sandwich 2 cookies together with about ⅓ cup ice cream in between; smooth edges with a knife. Immediately place on a foil- or wax paper-lined tray. Repeat with remaining cookies and ice cream. Freeze 1 hour, or until hard.

2. Meanwhile, prepare chocolate coating mixture. In a 2-cup glass measure, combine chocolate chips, milk, and butter. Heat in a microwave oven on High 2 to 2½ minutes, or until chocolate and butter are melted and smooth when stirred. Refrigerate until cold but not set, stirring a few times.

3. When ice cream sandwiches are frozen hard, remove from freezer and dip to coat half of each one with chocolate mixture; or spread chocolate over cookies with a spatula. Return to freezer and freeze until chocolate is set, about 1 hour. Then wrap individually in plastic wrap and store in freezer until serving time.

214 NO-BAKE PEANUT BUTTER AND MILK CHOCOLATE BARS

Prep: 45 minutes   Cook: 1½ to 2 minutes   Chill: 1 hour   Makes: 20

These are quick and delicious, easy enough for teenagers to make.

⅓ cup chocolate wafer cookie or graham cracker crumbs
1½ cups chunky peanut butter
1¼ cups powdered sugar
⅓ cup heavy cream or half-and-half

1 cup milk chocolate chips
1 tablespoon vegetable oil or solid vegetable shortening

1. Sprinkle cookie crumbs evenly over bottom of foil-lined 8-inch square baking pan.

2. In a medium bowl, mix together peanut butter, powdered sugar, and cream with a fork until well blended. Carefully spread evenly over cookie crust. Refrigerate until firm, about 30 minutes.

3. In a 1-cup glass measure combine chocolate chips and oil. Heat in a microwave oven on Medium 1½ to 2 minutes, or until mixture is melted and smooth when stirred.

4. Spread evenly over peanut butter layer. Refrigerate until chocolate is set, about 1 hour. Cut into 20 bars. Keep refrigerated.

215 CHOCOLATE CORNFLAKE RING FILLED WITH ICE CREAM

Prep: 20 minutes   Cook: 5 minutes   Chill: 4 hours   Serves: 10 to 12

This is an easy ice cream dessert—and kids of all ages love it.

6 cups cornflakes cereal
1 cup chopped pecans
6 ounces semisweet chocolate chips (1 cup)
3 cups packed brown sugar
6 tablespoons butter
6 tablespoons heavy cream

½ gallon favorite-flavor ice cream
1 (12-ounce) jar butterscotch sauce, heated
1 (12-ounce) jar chocolate sauce, heated

1. In a large bowl, combine cornflakes, pecans, and chocolate chips. In a medium saucepan, heat brown sugar, butter, and cream over medium heat, stirring often, until butter is melted. Cook for 2 minutes, stirring constantly. Pour over cornflake mixture and mix gently to combine. Press mixture into a buttered 8-cup ring mold. Refrigerate 4 hours, or until firm.

2. To serve, unmold and fill center with scoops of ice cream. Cut cornflake ring into slices and top with scoops of ice cream. Pass bowls of warm butterscotch and chocolate sauce on the side.

216 MOCK CRACKER TOFFEE
Prep: 20 minutes   Cook: 12 to 14 minutes   Makes: 40 or more pieces

As unbelievable as it may seem, there's a piece of soda cracker in each bite of this delicious toffee-like candy.

About 40 soda crackers	**1½ cups semisweet chocolate**
2 sticks (8 ounces) butter (do	**chips**
not substitute margarine)	**1 cup chopped walnuts**
1 cup packed brown sugar	

1. Preheat oven to 400°F. Place crackers side by side in a single layer without overlapping in a foil-lined 10 x 15-inch jelly-roll pan; set aside.

2. In a medium saucepan, combine butter and brown sugar. Heat to boiling over medium heat, stirring often. Cook, stirring, 2 minutes.

3. Pour butter mixture evenly over crackers and using a knife, spread until evenly covered. Bake 5 to 7 minutes, or until very bubbly.

4. Remove from oven and let stand 1 minute. Sprinkle chocolate chips evenly over crackers and let stand until melted, 5 minutes. With a knife, spread chocolate evenly over all. Sprinkle nuts on top. Let stand until cool. Then refrigerate until candies are cold and chocolate is set. Cut into about 40 pieces before serving.

---

217 CHOCOLATE-COVERED MARSHMALLOWS
Prep: 15 minutes   Cook: 1½ to 2 minutes   Chill 45 to 60 minutes
Makes: 12 to 14

6 ounces semisweet chocolate	**12 to 14 marshmallows**
chips (1 cup)	**Colored decors or sprinkles,**
1 tablespoon solid vegetable	**flaked coconut, M&M's,**
shortening	**or pecan halves**

1. In a 1-cup glass measure, heat together chocolate chips and shortening in a microwave oven on High about 1½ to 2 minutes, or until chocolate is melted and smooth when stirred.

2. Using a fork, dip each marshmallow into chocolate to cover completely. Drain off excess chocolate by pulling fork across rim of cup. Place marshmallows 1-inch apart on a wax paper-lined baking sheet; immediately sprinkle colored decors or other toppings on top. Refrigerate until chocolate is firm, 45 to 60 minutes. Store, covered, in refrigerator.

Variation: **CHOCOLATE-COVERED FORTUNE COOKIES**

Follow directions above, substituting 12 to 14 fortune cookies for marshmallows. Leave plain or sprinkle with toppings as desired. Remove from refrigerator 1 hour before serving.

218   CHOCOLATE-COATED POTATO CHIPS

Prep: 15 minutes   Cook: 1½ to 2 minutes   Serves: 6

Teenagers love these and can make them in a jiffy to serve at a party or for friends. The salty flavor teamed with chocolate is a winning combination.

6 ounces semisweet chocolate chips (1 cup)
1 tablespoon solid vegetable shortening

½ of a 6½-ounce bag ruffled potato chips

1. In a small shallow glass dish, combine chocolate chips and shortening. Heat in a microwave oven on High 1½ to 2 minutes, or until melted and smooth when stirred.

2. Dip chips, one at a time, into chocolate, coating one third to one half of each chip. Pull chip against edge of dish to remove excess chocolate. Place chips on wax paper-lined baking pan. Let stand at room temperature 15 minutes, then refrigerate until set.

219   CHOCOLATE PEANUT BUTTER SNACK SPREAD

Prep: 5 minutes   Cook: 1 to 1½ minutes   Makes: 1⅔ cups

This is great for gift-giving. Serve on crackers, shortbread, plain cookies, or fruit for a special after-school or evening treat.

6 ounces semisweet chocolate chips (1 cup)
¼ cup milk

1 cup roasted honey nut or regular-flavor chunky or smooth peanut butter

In a 1-quart glass measure, combine chocolate chips and milk. Heat in a microwave oven on High 1 to 1½ minutes, or until chocolate is melted and mixture is smooth when stirred. Stir in peanut butter until well blended. Store, covered, in refrigerator up to 1 month. Remove from refrigerator 1 hour before serving for easier spreading.

220   SPEEDY CHOCOLATE PEANUT BUTTER FUDGE

Prep: 10 minutes   Cook: 1½ to 2 minutes   Makes: 64 squares

This is fast and easy for budding kid chefs to put together.

¾ cup smooth or crunchy peanut butter
6 ounces semisweet chocolate chips (1 cup)

2 cups miniature marshmallows
¼ cup heavy cream or milk
1 teaspoon vanilla extract

1. In a 2-quart glass bowl, combine peanut butter, chocolate chips, marshmallows, cream, and vanilla. Place in a microwave oven and heat on High 1½ to 2 minutes, or until marshmallows are melted and mixture is smooth when stirred.

2. Turn into a foil-lined 8-inch square baking ban. Let cool ½ hour, then refrigerate until firm. Cut into 1-inch squares.

221   NUTTY CHOCOLATE-COVERED POTATO CHIPS

Prep: 10 minutes   Cook: 1½ minutes   Chill: 1 hour
Makes: about 36

Potato chips and chocolate are a tasty duo. Teenagers love these and can make them easily with the assistance of the microwave oven.

12 ounces semisweet chocolate chips (2 cups)
2 tablespoons cooking oil or solid vegetable shortening

2 cups crushed potato chips
½ cup chopped nuts
½ cup flaked or shredded coconut

1. In a 2-quart glass bowl, combine chocolate chips and oil. Heat in a microwave oven on High about 1½ minutes, until melted and smooth when stirred.

2. Stir in potato chips, nuts, and coconut until well coated. Drop by teaspoonfuls onto 2 wax paper-lined baking sheets. Refrigerate until set, about 1 hour. Store, covered, in refrigerator.

222   CHOCOLATE POPCORN SQUARES

Prep: 10 minutes   Cook: 1½ to 1¾ minutes   Chill: 5 to 6 hours
Makes: 25 squares

This is an easy recipe for kids to make. Microwave popcorn works well in this recipe.

6 ounces semisweet chocolate
   chips (1 cup)
⅓ cup heavy cream
1 teaspoon vanilla extract

4 cups popped popcorn (from
   3 tablespoons kernels)
1 cup chopped nuts

1. In a 2-quart glass bowl, combine chocolate chips and cream. Heat in a microwave oven on High 1½ to 1¾ minutes, or until melted and smooth when stirred. Stir in vanilla. Add popcorn and nuts and mix until evenly coated.

2. Turn into a foil-lined 8-inch square baking pan; press gently with back of spoon to spread evenly. Refrigerate 5 to 6 hours, or until firm. Cut into 25 squares. Cover and refrigerate until serving time.

223   BANANAS AMBROSIA WITH FUDGE SAUCE

Prep: 15 minutes   Cook: none   Serves: 6

1 cup sour cream
1 tablespoon orange juice
   concentrate
1 to 1¼ cups flaked coconut
3 medium or large bananas,
   cut diagonally into 6
   slices each

1 to 1⅓ cups hot fudge sauce
   (homemade or store-
   bought), heated
⅓ cup diced roasted almonds
   Whipped cream

1. In a small bowl, mix sour cream and orange juice concentrate until well blended. Place coconut into a small bowl.

2. Roll banana slices in sour cream mixture to coat, then immediately roll in coconut to coat completely. Place bananas on a plate; refrigerate at least ½ hour but no longer than 1½ hours.

3. To serve, place 3 banana slices on each of 6 individual dessert plates. Drizzle hot fudge sauce over bananas; then sprinkle almonds on top. Garnish with whipped cream, if desired.

224   WHITE CHOCOLATE-DIPPED PRETZELS
Prep: 20 minutes   Cook: 3½ to 4 minutes   Makes: 80

Teenagers enjoy these easy-to-make snacks. Melt the white chocolate in the microwave oven, but be sure to watch it closely to avoid scorching.

8 ounces imported white chocolate, broken up

½ of an 8-ounce package mini-pretzel twists (about 3 cups or 80 pretzels)

1. In a 1-quart glass bowl, heat white chocolate in a microwave oven on Medium 2 minutes; stir. Heat 1½ to 2 minutes longer, or just until melted and smooth when stirred.

2. Using a fork, dip pretzels one at a time into melted chocolate, tapping fork on edge of bowl to remove excess. Place on wax paper-lined baking sheets. Refrigerate until firm. Remove from pan and store in a covered container in refrigerator.

225   FROZEN CHOCOLATE BANANA POPS
Prep: 15 minutes   Cook: 1½ minutes   Freeze: 2¼ hours   Serves: 6

These are easy enough for kids to make, and they love them. Anytime you have extra ripe bananas on hand, cut and freeze them and you'll be ready to make these goodies.

3 ripe bananas
½ cup semisweet chocolate chips

⅓ cup crunchy or smooth peanut butter

1. Peel bananas; cut each crosswise in half. Insert a wooden pop-type stick into the cut end of each banana piece. Wrap tightly in plastic wrap or in a plastic freezer bag and freeze until firm. 2 hours or overnight.

2. In a small microwave-safe dish, combine chocolate chips and peanut butter. Heat in a microwave oven on High about 1½ minutes, until chocolate is melted when mixture is stirred. Using a knife, spread mixture evenly over bananas (some of mixture will harden immediately). Wrap in wax paper or plastic wrap and freeze until chocolate is firm and set, 15 to 20 minutes. Wrap well and store in freezer.

226 BROWNIE PIZZA

Prep: 15 minutes   Cook: 27 to 30 minutes   Makes: 12 to 14 slices

Kids and adults love brownies served this way for an innovative, fun offering. You can top these with nuts, chocolate pieces, coconut pieces, and even candies.

1 stick (4 ounces) butter	2 tablespoons light corn syrup
¾ cup granulated sugar	1 teaspoon vanilla extract
½ cup packed brown sugar	½ cup flour
2 (1-ounce) squares unsweetened chocolate, cut up	½ teaspoon baking powder
	6 ounces semisweet chocolate chips (1 cup)
2 eggs	1 cup chopped walnuts

1. Preheat oven to 350°F. In a 2-quart glass bowl, combine butter, granulated sugar, brown sugar, and unsweetened chocolate. Heat in a microwave oven on High 1½ to 2 minutes, or until butter and chocolate are melted and smooth when stirred. Let cool 5 minutes.

2. With a whisk or fork, beat in eggs, corn syrup, and vanilla until well blended. Add flour and baking powder; mix well. Stir in ½ cup chocolate chips.

3. Line a 12-inch pizza pan with a ½-inch-high rim with foil. Grease foil well. Spread batter evenly over pan. Sprinkle nuts and remaining ½ cup chocolate chips over batter. Bake 25 to 28 minutes, or until set. Do not overbake.

4. Let cool, then refrigerate until chilled. Cut pizza into 12 to 14 wedges. Peel off foil before serving.

Chapter 9

Chocolate Softies

This chapter is filled with those nostalgic American-style chocolate desserts of yesteryear that are enjoying a resurgence in popularity today. You know the ones—chocolate custard, chocolate bread pudding, chocolate mousse, chocolate soufflé, chocolate pots, fruit cobbler, chocolate trifle, chocolate rice pudding, and chocolate Bavarians. All are homey, old-fashioned comfort desserts created from simple, often inexpensive ingredients. These are the kind of soft, easy-to-eat desserts that were served in many a nursery and that have been thriving in new dress on restaurant menus these days. You might say these old softies are coming into their own.

Chocolate bread pudding is among my old-time dessert favorites and has been since I was a youngster. Every time my mother entertained on a large scale and had leftover bread crusts on hand (trimmings from making party sandwich loaves), she whipped up chocolate bread pudding. After years of not making it, the recipe eluded her, so several years ago I recreated it from memory and I think my facsimile version (which I've updated in this chapter with chopped pecans) comes fairly close. At any rate it tastes delicious warm with plenty of heavy unwhipped cream poured over all.

There's really no trick to making any of these homespun favorites, some of which have been updated here for chocolate lovers. Take the fruit cobbler, for instance; instead of the usual blonde topping, the version here contains chocolate. It's great-tasting and gives the raspberries and peaches a pleasant lift.

All of these old-fashioned desserts will soothe the spirits. There's nothing quite like spooning something nice and soft into your mouth. In case you've forgotten what it's like, hustle into the kitchen and rustle up Easy Chocolate Baked Custard, Chocolate Orange Mousse, Chocolate Raisin Rice Pudding, Marbled Chocolate Bavarian, Easy Chocolate Soufflé, or Chocolate Fudge Trifle, for starters. These downright unpretentious classics are just plain good.

227 CHOCOLATE PECAN BREAD PUDDING
Prep: 15 minutes   Cook: 40 to 45 minutes   Serves: 6 to 8

3 **cups milk**	1½ **teaspoons vanilla extract**
4 **(1-ounce) squares**	⅛ **teaspoon salt**
unsweetened chocolate,	¾ **cup chopped pecans**
cut up	6 **cups ¾-inch French or**
3 **eggs**	**Italian bread cubes**
1 **cup sugar**	**Heavy cream**

1. Preheat oven to 350°F. In a medium saucepan, heat milk and chocolate over medium heat, stirring constantly, until boiling and chocolate is melted.

2. In a large bowl, whisk eggs, sugar, vanilla, and salt until blended. Whisk in hot chocolate milk. Stir in pecans and bread until well mixed.

3. Turn batter into a well-greased 11 x 7-inch (1½-quart) baking dish; spread evenly. Bake, uncovered, 35 to 40 minutes, or until set. Serve warm or cold. Pass a pitcher of cream on the side.

228 CHOCOLATE COEUR A LA CREME
Prep: 35 minutes   Cook: 6 to 7 minutes   Chill: overnight
Serves: 8 to 10

A lovely chocolate cream cheese dessert molded in a heart shape is wonderful for a special Valentine's Day offering with raspberry sauce and fresh strawberries. Another time, accompany with assorted fresh fruits.

6 **ounces semisweet chocolate**	1 **tablespoon plus 1 teaspoon**
chips (1 cup)	**cornstarch**
1½ **cups heavy cream**	2 **tablespoons Grand Marnier**
1 **(8-ounce) package cream**	**or framboise**
cheese, softened	1 **pint whole strawberries**
⅓ **cup powdered sugar**	
1 **teaspoon vanilla extract**	
2 **(10-ounce) packages frozen**	
red raspberries in syrup,	
thawed	

1. Line a 1-quart coeur à la crème mold with a single layer of damp cheesecloth, allowing a 2- to 3-inch overhang all around.

2. In a 2-cup glass measure, combine chocolate chips and ½ cup cream. Heat in a microwave oven on High 1 to 1½ minutes, or until smooth when stirred. Let cool.

3. In a medium bowl, whip remaining 1 cup cream with an electric mixer on high speed to soft peaks; set aside.

4. In a medium bowl, combine cream cheese, powdered sugar, and vanilla. Beat with electric mixer on medium speed until smooth, about 1 minute. Beat in cooled chocolate mixture until well blended, 1 to 2 minutes. Fold in whipped cream.

5. Turn cheese mixture into prepared mold; spread evenly. Fold overhanging cheesecloth over top. Place mold on a wire rack set over a pan or shallow bowl. Refrigerate overnight to drain.

6. To prepare sauce, drain syrup from thawed raspberries into a small saucepan. Stir in cornstarch until free of lumps. Cook over medium heat, stirring constantly, until sauce clears and thickens. Sieve to remove seeds, if desired. Stir in liqueur and raspberries. Cover and refrigerate until chilled.

7. To serve, fold back cheesecloth and invert mold onto serving plate; remove mold and cheesecloth. Dip whole strawberries into raspberry sauce to glaze. Ring edges of cheese heart with glazed berries. Pass raspberry sauce separately to spoon over individual servings as desired.

---

229 CHOCOLATE FUDGE TRIFLE
Prep: 30 minutes   Cook: 2 minutes   Chill: 5 to 6 hours
Serves: 10 to 12

In this rich version, trifle pudding is given a dose of chocolate. For a festive presentation, assemble this dessert in an attractive clear glass serving bowl.

1 **(4-ounce) package instant chocolate fudge pudding and pie filling mix**
1 **cup milk**
2 **cups heavy cream, whipped**
6 **tablespoons seedless red raspberry jam**

1 **(10- to 12-ounce) loaf pound cake, cut into ½-inch-thick slices**
3 **tablespoons crème de cacao**
½ **cup chocolate sauce or chocolate fudge sauce**
½ **cup diced roasted almonds**

1. In a medium bowl, combine pudding mix with milk. Whisk until well blended, 1 to 2 minutes; mixture will thicken as mixed. Fold in half of whipped cream until well blended and no white streaks remain; set aside.

2. To assemble trifle, heat raspberry jam in microwave or over low heat until melted when stirred. In a 2- or 2½-quart glass serving bowl, arrange 4 or 5 slices of pound cake to cover bottom of dish and curve up sides of bowl slightly. Sprinkle 1 tablespoon crème de cacao over cake. Drizzle ¼ cup chocolate sauce and then 2 tablespoons jam on top. Using back of a spoon, spread jam around evenly. Add half of reserved pudding mixture and spread evenly.

3. Top with 3 or 4 cake slices to cover in a single layer. Repeat as above using 1 tablespoon crème de cacao, remaining ¼ cup chocolate sauce, 2 tablespoons jam, and remaining pudding mixture.

4. Top with 3 or 4 more cake slices. Drizzle remaining 1 tablespoon crème de cacao over cake and spread remaining 2 tablespoons raspberry jam on top. Cover trifle with remaining whipped cream, spreading evenly. Sprinkle almonds on top.

5. Cover trifle and refrigerate until well chilled, 5 to 6 hours or overnight. Use a large spoon to scoop out and serve.

230   ALMOND CHOCOLATE CREME BRULEE

Prep: 15 minutes   Cook: 10 to 12 minutes   Chill and freeze: 7 hours
Serves: 8

This bittersweet chocolate crème brûlée is heavenly. Be sure to freeze for one hour before popping under the broiler to caramelize the brown sugar, so the crème brûlée will remain chilled.

3   **cups heavy cream**
8   **egg yolks**
1   **cup granulated sugar**
½   **cup firmly packed unsweetened cocoa powder**

½   **teaspoon almond extract**
3   **ounces bittersweet chocolate, melted**
½   **cup sliced almonds**
¼   **cup plus 4 teaspoons brown sugar**

1. In a medium saucepan over medium heat, heat cream until bubbles start to form around edges of pan. In a large saucepan, whisk together egg yolks, granulated sugar, and cocoa. Slowly add hot cream to yolk mixture, whisking constantly. Place over medium heat and cook, stirring constantly, 5 to 7 minutes, or until mixture thickens. Temperature should be approximately 175° to 180°F on a candy thermometer. Do not boil. Remove from heat and add bittersweet chocolate; stir to blend well.

2. Divide mixture evenly among 8 ovenproof ½-cup custard or soufflé dishes. Sprinkle almonds over top, dividing evenly. Cover and refrigerate 6 hours or overnight. One hour before serving, place all dishes in freezer.

3. Just before serving, preheat boiler. Sprinkle top of each crème brûlée with 2 teaspoons brown sugar. Place dishes under boiler 5 to 6 inches from heat and broil 1½ to 2 minutes, just to caramelize sugar. Watch carefully since brown sugar burns easily. Serve immediately. Any leftover crème brûlée can be kept in refrigerator and eaten within a day.

231   CHOCOLATE POTS DE CREME WITH RASPBERRIES

Prep: 20 minutes   Cook: 47 to 59 minutes   Chill: 3 hours   Serves: 8

Raspberries and chocolate combine in individual pots for an elegant and rich ending to a meal. Serve with unsweetened whipped cream.

9   **ounces semisweet chocolate, chopped**
3   **cups heavy cream**
¼   **cup sugar**
8   **egg yolks**

2   **teaspoons vanilla extract**
40   **fresh raspberries (about ¾ pint)**
   Whipped cream

1. Preheat oven to 350°F. In a 2-quart bowl, combine chocolate and cream. Heat in a microwave oven on High 2 to 3 minutes, until chocolate is melted and mixture is smooth when stirred.

2. In a medium bowl, whisk sugar into egg yolks. Whisk half of chocolate mixture into yolks, and then pour yolks into chocolate mixture in glass measure, whisking to blend well. Heat in microwave oven on Low 3 to 4 minutes, stirring every minute, then on Medium 2 minutes, stirring twice, until slightly thickened. Stir in vanilla.

3. Place 5 raspberries into each of 8 (6-ounce) individual ramekins or chocolate pots. Top with chocolate mixture, dividing evenly. Place ramekins in a 2-inch deep baking pan and add enough water to reach halfway up sides of ramekins. Cover pan with foil.

4. Bake 40 to 50 minutes, or until almost set. Let cool ½ hour. Then refrigerate until chilled, at least 3 hours. Serve topped with whipped cream.

232 RASPBERRY WHITE CHOCOLATE MOUSSE IN BITTERSWEET CHOCOLATE CUPS

Prep: 40 minutes   Cook: 10 to 12 minutes   Chill: 6 to 7 hours
Serves: 10

8 ounces imported white
    chocolate
2 cups heavy cream

12 ounces bittersweet chocolate
2 cups fresh raspberries,
    washed and well-drained

1. Melt white chocolate in a double boiler over hot—not boiling—water or in a glass bowl in a microwave oven on Medium about 2 to 3 minutes, stirring several times. In a medium saucepan, heat cream to boiling; boil 30 seconds. Whisk cream into white chocolate until thoroughly blended and smooth. Refrigerate 5 to 6 hours, or overnight, until well chilled.

2. Meanwhile, prepare bittersweet chocolate cups. Place 10 paper muffin cups in muffin tins. In a microwave oven or over low heat, melt bittersweet chocolate until smooth and shiny when stirred. Using a table knife or pastry brush, coat inside of paper muffin cups with melted chocolate. Be sure coating is not too thin, or cups will break when paper is peeled away. Refrigerate until set and well chilled, 2 to 3 hours. Remove cups from muffin tin and peel off paper. Place chocolate cups on a baking sheet. Cover loosely and return to refrigerator.

3. Place white chocolate mousse in a large bowl. Beat with an electric mixer on high speed, until mixture is fluffy, stiff, and holds its shape when beaters are lifted, 4 to 6 minutes. Do not overbeat.

4. Reserve some raspberries for garnish and gently fold remaining raspberries into white chocolate mousse. Spoon into chocolate cups. Return to refrigerator and chill at least 1 hour and up to 4 hours before serving. Serve garnished with reserved raspberries.

NOTE: *White chocolate and raspberry mixture can also be served alone (without chocolate cups) in stemmed glasses for an attractive dessert.*

233   EASY CHOCOLATE BAKED CUSTARD
Prep: 15 minutes   Cook: 30 to 35 minutes   Serves: 4

⅓ cup unsweetened cocoa
    powder (preferably
    Dutch-processed)
⅓ cup sugar

½ cup heavy cream
3 egg yolks
1 cup sour cream
1½ teaspoons vanilla extract

1. Preheat oven to 325°F. In a medium bowl, combine cocoa powder, sugar, cream, and egg yolks. Stir until well blended. Stir in sour cream and vanilla until well mixed.

2. Divide mixture evenly among 4 (¾-to 1-cup) custard cups. Set cups in a 9-inch square baking pan (or larger, if necessary, depending on size of dishes used). Place pan on middle rack of oven. Add hot water to pan to reach 1 inch up sides of cups.

3. Bake 30 to 35 minutes, or until custard looks firm and set. Do not overbake. Transfer cups from water to rack to let cool. Serve warm or refrigerate several hours or overnight and serve chilled.

Variation: **RASPBERRY CHOCOLATE BAKED CUSTARD**

Place 2 tablespoons fresh raspberries, rinsed and well drained, in bottom of each cup before adding chocolate mixture. Proceed as directed above.

234   PEACH AND RASPBERRY CHOCOLATE COBBLER
Prep: 25 minutes   Cook: 40 to 45 minutes   Serves: 8

This is a chocolate adaptation of a recipe San Francisco pastry chef Jim Dodge shared. It's a delicious way to treat fresh fruits and have your chocolate too.

4 cups fresh raspberries
4 cups peeled, coarsely
    chopped fresh peaches
⅓ cup plus 2 teaspoons
    granulated sugar
1¼ cups flour
3 tablespoons dark brown
    sugar
3 tablespoons unsweetened
    cocoa powder

1 teaspoon baking powder
¼ teaspoon grated nutmeg
6 tablespoons butter, cold, cut
    into pieces
¼ cup heavy cream
    Whipped cream or vanilla
    ice cream

1. Preheat oven to 375°F. Place fruit in a 2- or 2½-quart shallow baking dish. Sprinkle with ⅓ cup granulated sugar and ¼ cup flour, tossing gently to mix and coat fruit.

2. In a food processor, combine remaining 1 cup flour, brown sugar, cocoa, baking powder, and nutmeg. Process to combine. Add butter pieces and process until size of small peas. Add cream and process until dough just forms ball.

3. Pat dough into a round on a lightly floured sheet of wax paper. Sprinkle lightly with flour; cover with another sheet of wax paper. With rolling pin, roll dough out to fit inside dimension of baking dish. Remove top sheet of wax paper. Turn dough upside down over fruit mixture; remove wax paper sheet. Tuck in any edges, if necessary (dough doesn't have to lay smooth). Brush top with ½ teaspoon water and sprinkle with remaining 2 teaspoons granulated sugar. With knife, cut 4 slashes in dough to allow steam to escape.

4. Bake 40 to 45 minutes, until fruit is bubbling around edges and top crust is moist but set. Let stand at least 15 minutes before serving. Serve warm or at room temperature, with whipped unsweetened cream or vanilla ice cream.

---

235 EASY CHOCOLATE SOUFFLE
Prep: 30 minutes   Cook: 30 to 35 minutes   Serves: 8

Serve this specialty for a dinner party finale and get ready for the guests' raves. These are light but rich, and they go well with red wine as well as dessert wine.

½ cup plus 1 tablespoon
   granulated sugar
9 ounces bittersweet
   chocolate, cut up

½ cup heavy cream
9 eggs, separated
Powdered sugar

1. Preheat oven to 350°F. Butter 8 (1-cup) soufflé dishes and sprinkle each with a light coating of granulated sugar, using 1 tablespoon total.

2. In a small saucepan, combine chocolate and cream. Heat over medium-low heat, stirring occasionally, until chocolate is melted.

3. In a medium bowl, beat egg yolks and ¼ cup granulated sugar with an electric mixer on high speed until light and lemon colored, about 5 minutes. Add yolks to chocolate and whisk to blend.

4. In a large bowl, using clean dry beaters, beat egg whites with electric mixer on high speed until foamy. Gradually beat in remaining ¼ cup granulated sugar until stiff but not dry. With a rubber spatula, gently fold chocolate mixture into egg whites until no streaks remain. Divide mixture evenly among prepared soufflé dishes.

5. Bake 20 to 25 minutes, or until soufflés are puffed on top and pulling away from sides of dishes. Sift powdered sugar over top. Serve immediately.

236   CHOCOLATE ORANGE MOUSSE

Prep: 20 minutes   Cook: none   Chill: 4 hours   Serves: 6

½ cup heavy cream
3 eggs,* separated
6 ounces semisweet chocolate
   chips (1 cup), melted

1 teaspoon vanilla extract
1 to 1½ teaspoons grated
   orange zest
Dash of salt

1. In a medium bowl, beat cream with an electric mixer on high speed until stiff; transfer to a small bowl. In same bowl, with same beaters and mixer on high speed, beat egg yolks until pale and lemon colored, 3 to 4 minutes. Gradually beat in melted chocolate until well blended. Beat in vanilla and orange zest.

2. In a medium bowl with clean beaters in mixer, beat egg whites with salt on high speed until stiff but not dry. Gently fold half of beaten egg whites into chocolate mixture, then fold in remaining whites until no white streaks remain. Fold in whipped cream.

3. Turn into a 1-quart serving bowl or 6 individual serving dishes (stemmed wine glasses work well). Cover and refrigerate 4 to 12 hours before serving.

    * CAUTION: *Because of the possible threat of salmonella—a bacteria that causes food poisoning—from raw eggs, U.S. Government officials recommend that the very young, the elderly, pregnant women, and people with serious illnesses or weakened immune systems not eat raw or lightly cooked eggs. Keep this in mind and consume raw or lightly cooked eggs at your own risk.*

237   MARBLED CHOCOLATE BAVARIAN

*Prep: 35 minutes   Cook: about 6 minutes   Chill: 5 hours
Serves: 8 to 10*

1 envelope unflavored gelatin
2¼ cups milk
4 eggs
⅔ cup sugar
6 (1-ounce) squares
   unsweetened chocolate,
   melted

4 ounces imported white
   chocolate
1 cup heavy cream, whipped
¼ cup toasted sliced almonds

1. Sprinkle gelatin over ¼ cup milk in a glass measure to soften; set aside.

2. In a large saucepan, whisk together remaining 2 cups milk, eggs, and sugar. Bring to a simmer over medium heat, whisking constantly, about 3 minutes. Reduce heat to low and cook, whisking constantly, 2 minutes. Remove from heat and stir in softened gelatin and melted unsweetened chocolate. Refrigerate Bavarian mixture or place over ice water, stirring occasionally, until it starts to hold its shape.

3. Melt white chocolate over low heat or in microwave oven. Let stand until cooled to room temperature.

4. Fold whipped cream into chilled unsweetened chocolate mixture. Spoon a third of chocolate Bavarian mixture into an oiled 2-quart decorative mold. Drizzle a third of cooled white chocolate over Bavarian mixture. Repeat layering 2 more times, ending with white chocolate. Refrigerate 5 hours or overnight. When ready to serve, unmold onto an attractive plate and sprinkle almonds on top.

238 WHITE CHOCOLATE BAVARIAN WITH TRUFFLES

Prep: 65 minutes   Cook: about 6 minutes   Chill: 6 hours   Serves: 8

3 ounces extra-bittersweet chocolate, such as Tobler	1¼ cups milk
¼ cup Irish cream liqueur or Grand Marnier	⅓ cup sugar
	3 egg yolks
3 tablespoons unsweetened cocoa powder, sifted	1 teaspoon vanilla extract
	4 ounces imported white chocolate, melted
1 envelope unflavored gelatin	1 cup heavy cream, whipped

1. To make truffles, in a small glass bowl, heat bittersweet chocolate in a microwave oven on Medium 55 to 60 seconds, or until melted and smooth when stirred. Stir in liqueur. Refrigerate until mixture is firm enough to shape into balls, about 40 minutes. Using 2 teaspoons for shaping, form mixture into 8 equal-size balls and roll in cocoa. Refrigerate truffles until ready to use.

2. Meanwhile, in a glass measure, sprinkle gelatin over ¼ cup milk to soften; set aside. In a large saucepan, whisk together remaining 1 cup milk, sugar, egg yolks, and vanilla. Bring to a simmer over medium heat, whisking constantly, about 3 minutes. Reduce heat to low and cook, stirring constantly, 2 minutes. Remove from heat and stir in melted white chocolate and softened gelatin. Refrigerate until mixture starts to hold its shape. Fold in whipped cream.

3. Spoon half of Bavarian into an oiled 1-quart decorative mold. Place truffles evenly around outside edge of mold. Spoon remaining Bavarian over truffles. Refrigerate 6 hours or overnight. When ready to serve, unmold and cut into 8 slices, with a truffle in each.

239   CHOCOLATE RAISIN RICE PUDDING
Prep: 25 minutes   Cook: 12 to 13 minutes   Serves: 6

To aid today's in-a-hurry cook, this simplified recipe is cooked stove-top in a double boiler rather than baked slowly in an oven. Try it when you have leftover rice.

2 cups cooked rice	2 eggs,* separated
1½ cups milk	½ cup sugar
½ cup raisins	¼ teaspoon cinnamon
2 (1-ounce) squares	⅛ teaspoon salt
unsweetened chocolate,	2 teaspoons vanilla extract
cut up	

1. In top of a double boiler, combine rice, milk, raisins, and chocolate. Place over simmering water and cook, stirring often, until chocolate is melted.

2. In a small bowl, whisk together egg yolks, ¼ cup sugar, cinnamon, salt, and vanilla. Quickly stir into rice mixture. Cook over medium heat, stirring constantly, until pudding thickens, 7 to 8 minutes.

3. Place rice mixture over ice water and let cool, stirring often, 10 to 15 minutes.

4. Meanwhile, in a medium bowl, beat egg whites with an electric mixer on high speed until soft peaks form. Gradually beat in remaining ¼ cup sugar and beat until stiff. Gently fold into pudding. Serve warm or refrigerate and serve cold.

    * CAUTION: *Because of the possible threat of salmonella—a bacteria that causes food poisoning—from raw eggs, U.S. Government officials recommend that the very young, the elderly, pregnant women, and people with serious illnesses or weakened immune systems not eat raw or lightly cooked eggs. Keep this in mind and consume raw or lightly cooked eggs at your own risk.*

240   CHOCOLATE CHIP PARFAIT CAKE
Prep: 30 minutes   Cook: 10 minutes   Chill: 3 to 4 hours
Serves: 10 to 12

1 (8-inch) chocolate cake layer	1 cup milk
(made from a mix	2 teaspoons vanilla extract
according to package	1 cup heavy cream
directions) *	⅔ cup chopped walnuts
1 envelope unflavored gelatin	½ cup miniature chocolate
½ cup sugar	chips
⅛ teaspoon salt	

1. Place cake layer on a serving platter. Arrange a 3-inch-wide collar made from a triple thickness of aluminum foil around sides of cake layer; it should extend about 2 inches above top of cake. Overlap ends and secure with a couple of staples or straight pins.

2. In a medium saucepan, mix gelatin, sugar, and salt. Gradually stir in milk. Place over medium-low heat and cook, stirring constantly, until gelatin dissolves and milk comes to a very gentle boil, about 10 minutes. Remove from heat. Stir in vanilla. Set over a bowl of ice water and let stand, stirring several times, until mixture begins to thicken slightly, about 5 minutes.

3. Meanwhile, beat cream until stiff. Fold whipped cream, nuts, and chocolate chips quickly into cooled gelatin mixture. Heap mixture on top of cake; spread evenly. Refrigerate until set, 3 to 4 hours or overnight.

4. Before serving, remove foil from sides of dessert, and slice.

* *Bake only one layer. Use remaining batter for cupcakes.*

---

241   CHOCOLATE ANGEL REFRIGERATOR DESSERT
Prep: 25 minutes   Cook: 1 to 1½ minutes   Chill: 6 hours
Serves: 8 to 10

12 ounces semisweet chocolate chips (2 cups)	2 tablespoons sugar
3 tablespoons milk or brewed coffee	1 pint heavy cream, whipped
1 teaspoon vanilla extract	1 (1½-pound) baked angel food cake, cut into ½-inch pieces
1 teaspoon grated orange zest	½ cup diced roasted almonds
3 eggs,* separated	

1. In a 2-quart glass bowl, combine chocolate chips and milk. Heat in a microwave oven on High 1 to 1½ minutes, or until chocolate is melted and smooth when stirred. Whisk in vanilla, orange zest, and beaten egg yolks until well mixed; let cool.

2. In a medium bowl, beat egg whites and sugar with an electric mixer on high speed until stiff peaks form. Fold into cooled chocolate mixture. Fold in whipped cream.

3. To assemble, place half of cake pieces in a buttered 9½-inch springform pan. Add half of chocolate mixture, then remaining cake pieces. Cover with remaining chocolate mixture, spreading evenly. Top with almonds, pressing in lightly. Cover and refrigerate 6 hours or overnight. At serving time, run a sharp knife around edge of cake to loosen. Remove side of springform.

* **CAUTION:** *Because of the possible threat of salmonella—a bacteria that causes food poisoning—from raw eggs, U.S. Government officials recommend that the very young, the elderly, pregnant women, and people with serious illnesses or weakened immune systems not eat raw or lightly cooked eggs. Keep this in mind and consume raw or lightly cooked eggs at your own risk.*

242   CHOCOLATE PATE
Prep: 10 minutes   Cook: 1½ to 2 minutes   Chill: 2 to 3 hours
Makes: about 1¾ cups

This is an interesting idea to serve for dessert with sweet crackers, fruits, cheese, and cookies. The recipe is actually very versatile. When chilled, it forms a firm, spreadable pâté, but when heated, you can use it as a sauce over cakes, fruits, and ice cream.

1 **cup heavy cream**
6 **ounces semisweet chocolate chips (1 cup)**
1 **(1-ounce) square unsweetened chocolate, cut up**

2 **tablespoons butter, softened**
1 **teaspoon vanilla extract or 1 tablespoon rum, Cognac, or Grand Marnier**

1. In a 1-quart glass bowl, combine cream, semisweet chocolate, and unsweetened chocolate. Heat in a microwave oven on High 1½ to 2 minutes, stirring once or twice, until chocolate is melted and smooth.

2. Stir in butter until melted and mixture is smooth. Stir in vanilla. Turn into a 2- or 2½-cup cheese or pâté crock or into 2 or 3 individual soufflé dishes. Refrigerate until firm, 2 to 3 hours. Once firm, cover with plastic wrap and refrigerate until 1 hour before serving time. Store in refrigerator and use within 5 days.

NOTE: *Pâté can also be heated in microwave oven on High 1½ to 2 minutes, until mixture reaches sauce consistency when stirred and is warm. Serve warm sauce over cakes, ice cream, or fruits.*

243   CHOCOLATE CREAM CHEESE SPREAD
Prep: 10 minutes   Cook: 1 to 1¼ minutes   Chill: 1 to 2 hours
Makes: 1¼ cups

Use as a dessert spread on crackers when serving fruit and cheese, on cut-up fresh fruits, or on scones, biscuits, breads, croissants, rolls, etc.

⅓ **cup heavy cream**
2 **(1-ounce) squares semisweet chocolate, cut up**

1 **(8-ounce) package cream cheese, softened**
1 **teaspoon grated orange zest**

1. In a 2-cup glass measure, combine cream and chocolate. Heat in a microwave oven on High 1 to 1¼ minutes, until melted and smooth when stirred; let cool to lukewarm.

2. In a medium bowl, beat cream cheese with an electric mixer on medium speed until smooth. Beat in chocolate mixture on medium-high speed until light and fluffy, about 2 minutes. Stir in orange zest. Turn into a small serving dish or bowl. Cover and refrigerate until firm, about 1 to 2 hours.

244   CHOCOLATE FRIED CREAM
Prep: 25 minutes   Cook: 8 to 12 minutes   Chill: overnight
Serves: 4 to 6

This dessert creation is a conversation piece—novel as well as delicious.

2 tablespoons flour	1¼ cups heavy cream
⅓ cup cornstarch	1 teaspoon chocolate extract
½ cup sugar	1 whole egg, lightly beaten
¼ cup firmly packed	1 (2-ounce) package slivered
unsweetened cocoa	blanched almonds,
powder	finely chopped
3 egg yolks	4 tablespoons butter
Dash of salt	Whipped cream

1. In top of a double boiler, over simmering water, whisk together flour, cornstarch, sugar, cocoa, egg yolks, salt, and cream. Cook over simmering water, whisking constantly, until mixture thickens, 5 to 7 minutes. Remove from heat and stir in chocolate extract. Spread in a greased 8-inch square baking pan. Refrigerate overnight.

2. Just before serving, cut chocolate cream into 8 to 12 diamond-shaped pieces about 2 x 2 inches. Dip each piece into beaten egg, then coat completely with chopped almonds.

3. In a large skillet, melt 2 tablespoons butter over medium heat until sizzling. Fry chocolate cream 4 to 6 pieces at a time, 1 to 2 minutes on one side, until light golden. Turn over and fry on other side 2 to 3 minutes longer. Repeat with remaining butter and cream diamonds. To serve, place 2 diamonds on each of 4 to 6 individual dessert plates and top with a dollop of whipped cream.

245 REFRIGERATOR CHOCOLATE DESSERT SQUARES

Prep: 15 minutes   Cook: none   Chill: overnight   Serves: 12

When you need a quick dessert and want to make it the night before, try this easy chocolate creation. It's an adaptation of one my mother has been serving successfully for years.

2 cups chocolate or vanilla
   wafer cookie crumbs
1 stick (4 ounces) butter, very
   soft
2 cups powdered sugar
1 teaspoon vanilla extract
3 (1-ounce) squares
   unsweetened chocolate,
   melted

2 eggs*
1 cup chopped roasted
   almonds
   Whipped cream

1. Scatter 1 cup cookie crumbs evenly over bottom of a buttered 11 x 7-inch glass dish. In a medium bowl, beat butter, powdered sugar, and vanilla with an electric mixer on medium speed until light and fluffy, 1 to 2 minutes. Beat in melted chocolate and eggs until well blended, about 2 minutes. Stir in chopped almonds.

2. Drop spoonfuls of chocolate mixture evenly over crumbs in dish. With a spatula, carefully spread out in an even layer. Sprinkle remaining 1 cup crumbs over top. Refrigerate overnight. Cut into 12 squares. Serve each topped with a spoonful of whipped cream.

* CAUTION: *Because of the possible threat of salmonella—a bacteria that causes food poisoning—from raw eggs, U.S. Government officials recommend that the very young, the elderly, pregnant women, and people with serious illnesses or weakened immune systems not eat raw or lightly cooked eggs. Keep this in mind and consume raw or lightly cooked eggs at your own risk.*

Chapter 10

Chocolate Rises

When you want a chocolate treat or dessert that's not too sweet, rely on chocolate muffins, coffeecakes, yeast coffeecakes or rolls, quick breads, and the like. There's nothing quite so wonderful as the aroma of fresh-baked coffeecakes, muffins, and the like wafting from the oven. They're fabulous with a cup of coffee or tea, morning, noon, or night or at brunches as well. All make great snacks any time of day.

Whether you're a veteran baker or a novice, these delectable recipes are designed to bring you and your family and friends easy pleasure. There are numerous possibilities—those made with plain or chocolate dough—in combination with a variety of winning flavors. Peanut butter, orange, lemon, apple, pumpkin, banana, and cinnamon are all compatible with chocolate in quick-rising as well as yeast-raised creations.

For fast-baking creations leavened without yeast, try a cache of muffins, such as Banana Chocolate Chip Muffins, Double Chocolate Muffins, Peanut Butter Chocolate Chip Muffins, or quick breads, such as Harvest Loaf, Chocolate-Nut Pumpkin Bread, or Chocolate Pecan Date Loaf, or even Chocolate Chip Orange Scones.

If you decide to tackle yeast baking, keep in mind that while it is not difficult, it is not something that can be rushed. There are so many delicious options, many of them showstoppers, including Chocolate Chip Swirl Coffeecake, Chocolate Race Track, Pecan Chocolate Yeast Cake, Chocolate Peanut Ring, Apple-Filled Chocolate Coffeecake, and Miniature Chocolate Caramel Sticky Buns, to name a few.

Basically, yeast breads can be prepared using two different methods—the modern, no-dissolve yeast method or the more traditional dissolved yeast method. In the no-dissolve method, undissolved yeast is mixed with some of the dry ingredients, eliminating the need to dissolve the yeast in warm water prior to mixing the dough. With this method, an electric mixer is generally used, and the liquid temperature is very warm, 125 to 130°F (use a yeast or candy thermometer for greatest accuracy). The warm liquids warm the dough, making the yeast work faster, which in turn, makes the dough rise faster.

In the more conventional, dissolved-yeast method, the yeast is sprinkled into warm water (105 to 115°F) and stirred until dissolved, then mixed with the flour, sugar, and other ingredients.

When working with yeast, it's imperative that liquids be used at the temperatures specified in recipes. Temperatures above 140°F will kill yeast, temperatures below 80°F will delay its growth and limit leavening power. While yeast can be purchased in both active dry or compressed (fresh) forms, active dry is preferred as it is readily available, easier to use (more convenient), and stays fresh for months without refrigeration. Compressed yeast (which should be dissolved in lukewarm water, about 95°F, rather than warm water) is perishable and must be kept refrigerated.

Many of the yeast doughs in this chapter can be kneaded with a dough hook attached to an electric mixer, but if you don't have such a tool, kneading by hand will suffice. Fold the rounded dough ball toward you on a floured board, then push it away with the heel of your hand in a rolling motion. Give the dough a quarter turn and repeat the folding, pushing, and rotating until the dough is smooth, satiny, and elastic, generally about 8 to 10 minutes.

To test yeast dough for doubling in size or bulk, press the tips of two fingers lightly and quickly ½ inch into the dough. If the indentation remains, the dough has doubled.

Don't let yeast baking intimidate you. Keep in mind that practice makes perfect. Depending on time schedules, preferences, and tastes, today's baker has a wide range of choices. Surprise your family and friends soon with some of these inspirations. And if you want to make a yeast-style coffee cake without the trouble of making yeast dough, rely on frozen white bread dough, as in the Quick Chocolate Poteca.

246   MINIATURE CHOCOLATE CARAMEL STICKY BUNS

Prep: 1 hour   Cook: 30 to 35 minutes   Makes: 36

1   envelope (¼ ounce) quick-rising yeast
⅓   cup granulated sugar
¼   cup packed unsweetened cocoa powder
2   to 2½ cups flour
1   teaspoon salt
¾   cup milk
1   stick plus 2 tablespoons butter

1   egg
1¼   cups packed brown sugar
½   cup chopped pecans
3   tablespoons light corn syrup
1   cup miniature semisweet chocolate chips (6 ounces)
1   tablespoon ground cinnamon

1. In a large bowl, combine yeast, granulated sugar, cocoa, 1½ cups flour, and salt; mix well. In a small saucepan, heat milk and 3 tablespoons butter to 125°F on a candy thermometer or hot to the touch. Add milk mixture to yeast mixture and beat with electric mixer on low speed until blended. Add egg and beat well.

2. If your mixer has a dough hook, remove beater and attach dough hook; add remaining ½ to 1 cup flour to make a fairly soft dough and knead on medium-high speed 5 minutes. If your mixer does not have a dough hook, remove dough to a lightly floured surface and knead in remaining flour by hand; continue kneading dough until smooth and elastic, 7 to 8 minutes. Cover and let rest 20 minutes.

3. Meanwhile, prepare caramel for pans: In a medium saucepan, combine 4 tablespoons butter, ½ cup brown sugar, pecans, and corn syrup. Cook over low heat, stirring, until sugar and butter are completely melted. Do not boil. Divide mixture evenly among 36 mini-muffin cups, 1¾ inches in diameter.

4. Make chocolate chip filling: Melt remaining 3 tablespoons butter; let cool. In a medium bowl, combine melted butter, remaining ¾ cup brown sugar, chocolate chips, and cinnamon; mix well.

5. Punch dough down. Divide dough in half. On a lightly floured board or pastry cloth, roll each dough half into a 9 x 18-inch rectangle. Spread each dough rectangle with half of chocolate chip filling to within ½ inch of edges, pressing down slightly. Starting from one long side, roll dough up jelly-roll fashion. Pinch seams and ends to seal. Using a sharp knife, cut each roll into 18 pieces. Place rolls, cut side up, on top of caramel mixture in mini-muffin cups.

6. Let rise in a warm, draft-free place 60 to 70 minutes, or until doubled. About 15 minutes before rising time has been completed, preheat oven to 350°F. Bake 20 to 25 minutes. Immediately invert pans onto foil-lined baking sheets. Let cool 15 minutes. Serve warm or wrap in foil and serve at room temperature.

247   CHOCOLATE PECAN DATE LOAF
Prep: 25 minutes   Cook: 55 to 60 minutes   Chill: 2 hours
Serves: 10 to 12

Because this loaf is so very moist, it should be refrigerated until well chilled before slicing or it will tend to fall apart.

1 stick (4 ounces) butter or margarine, softened	½ teaspoon ground allspice
1 cup sugar	1 teaspoon baking powder
¼ cup firmly packed unsweetened cocoa powder	½ teaspoon baking soda
	¼ teaspoon salt
	1 cup buttermilk
2 eggs	6 ounces semisweet chocolate chips (1 cup)
1½ cups flour	½ cup chopped pitted dates
2 teaspoons cinnamon	½ cup chopped pecans
1 teaspoon grated nutmeg	

1. Preheat oven to 350°F. Generously grease a 9 x 5 x 3-inch loaf pan.

2. In a medium bowl, beat together butter and sugar with an electric mixer on medium speed until light and fluffy, about 2 minutes. Add cocoa and beat until well blended. Add eggs, one at a time, beating well after each addition.

3. Sift together flour, cinnamon, nutmeg, allspice, baking powder, baking soda, and salt. Add to butter mixture alternately with buttermilk, beating just until blended. By hand, stir in chocolate chips, dates, and pecans. Turn into prepared pan.

4. Bake 55 to 60 minutes, or until a cake tester inserted in center comes out clean. Let loaf cool 30 minutes. Remove from pan, wrap immediately in plastic wrap, and refrigerate until chilled, at least 2 hours, before serving.

248   CHOCOLATE CHIP ORANGE SCONES
Prep: 20 minutes   Cook: 13 to 18 minutes   Makes: 12

These not-too-sweet breads are an ideal offering to accompany tea or coffee.

1¾ cups flour	½ cup miniature semisweet chocolate chips
⅓ cup sugar	¼ cup chopped candied orange peel
3 tablespoons unsweetened cocoa powder	½ cup cold heavy cream
2½ teaspoons baking powder	2 egg yolks
¼ teaspoon salt	1 egg white, lightly beaten
4 tablespoons cold butter or margarine, cut up	

1. Preheat oven to 400°F. In a medium bowl, combine flour, sugar, cocoa, baking powder, and salt. With 2 knives or a pastry cutter, cut in butter until pastry is crumbly. Stir in chocolate chips and orange peel.

2. In a small bowl, beat cream and egg yolks with a fork until well blended, then quickly stir into dry ingredients until dough is soft and holds together.

3. On a greased foil-lined baking sheet, drop dough by scant ¼ cupfuls into 12 mounds. Brush with egg white.

4. Bake 13 to 18 minutes, or until a toothpick inserted in centers comes out clean. Do not overbake to avoid drying out scones. Let cool on pan.

> **NOTE:** *Dough can also be prepared in a food processor: Combine flour, sugar, cocoa, baking powder, and salt. Process to mix. Add butter and process with on/off motion until mixture is crumbly. Add cream and egg yolks and process until dough holds together. Stir in chocolate chips and orange peel. Continue as directed in step 3.*

---

249   APRICOT CHOCOLATE COFFEECAKE
Prep: 35 minutes   Cook: 50 to 55 minutes   Serves: 12

Apricots and chocolate are one of the most compatible of duos, and this recipe proves it. This cake is ideal for morning coffee, brunch, snack, or dessert anytime.

½ cup chopped blanched almonds	5 eggs
2 sticks (8 ounces) butter or margarine, softened	2½ cups cake flour
1 (8-ounce) package cream cheese, softened	2 teaspoons baking powder
2¼ cups sugar	1 teaspoon baking soda
½ cup firmly packed unsweetened cocoa powder (preferably Dutch-processed)	½ teaspoon salt
	6 ounces dried apricots, chopped
	6 ounces semisweet chocolate chips (1 cup)

1. Preheat oven to 350°F. Generously grease a 12-cup bundt pan. Scatter ¼ cup almonds over inside of pan. In a large bowl, beat together butter, cream cheese, and 1¾ cups sugar with an electric mixer on medium speed until light and fluffy, about 2 minutes. Add cocoa and beat well. Add eggs, one at a time, beating well after each addition.

2. Sift together cake flour, baking powder, baking soda, and salt. Add to chocolate mixture. Beat with mixer on low speed until blended.

3. In a small bowl, mix together remaining ¼ cup almonds, remaining ½ cup sugar, apricots, and chocolate chips. Spoon half of cake batter into prepared pan. Sprinkle two thirds of apricot mixture over center of batter (mixture will burn if it touches the sides or middle tube of pan). Spoon on remaining batter and sprinkle remaining apricot mixture on top.

4. Bake 50 to 55 minutes, or until a cake tester inserted in center comes out clean. Let cake cool in pan 15 to 20 minutes, then invert onto a rack to let cool completely before serving.

250   CHOCOLATE WALNUT TEA BREAD
Prep: 20 minutes   Cook: 55 to 60 minutes   Makes: 1 (9-inch) loaf

Served sliced with tea or coffee, this delicious bread is great plain or spread with orange or strawberry whipped cream cheese.

1½ teaspoons instant coffee powder	2 (1-ounce) squares unsweetened chocolate, melted
1 cup boiling water	
1 cup sugar	2 cups flour
4 tablespoons butter or margarine	1 teaspoon baking soda
	½ teaspoon salt
1 egg	¾ cup chopped walnuts
1 teaspoon vanilla extract	

1. Preheat oven to 350°F. In a small bowl, dissolve coffee powder in boiling water. Set aside to cool slightly.

2. In a medium bowl, beat together sugar, butter, egg, and vanilla with an electric mixer on medium speed, until light and fluffy, 2 to 3 minutes. Beat in chocolate.

3. Combine flour with baking soda and salt. Add dry ingredients to chocolate mixture alternately with reserved coffee, beating well after each addition. Stir in walnuts. Turn batter into greased 9 x 5 x 3-inch loaf pan.

4. Bake 55 to 60 minutes, or until a cake tester inserted in center comes out clean. Let loaf cool in pan 10 minutes, then turn out onto rack to let cool completely.

---

251   CHOCOLATE-NUT PUMPKIN BREAD
Prep: 25 minutes   Cook: 1¼ hours   Serves: 10 to 12

1 stick (4 ounces) butter or margarine, softened	2 eggs
	1½ cups flour
¾ cup granulated sugar	1 teaspoon baking powder
¾ cup packed brown sugar	1 teaspoon baking soda
1 teaspoon ground cinnamon	½ teaspoon salt
½ teaspoon grated nutmeg	¼ cup milk
¼ teaspoon ground cloves	6 ounces semisweet chocolate chips (1 cup)
¼ teaspoon ground ginger	
1 cup canned pumpkin	¼ cup chopped pecans
½ cup firmly packed unsweetened cocoa powder	¼ cup currants or raisins
	Powdered sugar

1. Preheat oven to 350°F. Generously grease a 9 x 5 x 3-inch loaf pan.

2. In a large bowl, beat together butter, granulated sugar, and brown sugar with an electric mixer on medium speed until light and fluffy, about 2 minutes. Add cinnamon, nutmeg, cloves, ginger, pumpkin, and cocoa; beat well. Add eggs, one at a time, beating well after each addition.

3. Sift together flour, baking powder, baking soda, and salt. Add to chocolate mixture alternately with milk, beating until mixed. Stir in chocolate chips, pecans, and currants. Turn batter into prepared pan.

4. Bake 1¼ hours, or until a cake tester inserted in center comes out clean. Let loaf cool in pan 30 minutes, then transfer to a rack to let cool completely. Sift powdered sugar over top before serving.

---

252 HARVEST LOAF
Prep: 35 minutes   Cook: 60 to 70 minutes   Serves: 8 to 10

This loaf freezes well with or without the glaze. It's a good choice for holiday gift-giving.

1¾ cups flour
 1 teaspoon baking soda
 ½ teaspoon salt
1½ teaspoons cinnamon
 ½ teaspoon plus ⅛ teaspoon grated nutmeg
 ¼ teaspoon ground ginger
 ¼ teaspoon ground cloves
 1 stick (4 ounces) butter or margarine, softened
 1 cup granulated sugar

 2 eggs
 ¾ cup canned solid-pack pumpkin
 6 ounces semisweet chocolate chips (1 cup)
 ⅔ cup chopped walnuts or almonds
 ½ cup sifted powdered sugar
 1 to 2 tablespoons milk or heavy cream

1. Preheat oven to 350°F. Generously grease a 9 x 5 x 3-inch loaf pan. In a medium bowl, stir together flour, baking soda, salt, 1 teaspoon cinnamon, ½ teaspoon nutmeg, ginger, and cloves.

2. In a medium bowl, cream together butter and granulated sugar with an electric mixer on medium speed until light and fluffy, 2 to 3 minutes. Beat in eggs until well blended. Reduce mixer speed to low and add dry ingredients alternately with pumpkin, beginning and ending with dry ingredients. Stir in chocolate chips and ⅓ cup nuts. Turn into prepared pan. Sprinkle remaining ⅓ cup nuts over top.

3. Bake 60 to 70 minutes, or until a cake tester inserted in center comes out clean. Let loaf cool in pan 15 minutes, then unmold onto a rack and let cool completely.

4. In a small bowl, combine powdered sugar, remaining ½ teaspoon cinnamon, remaining ⅛ teaspoon nutmeg, and milk. Mix until smooth and of glazing consistency. Drizzle glaze over cooled loaf. Let stand at least 6 hours before slicing.

253 CHOCOLATE CHIP SWIRL COFFEECAKE
Prep: 25 minutes   Cook: 21 to 26 minutes   Serves: 8

This chocolate creation is a favorite at our house and a showstopper on a brunch table. It's a decadent, sweet coffeecake that makes great eating any time of day.

6 tablespoons butter	Mom's Sweet Yeast Dough
¾ cup packed brown sugar	(recipe follows)
1 tablespoon cinnamon	6 ounces semisweet chocolate
1½ tablespoons grated orange zest	chips (1 cup)
1½ cups chopped walnuts or pecans	

1. In a 1-quart glass bowl, melt butter in a microwave oven on High about 50 seconds. Stir in brown sugar, cinnamon, orange zest, and nuts until well mixed; set aside.

2. On a lightly floured board, with a rolling pin, roll out Sweet Yeast Dough to a 22 x 8-inch rectangle. Spread brown sugar-nut mixture evenly over dough to within 1 inch of edges. Sprinkle chocolate chips over nut mixture; press in lightly. Starting from a long side, roll up jelly-roll fashion. Moisten edges with water; pinch firmly to seal all edges closed. Turn seam side down. With a sharp floured knife, cut roll in half lengthwise. Turn cut sides up and carefully move to a buttered baking sheet. Loosely twist to braid the 2 rolls, keeping cut sides up. Bend braid into a 10-inch circle, pinching ends together firmly. Let rise in a warm place until almost doubled, 40 to 50 minutes.

3. Preheat oven to 350°F. Bake coffeecake 20 to 25 minutes, or until golden brown. Serve warm or at room temperature.

MOM'S SWEET YEAST DOUGH

My mother, Phyllis Hartanov, has a reputation for making fabulous yeast rolls. This is the yeast dough recipe she uses. It's easy, versatile, and requires no kneading. You can stash it in the refrigerator for up to two days. I usually prepare the dough the night before using and let it rise overnight in the refrigerator. Use to make Chocolate Chip Swirl Coffeecake (above) other coffeecakes, or sweet rolls.

1 envelope (¼ ounce) active dry yeast	½ cup sugar
	¾ teaspoon salt
¼ cup warm (not hot) water (105° to 115°)	3 eggs
	4 to 4½ cups flour
¾ cup milk	
1 stick (4 ounces) margarine, cut up	

1. In a 1-cup glass measure, sprinkle yeast over warm water. Stir to dissolve. Set aside.

2. In a 1-quart glass bowl, heat milk to boiling in a microwave oven on High 1½ to 2 minutes. Add margarine, sugar, and salt and stir until margarine melts. Let cool slightly.

3. In a large bowl, whisk eggs until well blended. Beat in milk mixture. Add yeast mixture and beat with a wooden spoon until well mixed.

4. Add flour, 1 cup at a time, blending well after each addition. Dough may still be slightly sticky after adding all flour. With floured hands, roll dough into a ball in bowl. Grease top of dough with a little shortening, then place a piece of plastic wrap on top of dough. Cover bowl with foil. Refrigerate overnight or for as long as 2 days. When ready to use, remove from refrigerator and punch dough down.

---

254 MARBLEIZED CHOCOLATE ORANGE LOAF
Prep: 25 minutes   Cook: 58 to 68 minutes   Serves: 8 to 10

Mix chocolate into half of the batter and swirl it with an orange batter for a delicious loaf cake. This recipe is an adaptation of one shared by my friend Harriet Part, who has enjoyed it since her childhood days.

2 **sticks (8 ounces) butter, softened**	1 **cup sour cream**
1 **cup plus 3 tablespoons sugar**	1 **tablespoon grated orange zest**
2 **teaspoons vanilla extract**	2 **(1-ounce) squares unsweetened chocolate, melted**
3 **eggs**	
1¾ **cups flour**	
¾ **teaspoon baking powder**	⅓ **cup orange juice**
¾ **teaspoon baking soda**	

1. Preheat oven to 350°F. Grease a 9 x 5 x 3-inch loaf pan. Dust with flour; tap out excess.

2. In a medium bowl, beat butter, 1 cup sugar, and vanilla with an electric mixer on medium speed until light and fluffy, 1 to 2 minutes. Add eggs, beating well after each addition. Beat 2 minutes. Beat in flour, baking powder, and baking soda. When partially mixed, beat in sour cream until mixture is smooth.

3. Remove half of batter to another bowl. To batter remaining in bowl, add orange zest and mix until blended. To batter removed to other bowl, beat in melted chocolate until well combined.

4. Spoon half of orange batter into prepared loaf pan. Drop half of chocolate batter by spoonfuls over top. Repeat layers. Using a knife, lightly swirl batter to marbleize.

5. Bake 55 to 65 minutes, or until a cake tester inserted in center comes out clean. Let cake cool 5 minutes in pan.

6. Meanwhile, in a small saucepan, heat orange juice and remaining 3 tablespoons sugar to boiling over medium heat. Boil 1 minute, or until sugar dissolves. Spoon hot syrup slowly over hot cake. Let cake cool completely in pan before unmolding and slicing.

255 QUICK CHOCOLATE POTECA
Prep: 35 minutes   Cook: 32 to 38 minutes   Serves: 10

You won't believe this terrific chocolate sweet, fashioned after the Yugo-slavian-style coffeecake known as *poteca*, is made with frozen bread dough. It's an ideal accompaniment to a cup of coffee.

5 tablespoons butter	**1 cup ground toasted walnuts** (see Note)
1 (1-pound) loaf frozen white bread dough, thawed	**¼ cup currants or raisins**
½ cup packed brown sugar	**6 ounces semisweet chocolate chips (1 cup)**
1 cup milk chocolate chips	**¼ cup heavy cream**
2 teaspoons grated lemon zest	

1. Melt 4 tablespoons butter. On a lightly floured surface, roll out bread dough with a rolling pin to a 12 x 18-inch rectangle. In a medium bowl, mix together brown sugar, milk chocolate chips, melted butter, lemon zest, walnuts, and currants. Spread over dough to within ¾ inch of edges. Starting from a long side, roll up dough tightly jelly-roll fashion. Pinch edges to seal.

2. Carefully lift roll onto a lightly greased baking sheet and form into a ring; pinch ends to hold together. Let rise in a draft-free area about 45 to 60 minutes, or until doubled in size.

3. About 15 minutes before rising is completed, preheat oven to 350°F. Bake 30 to 35 minutes. Let cool on baking sheet.

4. Meanwhile, in a small glass bowl, combine semisweet chocolate chips, cream, and remaining 1 tablespoon butter. Heat in a microwave oven on High 1 to 1½ minutes, or until chocolate and butter are melted and mixture is smooth when stirred. Let chocolate glaze cool slightly before using. When *poteca* is cool, drizzle chocolate glaze on top.

NOTE: *To toast walnuts lightly, place in a preheated 350°F oven about 5 minutes.*

256 CHOCOLATE RACE TRACK
Prep: 30 minutes   Cook: 36 to 42 minutes   Serves: 8

This is chocolate through and through and designed only for the most avid chocolate lovers. The recipe is fashioned after a commercial bakery creation.

Refrigerated Sour Cream Coffeecake Dough (recipe follows)	**1 teaspoon cinnamon**
1⅓ cups regular-size semisweet chocolate chips (8 ounces)	**1¼ cups miniature semisweet chocolate chips (7½ ounces)**
⅓ cup heavy cream	**Rich Chocolate Glaze (recipe follows)**

1. Prepare Refrigerated Sour Cream Coffeecake Dough. Refrigerate at least 3 hours or up to 2 days.

2. In a 1-quart glass bowl, combine regular-size chocolate chips and cream. Heat in a microwave oven on High 1 to 1¼ minutes, or until chocolate is melted and smooth when stirred. Stir in cinnamon. Let cool completely.

3. Preheat oven to 375°F. To assemble dessert, roll out dough on a lightly floured surface to a 15 x 18-inch rectangle. Spoon cooled filling onto center of dough and spread to within 3 inches of edges. Sprinkle 1 cup miniature chocolate chips on top. From long side, roll up dough jelly-roll fashion. Press seam to seal. Lift carefully into a greased 10-inch springform tube pan. Press ends together to seal. Do not let rise.

4. Bake 35 to 40 minutes, or until golden brown. Let cake cool in pan 15 minutes, then loosen sides, remove cake ring from pan, and let cool completely. When cool, cover with Rich Chocolate Glaze and sprinkle remaining ¼ cup miniature chocolate chips over top.

REFRIGERATED SOUR CREAM COFFEECAKE DOUGH

Prep: 15 minutes   Cook: none   Chill: 3 hours   Makes: enough for 1 coffeecake

This wonderful refrigerator sour cream yeast dough can be kept in the refrigerator up to two days before using.

4 cups flour	⅓ cup sugar
½ teaspoon salt	3 eggs
2 sticks (8 ounces) cold butter	1 cup sour cream
2 (¼-ounce) packages active dry yeast	1½ teaspoons vanilla extract
¼ cup warm water (105° to 115°)	

1. In a food processor, combine flour and salt. Cut butter over top in ¼-inch slices, distributing evenly. Turn machine on and off quickly 8 times, or until mixture resembles very coarse meal.

2. In a small bowl, soften yeast in warm water 5 minutes. Stir in sugar. Blend eggs with sour cream and vanilla and mix with yeast mixture until well blended. Add to processor and turn motor on and off 2 or 3 times, or until dough is formed.

3. Transfer to a covered container and store in refrigerator at least 3 hours and no longer than 2 days. Remove dough when ready to make Chocolate Race Track (above).

RICH CHOCOLATE GLAZE

½ cup semisweet chocolate chips	1 tablespoon milk
1 tablespoon butter	2 teaspoons light corn syrup
	1 teaspoon vanilla extract

In a 1-cup glass measure, combine chocolate chips, butter, milk, and corn syrup. Heat in a microwave oven on High 40 to 60 seconds, or until melted and smooth when stirred. Stir in vanilla. Let cool slightly before using.

257   MINI-CHIP STRUDEL SLICES
Prep: 20 minutes   Cook: 13 to 15 minutes   Makes: 28

These attractive gems are easy to make with packaged puff pastry. They are small enough to offer guests any time of day with a cup of coffee.

½ **cup semisweet chocolate chips**
½ **cup chopped walnuts or pecans**
⅓ **cup sugar**
1 **teaspoon cinnamon**

1 **(17¼-ounce) package frozen puff pastry (2 sheets), thawed 30 minutes**
1 **egg**
1 **teaspoon water**

1. Preheat oven to 375°F. In a small bowl, mix together chocolate chips, nuts, sugar, and cinnamon.

2. On a lightly floured pastry cloth, using a rolling pin, roll each puff pastry sheet into a 14 x 11-inch rectangle. Sprinkle each sheet with half of chocolate-nut mixture, spreading to within ½ inch of edges. Roll up dough from long side, jelly-roll fashion.

3. In a cup, beat together egg and water. Brush over top of rolls. With a sharp knife, cut rolls crosswise into 1-inch pieces. Separate pieces and place 1-inch apart on ungreased baking sheets.

4. Bake 13 to 15 minutes, or until tops are golden. Let cool 5 minutes on pans, then loosen and remove to racks to let cool completely.

258   CHOCOLATE PEANUT RING
Prep: 30 minutes   Cook: 20 minutes   Serves: 8 to 10

Here's a specialty designed with peanut butter and chocolate fans in mind. It's a great chocolate treat any time of day.

1 **envelope (¼ ounce) active dry yeast**
⅓ **cup plus ½ teaspoon granulated sugar**
½ **cup warm water (105° to 115°)**
1 **egg**

4 **tablespoons butter, melted**
½ **teaspoon salt**
2 **to 2½ cups flour**
1 **cup chunky peanut butter**
¼ **cup packed brown sugar**
12 **ounces semisweet chocolate chips (2 cups)**

1. Sprinkle yeast and ½ teaspoon granulated sugar over warm water in a glass measure; stir and set aside.

2. In a large bowl, beat together egg, remaining ⅓ cup granulated sugar, butter, and salt with an electric mixer on low speed. Add 1 cup flour, beating well. Add yeast and beat well. If your mixer has a dough hook, remove beater and attach dough hook. Add remaining 1 to 1½ cups flour (until dough is no longer sticky) and knead by machine 5 minutes. If your mixer does not have a dough hook, remove dough and knead in remaining flour by hand until dough is smooth and elastic, 7 to 8 minutes. Place dough in a greased bowl, cover, and let rise until doubled, about 1½ hours.

3. Punch dough down. On a lightly floured pastry cloth or board, roll dough out to an 18 x 12-inch rectangle. In a small bowl, stir together peanut butter, brown sugar, and chocolate chips. Spread peanut filling over dough to within 1 inch of edges. Starting from 1 long side, roll up jelly-roll fashion and pinch edges to seal. Place roll on a lightly greased baking sheet and form into a ring. Pinch ends together to seal. With a sharp knife, slash dough at 2-inch intervals cutting two thirds of the way into the ring and halfway to the bottom. Cover with a towel; let rise in a draft-free area until doubled, about 1½ hours.

4. About 15 minutes before rising has been completed, preheat oven to 350°F. Bake ring about 20 minutes, or until golden brown. Serve at room temperature.

---

259   DOUBLE CHOCOLATE MUFFINS
Prep: 10 minutes   Cook: 17 to 23 minutes   Serves: 12

These are great with coffee for a morning pick-me-up or for a lunch-time dessert or afternoon snack.

1 stick (4 ounces) butter or margarine	2 teaspoons vanilla extract Dash of salt
3 (1-ounce) squares unsweetened chocolate, cut up	1 cup buttermilk 2 cups flour 1 teaspoon baking soda
1 cup sugar 1 egg	6 ounces semisweet chocolate chips (1 cup)

1. Preheat oven to 400°F. In a 2-quart glass bowl, combine butter and unsweetened chocolate. Heat in microwave oven on High 2 to 2½ minutes, until melted and smooth when stirred. Let cool to lukewarm.

2. Stir in sugar, egg, vanilla, salt, and buttermilk, until thoroughly blended. Mix together flour and baking soda and stir into chocolate mixture just until combined. Stir in chocolate chips.

3. Spoon batter into 12 paper-lined 2½-inch muffin cups, filling to top.

4. Bake 15 to 20 minutes, or until a cake tester inserted in center comes out clean. Let muffins cool in pans 5 minutes, then transfer to racks to cool completely. Serve warm or cool.

Variation: **DOUBLE CHOCOLATE ORANGE MUFFINS**

Stir in 2 teaspoons grated orange zest along with vanilla. Proceed as directed above.

260 PEANUT BUTTER CHOCOLATE CHIP MUFFINS

Prep: 15 minutes   Cook: 20 to 25 minutes   Makes: 12

When you want a morning or afternoon sweet to serve with coffee, these are a good choice.

⅔ cup smooth or crunchy
    peanut butter
2 tablespoons butter, melted
¾ cup sugar
2 eggs
1½ teaspoons vanilla extract

1½ cups flour
1½ teaspoons baking powder
½ teaspoon baking soda
½ cup milk
6 ounces semisweet chocolate
    chips (1 cup)

1. Preheat oven to 350°F. In a large mixing bowl, combine peanut butter and melted butter; stir until well blended. Mix in sugar, eggs, and vanilla. Combine flour with baking powder and baking soda. Add to peanut butter mixture along with milk and chocolate chips. Stir just until combined.

2. Spoon batter into 12 paper-lined 2½- to 3-inch muffin tins. Bake 20 to 25 minutes, or until muffins spring back when lightly touched in center. Serve warm or at room temperature.

261 BANANA CHOCOLATE CHIP MUFFINS

Prep: 10 minutes   Cook: 20 to 22 minutes   Makes: 12

This is one of my daughter's all-time favorites; whip it up when you have a few ripe bananas around.

2 large or 3 medium ripe
    bananas
⅔ cup sugar
2 eggs
6 tablespoons butter, melted
1 teaspoon vanilla extract

2 cups flour
2 teaspoons baking soda
¼ cup buttermilk
⅔ cup semisweet chocolate
    chips
½ cup chopped pecans

Preheat oven to 350°F. In a medium bowl, mash bananas with a fork. Add sugar and eggs and mix well. Stir in melted butter and vanilla. Add flour, baking soda, and buttermilk. Stir with a fork just enough to combine. Stir in chocolate chips and pecans. Spoon batter into 12 paper-lined 2¾-inch muffin cups, filling almost full. Bake 20 to 22 minutes, or until golden and a cake tester inserted in center comes out clean. Let muffins stand in pans 5 minutes; then transfer to racks to let cool completely.

Variation: **CHOCOLATE CHOCOLATE CHIP BANANA MUFFINS**

Melt 3 (1-ounce) squares unsweetened chocolate with butter over very low heat or in microwave oven and add to batter along with butter.

262   APPLE-FILLED CHOCOLATE COFFEECAKE
Prep: 35 to 40 minutes   Cook: 1 hour   Serves: 12

2 (¼-ounce) envelopes active
   dry yeast
½ cup plus ½ teaspoon sugar
¾ cup warm water (105° to
   115°)
1 stick (4 ounces) butter,
   melted
½ cup warm milk (110°)

½ cup firmly packed
   unsweetened cocoa
   powder
1 teaspoon salt
2 eggs, lightly beaten
5 to 5½ cups flour
   Apple Filling (recipe
   follows)

1. Sprinkle yeast and ½ teaspoon sugar over warm water in a glass measure; stir and set aside.

2. In a large bowl, combine melted butter, milk, remaining ½ cup sugar, cocoa, salt, and eggs. Beat with an electric mixer on low speed. Add 3 cups flour and beat well. Beat in yeast mixture until well mixed. If your mixer has a dough hook, remove beater and attach dough hook; add remaining 2 to 2½ cups flour to make a soft dough. Knead on medium-high speed 5 to 7 minutes. If your mixer does not have a dough hook, remove dough to a lightly floured surface and knead in remaining flour by hand. Continue kneading about 10 minutes, until smooth and elastic. Place dough in a greased bowl, cover, and let rise until doubled in bulk, about 1 hour.

3. Punch dough down. On a lightly floured pastry cloth or board, roll out dough to a 14 x 20-inch rectangle. Spread with Apple Filling to within 1 inch of edges. Starting from one long side, roll up tightly jelly-roll fashion, pinching seam and ends to seal. Place in a lightly greased 10-inch tube pan and pinch ends together to seal. Let rise until doubled, about 1½ hours.

4. About 15 minutes before rising has been completed, preheat oven to 350°F. Bake about 1 hour, or until golden brown. Let cool in pan 10 minutes, then invert onto a wire rack. Serve warm or at room temperature.

APPLE FILLING

3 tablespoons butter
2 green apples, peeled, cored,
   and cut into ½-inch pieces
½ cup chopped pecans
½ cup packed brown sugar
¼ cup packed unsweetened
   cocoa powder

1 tablespoon ground
   cinnamon
½ cup golden raisins
6 ounces semisweet chocolate
   chips (1 cup)

1. In a medium skillet, melt butter over low heat. Add apples and pecans and cook, stirring constantly, over high heat 2 minutes. Remove from heat and let cool.

2. When cool, mix in brown sugar, cocoa, cinnamon, raisins, and chocolate chips.

263   CHOCOLATE CHIP CREAM CHEESE STRUDEL

Prep: 40 minutes   Cook: 25 to 30 minutes   Serves: 8

6 ounces cream cheese, softened
¼ cup granulated sugar
1 egg yolk
1½ teaspoons grated orange zest
1 teaspoon vanilla extract
½ cup semisweet chocolate chips

½ of a 16-ounce package filo dough sheets (thaw in refrigerator if frozen)
1 stick (4 ounces) unsalted butter, clarified (see Note)
⅓ cup packaged dry plain bread crumbs
Powdered sugar

1. In a medium bowl, combine cream cheese, granulated sugar, egg yolk, orange zest, and vanilla. Beat with an electric mixer on medium speed until light and fluffy, 2 to 3 minutes. By hand, stir in chocolate chips. Set aside.

2. Preheat oven to 375°F. Open filo sheets and unfold; leave stacked with long sides horizontally in front of you. Place on a large sheet of wax paper. Fold wax paper and filo sheets in half (to the right) like a book. Turn back (to the left) the first filo sheet (it will actually be ½ sheet) onto the wax paper and quickly brush with clarified butter. Sprinkle with a few bread crumbs. Turn the next filo sheet back on top of the first, brush with butter, and sprinkle with bread crumbs. Work quickly, repeating procedure until you get to the center, and all sheets on the left are buttered.

3. Now fold wax paper and all filo sheets on the right to the left like a book. Starting from the back cover of the book, repeat procedure, moving filo sheet to right, brushing with butter, and sprinkling with bread crumbs.

4. When you reach the center again and all sheets are flat, spread cheese filling down long side of dough closest to you, spreading over lower third of dough. Fold in the ends at the right and left edges. Roll up strudel (from long side closest to you) jelly-roll fashion, using paper to help lift and roll.

5. Place strudel seam side down on an ungreased foil-lined jelly-roll pan. Brush with a little of remaining clarified butter. Bake 15 minutes; brush top with remaining clarified butter. Bake 10 to 15 minutes longer, or until crisp and golden brown. Let cool 40 to 60 minutes, then sift powdered sugar on top. To serve, cut into 1-inch or larger slices.

NOTE: *To clarify butter, in a small skillet, melt butter over low heat. Let stand a few minutes. Skim off and discard white foam that rises to top and do not use any milky residue that sinks to bottom of skillet. The clear yellow liquid is clarified butter.*

264   PECAN CHOCOLATE YEAST CAKE
Prep: 25 minutes   Cook: 40 to 45 minutes   Serves: 12

2   sticks (8 ounces) butter or
      margarine
1   cup milk
¼   cup unsweetened cocoa
      powder
1   (1-ounce) square
      unsweetened chocolate
1   envelope (¼ ounce) quick-
      rising yeast

1½   cups sugar
2½   cups flour
1   teaspoon baking soda
½   teaspoon salt
3   eggs
1   cup chopped toasted pecans
    Cream cheese and berry
      preserves, as
      accompaniment

1. In a medium saucepan, combine butter, milk, cocoa, and unsweetened chocolate. Place over medium-low heat and heat, stirring occasionally, until butter is melted, chocolate is thoroughly incorporated, and mixture is hot to touch (125°F on a candy thermometer).

2. In a large bowl, mix together dry yeast, sugar, flour, baking soda, and salt. Add chocolate mixture and eggs. Beat with an electric mixer on low speed until well mixed. By hand stir in pecans. Turn batter into a well-greased 12-cup bundt pan. Let rise, uncovered, in a draft-free place 2 hours, or until imprint made by poking a finger ½ inch into dough remains.

3. Meanwhile, preheat oven to 350°F. Bake 40 to 45 minutes, or until cake sounds hollow when tapped. Let cake cool in pan 20 minutes, then invert onto a wire rack. Serve warm, with cream cheese and berry preserves.

265   CHOCOLATE-FILLED CRESCENT ROLLS
Prep: 15 minutes   Cook: 11 to 13 minutes   Serves: 8

2   tablespoons butter
3   tablespoons brown sugar
2   teaspoons grated orange zest
½   teaspoon cinnamon
½   cup semisweet chocolate
      chips

⅓   cup chopped walnuts
1   (8-ounce) package quick
      refrigerated crescent
      dinner rolls
1   to 2 teaspoons milk

1. Preheat oven to 375°F. In a small glass bowl, melt butter in a microwave oven on High 20 to 30 seconds. Stir in brown sugar, orange zest, and cinnamon. Let cool; then mix in chocolate chips and walnuts.

2. Unroll dough and separate into 8 triangles. Spread about 1 heaping tablespoon chocolate mixture over each triangle. Roll up from wide end (opposite the point), stretching dough a little as you roll. Place rolls, point side down, on an ungreased baking sheet. Curve into a crescent shape. Brush tops with a little milk.

3. Bake 10 to 12 minutes, or until golden brown. Wait 2 to 3 minutes, then transfer to a rack to let cool. Serve warm or at room temperature.

266   MINI CHOCOLATE PUFFS
Prep: 15 minutes   Cook: 10 to 12 minutes   Makes: 30

Prepared puff pastry, available in the freezer section of your supermarket, make these little chocolate pick-ups a snap.

1   (17¼-ounce) package frozen
    puff pastry (2 sheets),
    thawed 30 minutes
⅔ cup miniature semisweet
    chocolate chips

⅓ cup chopped pecans
1   egg white, lightly beaten

1. Preheat oven to 400°F. With a rolling pin, on a floured board, roll out each pastry sheet, 1 at a time, to a 9 x 15-inch rectangle. Cut each pastry sheet into 15 (3-inch) rectangles.

2. Place 1 teaspoon chocolate chips and ½ teaspoon pecans in center of each dough square. Moisten edges with egg white and fold in half diagonally to form a triangle. Press edges together firmly to seal. Place on buttered baking sheets. Brush tops with egg white.

3. Bake 10 to 12 minutes, or until golden brown. Serve warm.

267   CHOCOLATE CHIP CHEESE TRIANGLE PUFFS
Prep: 35 minutes   Chill: 20 to 30 minutes   Cook: 15 to 17 minutes
Makes: 1 dozen

These are a wonderful sweet to serve with a cup of coffee any time of day.

1   (8-ounce) package cream
    cheese, softened
3   tablespoons plus 2
    teaspoons sugar
1   tablespoon orange juice
1   teaspoon grated orange zest

½ cup miniature semisweet
    chocolate chips
1   (17¼-ounce) package frozen
    puff pastry (2 sheets),
    thawed 30 minutes
1   egg white

1. To make filling, in a small bowl, mix together cream cheese, 3 tablespoons sugar, orange juice, and orange zest until smooth and creamy. Stir in chocolate chips. Refrigerate or freeze 15 minutes to firm up mixture slightly.

2. With a rolling pin, roll out each pastry sheet, 1 at a time, on a floured pastry cloth to a 10 x 15-inch rectangle. Cut dough in half lengthwise. Then cut crosswise at 5-inch intervals so you end up with 6 (5-inch) squares from each pastry sheet.

3. Place 1 tablespoon of cheese mixture in center of each dough square. Moisten edges with some of egg white and fold in half diagonally to form a triangle. Press edges together firmly to seal. Place on a foil-lined baking sheet. Brush tops with more egg white and sprinkle remaining 2 teaspoons sugar on top. Refrigerate 20 to 30 minutes.

4. Preheat oven to 400°F. Bake triangles 15 to 17 minutes, or until golden brown. Serve warm or at room temperature. Pastries can also be prepared and baked ahead and recrisped in oven a few minutes just before serving.

---

268   RICOTTA-CHOCOLATE FRUIT CALZONE
Prep: 20 minutes   Cook: 15 to 16 minutes   Serves: 6

Although calzone is usually made with pizza dough, this version (an adaptation of one found on a Southern California restaurant menu), designed to be eaten for dessert, uses frozen puff pastry.

½   cup ricotta cheese
¼   cup powdered sugar
½   teaspoon vanilla extract
1   to 1½ tablespoons heavy
      cream
6   tablespoons miniature
      semisweet chocolate
      chips

1   (17¼-ounce) package frozen
      puff pastry (2 sheets),
      thawed
8   fresh strawberries, sliced
1   egg, beaten

1. Preheat oven to 400°F. In a medium bowl, combine ricotta cheese, powdered sugar, vanilla, and cream. Beat with an electric mixer on medium-high speed until light and almost smooth, 1 to 2 minutes. Stir in chocolate chips.

2. Unfold puff pastry sheets on a lightly floured pastry cloth and trim corners of each to make a 9- to 9½-inch round. Place rounds on a baking sheet. Spoon half of ricotta filling mixture on half of each pastry round to within 1 inch of edges. Top each with half of strawberry slices. With a pastry brush or fingers, spread some of beaten egg around edges of pastry. Fold pastry round in half like a turnover to form a half-moon shape. Pinch edges to seal. Brush top of calzones with more beaten egg.

3. Bake 15 to 16 minutes, or until golden brown. Sprinkle additional powdered sugar over top of calzones. Cut each calzone into 3 pieces and serve warm.

269   MOCK ALMOND-CHIP CROISSANTS
Prep: 10 minutes   Cook: 12 minutes   Serves: 8

½ **cup almond paste**
1 **egg, separated**
1 **tablespoon milk**
¼ **cup miniature semisweet chocolate chips**

1 **(8-ounce) package quick refrigerated crescent dinner rolls**

1. Preheat oven to 375°F. In a small bowl, beat almond paste, egg yolk, and milk with an electric mixer on medium speed until well blended. Stir in mini-chocolate chips.

2. Unroll dough; separate into 8 triangles. Place 1 scant tablespoon almond paste mixture at long end opposite point of triangle and roll dough up to point of triangle. Place rolls, point side down, on an ungreased baking sheet. Lightly beat egg white with a fork and brush over tops of croissants.

3. Bake 12 minutes, or until croissants are golden brown. Serve warm or at room temperature.

Chapter 11

Chocolate Frostings, Sauces, and Beverages

What is a well-dressed chocolate dessert wearing these days? Why of course a taste-tempting chocolate frosting or luxurious sauce. Chocolate frostings and sauces are those extra-special embellishments that make a cake or a scoop of ice cream something special; they add the finishing touch or gild the lily. Choices in this chapter range from basic to sophisticated, but all are chocolate-based.

For a versatile frosting, try Quick Chocolate Butter Cream Frosting that's simply a combination of butter, powdered sugar, cocoa, cream, and vanilla. To change the flavor, you might want to zip it up with a splash of liqueur such as Grand Marnier sometime. Another interesting frosting option for all kinds of chocolate cakes is a mousse-like mixture prepared with a package of chocolate pudding mix, milk, rum, and whipped cream. It's reminiscent of a chocolate pastry cream, but without all the muss and fuss.

Topping and sauce possibilities include variations on the hot fudge sauce theme along with a raspberry jam topping dotted with bittersweet chocolate chunks, a Chocolate Crème Anglaise and a Chocolate Pronto Crème Fraîche made in a jiffy with whipped cream, powdered sugar, sour cream, and cocoa. You can make a delicious dessert for chocolate fans by simply spooning some over fresh in-season fruits. Sauces lend themselves to do-ahead preparation; simply store them in the refrigerator. For the most part you can reheat sauces, if necessary, in the microwave oven.

Besides the frosting and sauce recipes that follow, you'll find many more sprinkled throughout this volume. Look in the index to find them. Mix and match to suit your personal taste. Many of the frostings can be used interchangeably with different cakes.

Chocolate is at home in all sorts of beverages that can be served around the clock—morning, noon, or night. It's not surprising, since chocolate was enjoyed as a drink in Mexico hundreds of years ago. It was during his conquest of Mexico that Hernando Cortez, the Spanish explorer, found the Aztec Indians using cacao beans in the preparation of a royal drink known as chocolatl, which was unsweetened. Later, the Spaniards mixed the beans with sugar, vanilla, and spices and the resulting concoction became the drink of the nobility in Spain.

Children devour the special pick-me-up treats including the Chocolate Chocolate Milk Shake, Chocolate

Orange Frost, Quick Hot Chocolate, and a special concoction made with banana, milk, cocoa drink mix, and ice. For adults, refreshing after-dinner sweet options include a Frosty Chocolate-Cappuccino, Hot Mocha Brandy, and Chocolate Delight. Chocolate Crème Liqueur is a reasonable facsimile of some of the commercial crème liqueurs; it's delicious for dessert served over ice. And it makes a terrific gift as well.

---

270 CHOCOLATE CREAM FROSTING
Prep: 10 minutes   Cook: none   Makes: 4 cups

Here's a quick way to make chocolate pastry cream or a mousse-like frosting with a package of pudding mix and whipped cream. The recipe makes enough to fill and frost a 9-inch 2-layer cake. Be sure to keep the frosting and cake refrigerated.

1   cup heavy cream
¾   cup milk
¼   cup dark rum, Grand
    Marnier, brewed coffee,
    or orange juice

1   (4-ounce) package instant
    chocolate fudge flavor
    pudding and pie filling
    mix

1. In a medium bowl, beat cream with an electric mixer on high speed until stiff; set aside. In a medium bowl, combine milk and rum; add pudding mix. Beat with an electric mixer on low speed until well blended, 1 to 1½ minutes.

2. Fold whipped cream into pudding mixture until no white streaks remain. Use immediately to fill and frost cake.

---

271 CHOCOLATE CHUNK RASPBERRY JAM TOPPING
Prep: 10 minutes   Cook: none   Makes: 2 cups

This is a nifty way to make a delicious jiffy topping for cake slices or ice cream. Make it up ahead and store it in the refrigerator. Packaged in an attractive container, it makes a terrific hostess gift any time of year.

1   (16-ounce) jar seedless red
    raspberry jam
⅓   cup Chambord, Grand
    Marnier, or dark rum

6   ounces bittersweet,
    semisweet, or imported
    white chocolate, cut into
    ½-inch chunks

In a small bowl, stir together jam and Chambord until well blended and smooth. Stir in chocolate chunks. Store in a tightly covered container in refrigerator. Serve spooned over ice cream, cake slices, or chocolate mousse.

272   CHOCOLATE PRONTO CREME FRAICHE
Prep: 10 minutes   Cook: none   Makes: about 1¾ cups

This is a good substitute for crème fraîche whenever you want a whipped topping that's not too sweet.

1 cup heavy cream	3 tablespoons powdered
2 to 3 tablespoons	sugar
unsweetened cocoa	¼ cup sour cream
powder	½ teaspoon vanilla extract

In a medium bowl, whip cream with cocoa powder and sugar until stiff. Add sour cream and vanilla and beat just until blended. Cover and refrigerate for up to 2 days before serving.

Variation: **PRONTO CREME FRAICHE**

Omit cocoa powder and vanilla; reduce powdered sugar to 2 tablespoons.

273   CHOCOLATE CREME ANGLAISE
Prep: 15 minutes   Cook: 8 minutes   Chill: 3 hours
Makes: about 2 cups

2 cups milk	2 teaspoons vanilla extract
4 egg yolks	or 1 tablespoon Grand
½ cup sugar	Marnier or Cognac
2 ounces semisweet chocolate,	
coarsely chopped	

1. In a heavy 2½-quart saucepan, scald milk over medium heat. Meanwhile, in a medium bowl, whisk together egg yolks and sugar. Gradually whisk in hot milk. Return custard to saucepan, reduce heat to low, and cook, stirring constantly with a wooden spoon, until custard thickens enough to coat back of spoon, 170° to 175°F on a candy thermometer. Do not boil, or custard will curdle.

2. Immediately strain hot custard through a sieve into a medium bowl placed over ice water. Add chopped chocolate and stir until melted and smooth.

3. Set bowl in a saucepan of ice water and stir occasionally, until cooled, about 5 minutes. Stir in vanilla. Cover and refrigerate until chilled, at least 3 hours, before serving.

Variation: **CREME ANGLAISE**

To make the traditional vanilla version of the sauce, omit the chocolate in step 2.

274   FUDGY CHOCOLATE SAUCE

Prep: 5 minutes   Cook: 2½ minutes   Makes: about 1¾ cups

1 (14-ounce) can sweetened
   condensed milk
3 (1-ounce) squares
   unsweetened chocolate,
   broken up

¼ cup milk
½ teaspoon vanilla extract
   Dash of salt

1. In a 1-quart glass bowl, combine sweetened condensed milk, chocolate, and milk. Heat in a microwave oven on High about 2½ minutes, stirring twice during cooking time, until mixture is smooth, blended, and thickened. Whisk in vanilla and salt.

2. Serve hot or cold over ice cream. Refrigerate any leftovers and reheat in microwave oven as needed.

275   CHOCOLATE DELIGHT

Prep: 5 minutes   Cook: 3 to 4 minutes   Serves: 2 or 3

Here's a wonderful sweet nightcap that is special enough to serve discriminating guests; you might never guess it has a milk base.

2 cups milk
¼ cup sweet ground chocolate
   and cocoa mix, such as
   Ghirardelli
2 tablespoons coffee-flavored
   liqueur

2 tablespoons crème de cacao
   or other chocolate-
   flavored liqueur
2 tablespoons brandy
   Whipped cream

In a 1-quart glass measure, heat milk in a microwave oven on High 3 to 4 minutes, or until boiling. Whisk in cocoa mix, coffee liqueur, crème de cacao, and brandy until well mixed. Serve in 2 or 3 coffee cups or mugs. Garnish with whipped cream. Serve immediately.

276   CHOCOLATE WHIPPED CREAM

Prep: 10 minutes   Cook: none   Makes: about 2 cups

Sometimes nothing else but chocolate whipped cream will do for crowning a special dessert. Follow these easy steps to make it.

3 tablespoons unsweetened
   cocoa powder
2 tablespoons powdered
   sugar

1 cup heavy cream
1 teaspoon vanilla extract

In a small bowl, whisk together cocoa and powdered sugar until well blended. Place cream in a medium bowl and whisk in cocoa and powdered sugar. Whisk in vanilla. With chilled beaters, beat cream with an electric mixer on high speed until stiff or desired consistency.

277 QUICK CHOCOLATE BUTTER CREAM FROSTING

Prep: 10 minutes   Cook: none   Makes: scant 2 cups

Here's a good basic chocolate butter cream, which makes enough to frost the top of a 9 x 13-inch cake or to fill and frost a 2-layer 8-inch cake. For a 2-layer 9-inch cake, make 1½ recipes.

1 stick (4 ounces) butter,
   softened
2 cups powdered sugar
¼ cup unsweetened cocoa
   powder

¼ cup heavy cream
1 teaspoon vanilla extract
Dash of salt

In a medium bowl, beat butter with an electric mixer on medium speed 1 minute. Add powdered sugar, cocoa, cream, vanilla, and salt. Beat on low speed until well mixed, then beat on medium speed until fluffy, 1 to 2 minutes.

278 HOT FUDGE SAUCE

Prep: 5 minutes   Cook: 30 minutes   Makes: 1¼ cups

This is an adaptation of the delicious fudge sauce I grew up on. We've been making it in our family for years.

2 (1-ounce) squares
   unsweetened chocolate,
   cut up
1 cup milk

1 cup sugar
Dash of salt
2 tablespoons light corn syrup
¾ teaspoon vanilla extract

1. In a medium saucepan, combine chocolate and milk. Heat to boiling over low heat, stirring constantly. Cook, stirring, until mixture is smooth and blended, about 5 minutes.

2. Add sugar, salt, and corn syrup. Increase heat to medium and cook, stirring, until sugar is dissolved and mixture boils. Continue boiling, without stirring, until sauce reaches 220°F on a candy thermometer or until ½ teaspoon dropped into a glass of cold water forms a soft mass, about 20 minutes. Stir in vanilla.

3. Serve hot or cold over ice cream or cake. Store sauce in a covered jar in refrigerator.

279   DARK CHOCOLATE FUDGE SAUCE
Prep: 10 minutes   Cook: 2½ to 3½ minutes   Makes: 1¾ cups

This yummy dark sauce can be kept refrigerated for two weeks. Serve warm or hot, over ice cream, cake, fruit, or whatever strikes your fancy.

½   cup packed brown sugar
⅓   cup granulated sugar
¾   cup unsweetened cocoa
       powder (preferably
       Dutch-processed)

¾   cup heavy cream
3   tablespoons butter
1   teaspoon vanilla extract
       Dash of salt

1. In a 1-quart glass bowl, combine brown sugar, granulated sugar, cocoa, and cream. Mix well. Add butter. Heat in microwave oven on High 1½ to 2 minutes, stirring once, until well mixed. Heat 1 to 1½ minutes longer, or until bubbly and sugars are dissolved. Stir in vanilla and salt.

2. Serve hot over ice cream, cake, fruits, etc. Or cool and store in refrigerator up to 2 weeks. Reheat in microwave oven on Low 1 to 2 minutes, stirring twice, until of good pouring consistency.

280   MOCHA CHOCOLATE SAUCE
Prep: 5 minutes   Cook: 2 minutes   Makes: about 2 cups

Anytime you need a thin chocolate sauce for gilding plates for terrines, cake slices, frozen desserts, or ice cream, try this sauce. It's fast and easy and will keep a week in the refrigerator. If you don't like coffee flavor, simply substitute a little vanilla extract for the coffee powder.

¼   cup sugar
1   tablespoon instant espresso
       powder
2   tablespoons butter

1½   cups semisweet chocolate
       chips (9 ounces)
2   tablespoons corn syrup

1. In a 1-quart glass bowl, combine sugar, espresso powder, and 1 cup water. Heat to boiling in a microwave oven on High 2 minutes, stirring twice, until sugar is dissolved.

2. Add butter and chocolate chips and stir until melted and smooth. Stir in corn syrup. Serve immediately or store, covered, in refrigerator 1 week. Reheat in microwave oven 30 to 60 seconds before serving, just to bring to room temperature or to warm slightly.

281   ALL-PURPOSE CHOCOLATE SYRUP
Prep: 5 minutes   Cook: 2 to 2½ minutes   Makes: 1¼ cups

This is a good homemade facsimile of store-bought chocolate syrup. Use when chocolate syrup is called for in beverages and dessert recipes. Also, you can use whenever a thin chocolate sauce is needed to accompany a dessert, such as bread pudding or ice cream desserts.

½ cup unsweetened cocoa
   powder
½ cup sugar

⅓ cup light corn syrup
1 teaspoon vanilla extract

1. In a 1-quart glass bowl, stir together cocoa and sugar. Gradually whisk in ½ cup hot water and corn syrup. Heat in a microwave oven on High 2 to 2½ minutes, stirring twice, until sugar is dissolved and mixture is smooth.

2. Stir in vanilla. Let cool. Store, covered, in refrigerator.

282   CHOCOLATE ORANGE FROST
Prep: 5 minutes   Cook: none   Makes: 1 cup

Thick and frosty, this is a favorite with children.

1 cup chocolate ice cream
½ cup orange juice

1 tablespoon chocolate-
   flavored syrup

In a blender container, combine ice cream, orange juice, and chocolate syrup. Whir on medium speed until blended, 20 to 30 seconds, then blend on high speed for 10 seconds. Serve immediately in a tall glass.

283   HOT MOCHA BRANDY
Prep: 5 minutes   Cook: 2 to 2½ minutes   Serves: 1

1 cup milk
2 teaspoons instant espresso
   powder
2 tablespoons sweet ground
   chocolate and cocoa mix,
   such as Ghirardelli

1½ tablespoons brandy
1½ tablespoons coffee-flavored
   liqueur
Whipped cream

In a 2-cup glass measure, heat milk and espresso powder in a microwave oven on High 2 to 2½ minutes, or until boiling. Whisk in cocoa mix, brandy, and coffee liqueur until well mixed. Pour into a mug or stemmed glass. Garnish with whipped cream. Serve immediately.

284   CHOCOLATE CREME LIQUEUR
Prep: 10 minutes   Cook: none   Makes: 2 pints

This makes a good gift or a delicious dessert drink. It's similar to some of the commercial cream liqueurs, but this version is less expensive than its store-bought counterparts and delicious, too! Serve over ice.

2   cups heavy cream
1   (14-ounce) can sweetened condensed milk
1   cup whiskey
¼   cup unsweetened cocoa powder

1½   tablespoons vanilla extract
1   tablespoon instant espresso powder
1   tablespoon coconut extract

1. In a food processor, combine cream, sweetened condensed milk, whiskey, cocoa, vanilla, espresso powder, and coconut extract. Process until well blended and smooth.

2. Serve immediately over ice. Or place in glass container, cover tightly, and store in refrigerator up to 3 weeks. Stir before serving.

285   FROSTY CHOCOLATE-CAPPUCCINO
Prep: 5 minutes   Cook: none   Serves: 3 or 4

Here's a refreshing after-dinner drink made with ice cream.

¼   cup milk
⅓   cup brandy
2   teaspoons instant espresso or coffee powder

1   quart chocolate ice cream
Sweetened whipped cream and ground cinnamon

1. In a blender or food processor, combine milk, brandy, and coffee powder. Add ice cream. Whir just until well blended, 30 to 60 seconds.

2. Pour into 3 or 4 stemmed glasses or goblets. Garnish with whipped cream and a sprinkling of cinnamon.

286   CHOCOLATE PICK-ME-UP
Prep: 5 minutes   Cook: none   Makes: 1½ cups

This is a tasty treat morning, noon, or night.

1   banana, cut up
¾   cup milk or chocolate milk

3   tablespoons sweetened cocoa drink mix
2   ice cubes

In a blender container, combine banana, milk, cocoa mix, and ice cubes. Whir on low speed until blended, 20 to 30 seconds, then blend on high speed until smooth. Serve immediately in 1 or 2 glasses.

287   CHOCOLATE MONKEY DRINK
Prep: 10 minutes   Cook: none   Serves: 2 to 3

This sweet after-dinner dessert drink, which teams ice cream, bananas, and chocolate, tastes like chocolate-covered bananas. For nondrinkers, leave out the liqueurs.

2 generous scoops chocolate
    ice cream
½ cup chocolate syrup
1 banana, cut up
3 tablespoons crème de cacao

3 tablespoons banana liqueur
2 cups crushed ice
Maraschino cherries,
    banana slices, and
    whipped cream

1. In a blender or food processor, blend together ice cream, chocolate syrup, banana, crème de cacao, banana liqueur, and crushed ice until smooth.

2. Pour into 2 or 3 stemmed glasses. Garnish each glass with a maraschino cherry, banana slice, and whipped cream. Serve immediately.

288   CHOCOLATE CHOCOLATE MILKSHAKE
Prep: 10 minutes   Cook: none   Serves: 2 to 3

1½ pints chocolate ice cream
1 cup cold milk
½ cup chocolate-flavored
    syrup

Store-bought whipped
    cream (in a pressurized
    container)

1. In a blender or food processor, combine ice cream, milk, and chocolate syrup. Blend until creamy and thick, 30 to 60 seconds. If a thinner shake is desired, add more milk.

2. To serve, squirt about 2 tablespoons whipped cream into bottom of each of 2 or 3 tall glasses. Top with shake. Squirt top of each shake with more whipped cream. Serve immediately.

289   QUICK HOT CHOCOLATE
Prep: 5 minutes   Cook: 1½ to 2 minutes   Serves: 1

When you want hot chocolate fast, use homemade chocolate syrup and the microwave oven.

1 cup milk
2 tablespoons All-Purpose
    Chocolate Syrup (page
    207)

1 tablespoon miniature
    marshmallows

In a large microwave-safe mug, combine milk and chocolate syrup. Stir to blend well. Heat in a microwave oven on High 1½ to 2 minutes, or until very hot. Sprinkle marshmallows on top. Serve immediately.

Chapter 12

Chocolate Confections

There's no mystery to making a good batch of fudge or truffles—or most any candy for that matter. All it requires is a little time, patience, and confidence in the kitchen and some delicious recipes, such as those included here.

To get busy cooks in and out of the kitchen fast and stay in tune with today's quick-paced life-styles, I've kept these candy recipes simple and fuss-free. Budding candy-makers won't have to spend hours over a hot stove to produce tasty results. One taste of Peanut Butter Bon Bons, Chocolate Peanut Butter Ribbon Fudge, and Rocky Road Mosaics will convince you of that. Only a few, such as the Chocolate Caramels and English Butter Chocolate Toffee, require a candy thermometer and longer cooking times.

None of these recipes require tempering the chocolate, a professional technique of melting and cooling chocolate at specific temperatures so that it cools and hardens quickly with a smooth, high-gloss, unstreaked finish when used for dipping or coating. It is laborious and involved. Instead, for coating my simple candies, I've carefully melted chocolate with a little solid vegetable shortening. It's also feasible to use coating chocolates available at candy-making or cake-decorating supply stores, as they dry shiny, but be aware that because they are not real chocolate, the flavor will be different.

The fudges are all the no-cook or quick-cook variety—made in no time flat with marshmallow creme, sweetened condensed milk, or cream cheese. For the fudges that require some cooking as well as for the caramels and toffee, be sure to use a heavy-bottomed saucepan to avoid scorching and burning.

For best results, use the best-quality ingredients including butter rather than margarine. For attractive presentation, place candies in paper or foil candy cups available at cake-decorating and candy supply stores.

Many of these candies are so fast to prepare that they lend themselves to last-minute or spur-of-the-moment homemade gifts, so keep that in mind when the holiday season rolls around.

290   EASY TURTLE CANDIES

Prep: 20 minutes   Cook: 6 to 8 minutes   Chill: 30 to 60 minutes
Makes: 24

Use store-bought caramels to make turtle candies simply. Children can help prepare this recipe, which makes a great gift any time of the year.

- 1   cup pecan halves
- 24   square light caramels, unwrapped (½ of a 14-ounce package)
- ½   cup semisweet chocolate chips
- 2   teaspoons vegetable oil

1. Preheat oven to 325°F. Line a baking sheet with foil. Grease foil well. Arrange pecans in clusters of 4, flat sides down, ½ inch apart. Place 1 caramel on top of each cluster of pecans, pressing into pecans to flatten slightly and hold pecans together.

2. Place in oven and bake 5 to 7 minutes, or until caramels are soft. Remove from oven and carefully flatten each caramel with a buttered knife.

3. In a 1-cup glass measure, combine chocolate chips and oil. Heat in a microwave oven on High 45 to 60 seconds, until melted and smooth when stirred. Spoon chocolate over turtles to cover caramels. Refrigerate 30 to 60 minutes, until set. Store and serve at room temperature.

---

291   WHITE CHOCOLATE HAZELNUT-APRICOT TRUFFLES

Prep: 20 minutes   Cook: 13 to 14 minutes   Chill: 2 to 3 hours
Makes: 28

Mingle the flavors of toasted hazelnuts and dried apricots with white chocolate for this terrific sweet.

- 1¼   cups hazelnuts
- 24   ounces imported white chocolate, cut up
- 6   tablespoons heavy cream
- ¼   cup finely chopped dried apricots

1. Preheat oven to 350°F. Spread out hazelnuts on a baking sheet. Bake 10 minutes, or until nuts are light brown and dark skins are cracked. Rub nuts in a terrycloth towel to remove as much of skins as possible. In a food processor, finely chop hazelnuts.

2. In a 1-quart glass measure, combine 12 ounces white chocolate and cream. Heat in a microwave oven on Medium 3 to 4 minutes, stirring twice, until chocolate is melted and smooth. Stir in ¾ cup hazelnuts and apricots.

3. Refrigerate, covered, 1 to 2 hours, or until mixture is firm enough to hold its shape. (If mixture gets too hard, let stand at room temperature ½ hour or until still firm but soft enough to shape.)

4. Using a 1¼-inch automatic-release ice cream-style scoop, scrape up truffle mixture into 28 (1¼-inch) balls (or use 1 tablespoon for each ball and roll between palms of hands into a smooth ball). Place on a wax paper-lined baking sheet and refrigerate until firm, 1 hour or longer.

5. In a small glass dish, place remaining 12 ounces white chocolate. Heat in microwave oven on Medium 3 to 3½ minutes, stirring often, until melted, smooth, and warm.

6. Using a fork, dip truffles quickly, one at a time, in chocolate, tapping fork on edge of dish to remove any excess. Place on wax paper-lined baking sheet and sprinkle tops with remaining hazelnuts. Store in an airtight container in refrigerator up to 2 weeks or in freezer 1 month. Serve in paper candy cups.

   NOTE: *Truffles can be dipped in bittersweet chocolate instead of white chocolate, if desired.*

---

292 CHOCOLATE FRUIT AND NUT ROLL
Prep: 15 minutes   Cook: 15 minutes   Chill: 1 hour
Makes: 6 rolls/2½ pounds candy

A not-too-sweet candy that's delicious.

2¾ cups chopped pecans	2 tablespoons grated orange
1½ cups sugar	zest
1 cup heavy cream	12 ounces semisweet chocolate
¼ cup light corn syrup	chips (2 cups)
1 (6-ounce) package dried	
apricots, chopped	

1. Line a cookie sheet with foil. Butter foil. Finely chop ¾ cup pecans; set aside.

2. In a large saucepan, combine sugar, cream, and syrup. Bring to a boil over high heat, stirring constantly. Reduce heat to medium-high and cook, stirring occasionally, just until mixture starts to turn amber color, or until a candy thermometer reaches 250°F, about 10 minutes. Remove from heat and immediately stir in remaining 2 cups pecans, dried apricots, and orange zest. Pour out onto prepared pan, spreading to about ½-inch thickness with back of wooden spoon. Let stand until cool enough to handle.

3. Sprinkle chocolate chips over caramel-fruit-and-nut mixture. With buttered hands, fold in chocolate. Some of the chocolate will melt. Divide candy into 6 equal pieces. Roll each piece into a 5 x 1½-inch log. Roll in reserved finely chopped pecans to coat completely. Refrigerate at least 1 hour to set. To serve, cut into ⅜- to ½-inch slices. Store, tightly covered, in refrigerator.

293 CHOCOLATE PEANUT BUTTER RIBBON FUDGE

Prep: 20 minutes   Cook: 15 minutes   Serves: 25

Wait until you taste this—it's fabulous, easy, and makes a wonderful gift.

1 cup peanut butter
1 stick (4 ounces) plus
    2 tablespoons butter, cut
    into tablespoons
2 tablespoons powdered
    sugar
12 ounces semisweet chocolate
    chips (2 cups)

½ of a 7-ounce jar
    marshmallow creme
2 teaspoons vanilla extract
2 cups granulated sugar
1 (5-ounce) can evaporated
    milk

1. In a small glass bowl, combine peanut butter and 2 tablespoons butter. Heat in a microwave oven on High 30 to 60 seconds, stirring once, until butter is melted and peanut butter is soft. Stir in powdered sugar until well blended; set aside.

2. In a large bowl, combine chocolate chips, remaining 1 stick butter, marshmallow creme, and vanilla; set aside.

3. In a large saucepan, combine granulated sugar and evaporated milk. Heat over low heat, stirring constantly, until mixture comes to a boil. Boil 6 minutes, stirring constantly. Pour over chocolate mixture in bowl and stir briskly until chocolate and butter melt and mixture is well blended.

4. Turn half of chocolate mixture into a well-buttered 8-inch square pan. Carefully spoon reserved peanut butter mixture over chocolate layer, spreading evenly. Carefully place remaining chocolate mixture over peanut butter mixture and spread evenly. Refrigerate until set. Cut into 25 squares.

294 CHOCOLATE-DIPPED COCONUT BALLS

*Prep: 45 minutes   Chill: 1 to 2 hours   Cook: 4 to 4½ minutes
Makes: 70*

This is one of my sister's favorite holiday recipes. They're good keepers, so make them ahead and store in an airtight container in the refrigerator.

1 (1-pound) box powdered
    sugar
4 cups flaked or shredded
    coconut
2 cups finely chopped walnuts
    or pecans
1 stick (4 ounces) butter,
    melted

1 teaspoon vanilla extract
⅔ cup sweetened condensed
    milk (½ of a 14-ounce can)
18 ounces semisweet chocolate
    chips (3 cups)
1½ tablespoons vegetable oil

1. In a large bowl, combine powdered sugar, coconut, and walnuts. Mix well. In a small bowl, stir together melted butter, vanilla, and sweetened condensed milk until well blended. Stir into coconut mixture, blending until mixed.

2. Form mixture into 70 (1-inch) balls. Place on 2 wax paper-lined baking sheets and refrigerate until firm, 1 to 2 hours.

3. In a medium glass bowl, combine chocolate and oil. Heat in a microwave oven on Medium 4 to 4½ minutes, until chocolate is melted and smooth when stirred.

4. With a fork, dip chilled balls, 1 at a time, into melted chocolate. Let excess drip off, then place on wax paper-lined baking sheets. Let stand at room temperature until set, about 1 hour. Store in an airtight container in refrigerator for up to 4 weeks.

---

295 ROCKY ROAD MOSAICS
Prep: 10 minutes   Cook: about 1 minute   Makes: 32

Although a bit messy to make, these quick confection slices are colorful and an attractive addition to cookie or candy trays.

6 **ounces semisweet chocolate chips (1 cup)**	3 **cups colored miniature marshmallows**
4 **tablespoons butter or margarine**	⅓ **cup flaked or shredded coconut**
1 **teaspoon vanilla extract**	2 **tablespoons graham cracker crumbs**
1 **cup plus 2 tablespoons chopped walnuts**	

1. In a 2-quart glass bowl, combine chocolate chips and butter. Heat in a microwave oven on High about 1 minute, until melted and smooth when stirred.

2. Mix in vanilla. Let cool to lukewarm. Stir in 1 cup walnuts and marshmallows.

3. Sprinkle coconut onto a large sheet of wax paper in a 10 x 6-inch rectangle. Spoon half of marshmallow mixture in a log shape down center of coconut. Even up and press mixture together with fingertips. Lifting wax paper to help, shape mixture into a log measuring about 8 to 9 inches long and 1¾ inches in diameter, covering completely with coconut.

4. In a small bowl, mix together remaining 2 tablespoons walnuts and graham cracker crumbs. On another sheet of wax paper, sprinkle mixture in a 10 x 6-inch rectangle. Spoon remaining marshmallow mixture into a log shape on top of crumb-nut mixture. Lifting wax paper, shape into log as above. Wrap logs tightly in wax paper and refrigerate or freeze until chocolate has hardened. With a sharp knife, cut each log into 16 (½-inch) slices. Store in refrigerator.

296   KAHLUA PECAN FUDGE

Prep: 20 minutes   Cook: 10 minutes   Makes: 36 pieces

This spirited fudge is creamy and rich. It's perfect for gift-giving any time of year. Vary the liqueur to suit personal taste.

3 cups miniature marshmallows	1 (5-ounce) can evaporated milk
12 ounces semisweet chocolate chips (2 cups)	1⅓ cups sugar
2 (1-ounce) squares unsweetened chocolate, cut up	4 tablespoons butter
	1 cup chopped pecans
	¼ cup Kahlua or other coffee liqueur

1. In a large bowl, combine marshmallows, chocolate chips, and unsweetened chocolate; set aside.

2. In a heavy 3-quart saucepan, combine evaporated milk, sugar, and butter. Heat to boiling over medium heat, stirring often. Boil, stirring constantly, 6 minutes. Remove from heat and pour over chocolate-marshmallow mixture. Stir until chocolate and marshmallows are completely melted and mixture is smooth. Stir in nuts and Kahlua until well blended.

3. Turn into a buttered 8-inch square pan. Let stand until cool. Then refrigerate until firm. Cut into 36 squares. Store in an airtight container in refrigerator or freeze.

297   CHOCOLATE BUTTERSCOTCH MACADAMIA FUDGE

Prep: 20 minutes   Cook: 10 minutes   Makes: 36 pieces

12 ounces semisweet chocolate chips (2 cups)	2 cups sugar
1 stick (4 ounces) butter, cut into slices	1 (5-ounce) can evaporated milk
½ of a 7-ounce jar marshmallow creme	1 to 1½ cups coarsely chopped macadamia nuts
2 teaspoons vanilla extract	1½ cups butterscotch-flavored chips (9 ounces), melted

1. In a large mixing bowl, combine chocolate chips, butter slices, marshmallow creme, and vanilla; set aside.

2. In a large saucepan, combine sugar and evaporated milk. Cook over low heat, stirring constantly, until mixture comes to a boil. Boil for 6 minutes, stirring constantly. Pour over chocolate chip mixture in bowl and stir quickly until well blended. Stir in nuts.

3. Turn chocolate mixture into a well-buttered 8- or 9-inch square baking pan. Spoon on melted butterscotch chips and using a knife, swirl into chocolate mixture. Refrigerate until set. Cut into 36 squares. Store, covered, in refrigerator.

298 GERMAN CHOCOLATE FUDGE
Prep: 15 minutes   Cook: 10 minutes   Makes: about 2¾ pounds

This light chocolate fudge is flecked throughout with shredded coconut and chopped pecans. Omit them and you'll have a recipe better known as Mamie's Million-Dollar Fudge, which is alleged to have been one of Mrs. Eisenhower's favorite recipes.

6 ounces semisweet chocolate chips (1 cup)	1 (5-ounce) can evaporated milk
1 (4-ounce) bar sweet cooking chocolate, cut into small pieces	1 tablespoon butter Dash of salt
1 (7-ounce) jar marshmallow creme	1 cup flaked or shredded coconut
2 cups sugar	1 cup coarsely chopped pecans

1. In a large bowl, combine chocolate chips, sweet chocolate pieces, and marshmallow creme; set aside.

2. In a heavy 3-quart saucepan, combine sugar, evaporated milk, butter, and salt. Heat to boiling over medium-high heat, stirring often. Cook, stirring constantly, 5 minutes. Remove from heat and pour over chocolate mixture in bowl. Stir vigorously until chocolate is melted and well mixed. Quickly stir in coconut and pecans. Turn into a buttered 8-inch square baking pan; spread evenly.

3. Cool, then refrigerate until well chilled and firm. Cut into squares. Store, covered, in refrigerator or freeze.

299 APRICOT MINI-CHIP SWEETIES
Prep: 10 minutes   Cook: 10 to 12 minutes per batch   Makes: 30

A cinch to prepare and with chocolate in each bite, these make a unique addition to a sweet tray.

1 (6-ounce) package dried apricots, chopped	½ cup powdered sugar
¾ cup chopped pecans	1 tablespoon flour
¾ cup miniature semisweet chocolate chips	1 egg white

1. Preheat oven to 350°F. In a medium bowl, combine apricots, nuts, chocolate chips, powdered sugar, and flour. Mix well with a fork. Stir in unbeaten egg white, mixing thoroughly.

2. Drop mixture by teaspoonfuls (it may be necessary to press mixture together with fingers) 1½ inches apart on well-greased foil-lined cookie sheets. Bake 10 to 12 minutes. Watch carefully to avoid overbaking bottom of sweets.

3. Let cool 5 minutes on pan, then carefully loosen using spatula and transfer to racks to cool completely.

300   PEANUT BUTTER BON BONS

Prep: 20 minutes   Chill: 1 hour   Cook: 1 minute   Makes: 36

These candies have been a family favorite for years. Store them in the refrigerator. Bet you can't eat just one of them!

1 cup chunky peanut butter
2 tablespoons butter, melted
1 cup sifted powdered sugar
1 cup chopped walnuts

6 ounces semisweet chocolate chips (1 cup)
2 tablespoons solid vegetable shortening

1. In a medium bowl, combine peanut butter, butter, and powdered sugar. Blend with a fork until well mixed. Stir in walnuts.

2. Shape mixture into 36 (1-inch) balls. Place on a baking sheet and refrigerate 1 hour.

3. In a 2-cup glass measure, combine chocolate chips and shortening. Heat in a microwave oven on High about 1 minute, or until melted and smooth when stirred.

4. Using a fork, dip balls, one at a time, in melted chocolate; shake off excess. Place on a wax paper-lined baking sheet. Refrigerate until set. Store, covered, in refrigerator.

301   CHOCOLATE ORANGE BON BONS

Prep: 25 minutes   Cook: about 1 minute   Chill: 1 hour
Makes: 40 candies

These no-bake goodies are a breeze to make and keep on hand for an unexpected treat when friends drop by.

1 (9-ounce) package chocolate wafer cookies
¼ cup powdered sugar
⅓ to ½ cup Cointreau, Grand Marnier, or orange juice
6 ounces semisweet chocolate chips (1 cup), melted

3 tablespoons light corn syrup
½ cup finely chopped walnuts or pecans
8 ounces imported white chocolate, melted

1. In a food processor, grind cookies until consistency of fine crumbs. Add powdered sugar and Cointreau and process until well mixed.

2. In a small glass bowl, combine chocolate chips and corn syrup. Heat in microwave oven on High 45 to 60 seconds, or until melted and smooth when stirred. Add to food processor and process until mixed. Mixture will be stiff. Transfer from processor to a medium bowl. Stir in nuts.

3. Shape mixture into 40 (1-inch balls). Place on a wax paper-lined baking sheet. Refrigerate 1 hour. Dip half of each ball into melted white chocolate; place ½-inch apart on wax paper-lined baking sheet. Refrigerate until firm. Store in an airtight container in refrigerator 1 to 2 weeks.

302 ENGLISH BUTTER CHOCOLATE TOFFEE

Prep: 20 minutes   Cook: 45 to 55 minutes   Makes: about 1 pound

This recipe is not difficult to make, but it does require a candy thermometer.

2 sticks (8 ounces) butter	6 ounces semisweet chocolate,
1 cup sugar	melted
1 tablespoon corn syrup	¾ cup diced roasted almonds
1 teaspoon vanilla extract	

1. In a large heavy 4½-quart saucepan, combine butter, sugar, corn syrup, and 3 tablespoons water. Heat over medium heat, stirring often, until butter melts. Cover and heat to boiling over medium-high heat. Boil 1 minute. Remove cover; place a candy thermometer in pan. Cook over medium-high heat until syrup reaches 300°F, stirring often after mixture reaches 250°F to prevent scorching. If mixture begins to darken at sides of pan, reduce heat to medium.

2. Stir in vanilla. Pour toffee immediately into a well-buttered 9-inch square metal pan (do not use glass, or candy will be too difficult to remove). Let cool completely at room temperature.

3. Turn toffee out of pan onto a sheet of wax paper or foil. Spread half of melted chocolate over toffee and sprinkle half of almonds on top, pressing lightly into chocolate. Let stand until chocolate is almost set. Turn over and spread uncoated side with remaining chocolate and sprinkle with remaining nuts. Let stand overnight until chocolate is set and completely dry. Break into pieces. Store in an airtight container at room temperature.

303 CHOCOLATE CREAM CHEESE RASPBERRY FUDGE

Prep: 10 minutes   Cook: none   Chill: 3 hours   Makes: 25 pieces

1 (8-ounce) package cream cheese, softened	1 teaspoon vanilla extract
	Dash of salt
3 cups powdered sugar	4 (1-ounce) squares
2 tablespoons Chambord or other raspberry-flavored liqueur	unsweetened chocolate, melted
	1 cup chopped pecans

1. In a medium bowl, mix together cream cheese and powdered sugar until smooth. Mix in Chambord, vanilla, and salt until well blended. Stir in melted chocolate until thoroughly mixed. Mix in nuts.

2. Spread evenly in a buttered 8-inch square baking pan. Refrigerate several hours, or until firm. Cut into 25 squares. Store, covered, in refrigerator.

304   CHOCOLATE CARAMELS
Prep: 15 minutes   Cook: 40 to 50 minutes   Makes: 36

These are dark and chewy. To hasten the caramelization of the sugar, use a can of sweetened condensed milk. Wrap individually in colored food-safe plastic wrap for festive giving.

2   **sticks (8 ounces) butter**
1   **cup granulated sugar**
1   **cup packed brown sugar**
1   **cup light corn syrup**
1   **(14-ounce) can sweetened condensed milk**

2   **(1-ounce) squares unsweetened chocolate**
1   **teaspoon vanilla extract**
     Dash of salt

1. Butter an 8-inch square baking pan. In a heavy 2½-quart saucepan, combine butter, granulated sugar, brown sugar, and corn syrup. Cook over medium heat, stirring constantly, until butter melts and mixture comes to a boil. Mix in sweetened condensed milk and chocolate, and stir constantly until chocolate is melted. Cook over medium to medium-low heat, stirring often, until mixture reaches 245°F on a candy thermometer, about 40 minutes.

2. Remove from heat and stir in vanilla and salt. Quickly turn into prepared pan. Let stand at room temperature until cool. Cut caramels into 36 squares and wrap each individually in plastic wrap, twisting ends. Or place each caramel in a paper candy cup. Store at room temperature and use within a week or two.

305   ALMOND CHOCOLATE SLICES
Prep: 10 minutes   Cook: 10 to 15 minutes   Chill: 3 hours
Makes: 50

A cruise ship chef shared this recipe with me some years back. These are great to serve on a dessert tray with other sweets. They're sheer simplicity, but delicious.

3   **cups sliced blanched almonds**
14   **ounces semisweet, bittersweet, or imported white chocolate, cut up**

¾   **cup heavy cream**
1   **tablespoon corn syrup**

1. Preheat oven to 325°F. Spread out almonds on a baking sheet and toast in oven 7 to 10 minutes, until light brown.

2. In a medium saucepan, over medium-low heat, heat together chocolate and cream, stirring often, until chocolate is melted and mixture is smooth. Remove from heat and stir in corn syrup and toasted almonds.

3. Turn mixture into a wax paper-lined 8-inch square baking pan. Refrigerate until firm, several hours or overnight. For ease in cutting, turn chilled chocolate square out onto a cutting board, top side up, and cut into 50 sticks 1¼ x ¾ inch. Store, tightly wrapped, in refrigerator.

---

306   CHOCOLATE LEAVES
Prep: 25 minutes   Cook: 1½ to 5 minutes   Chill: 25 to 30 minutes
Makes: 14 to 15

If you've never made chocolate leaves, give them a whirl. They gussy up a dessert with very little effort, and people are always impressed. Although chocolate leaves may look difficult and intimidating to make, they're really a snap once you've had a little practice. Be sure to spread the leaves with a thick coating of chocolate. If it's too thin, the chocolate leaves will crumble and break when you separate the leaf from the chocolate.

**14 to 15 nontoxic stiff leaves
with well-defined veins
and with ¼ to ½ inch of
stem attached: lemon,
orange, rose, or camellia,
for example**

**3 ounces semisweet,
bittersweet, or imported
white chocolate or coating
chocolate**

1. Wash leaves and dry thoroughly with a towel. Carefully melt chocolate in top of a double boiler or in a small glass bowl in a microwave oven until melted and smooth. Using a narrow metal spatula or a dull knife, spread a thick layer of chocolate on underside of each leaf to within ¹⁄₁₆ inch of edge. Do not let chocolate go over edges of leaves. Place leaves, chocolate side up, on a wax paper-lined plate or tray. Refrigerate until chocolate is firm, 25 to 30 minutes, or longer.

2. To remove chocolate from leaf, grasp stem of leaf and gently peel off leaf to separate. Touch chocolate as little as possible to avoid fingerprints and smudging. Discard green leaves. Refrigerate or freeze chocolate leaves in an airtight container until ready to use.

Chapter 13

Chocolate in the Cookie Jar

Who doesn't love chocolate cookies? For many, cookies bring back treasured childhood memories. One of America's most beloved cookies, the legendary Original Toll House Cookie, is sprinkled with chocolate throughout. Another one of our favorites, the brownie, which has a special place in the cookie hall of fame, is usually synonymous with chocolate in a myriad of forms and flavors, from bittersweet to white.

Some people like their cookies soft and moist, others prefer them crisp and chewy, and still others enjoy them buttery rich and sweet. But at one time or another all of us cookie monsters—young and old alike—dream of raiding a cookie jar filled with wonderful homemade cookies, with their various tastes—especially chocolate.

Cookies come in an endless variety of sizes and shapes, including bar, drop, refrigerator, molded, pressed, and rolled. Bar cookies are my favorites because they are the easiest to bake, especially when time is at a premium. Because all of the dough is baked at once and then cut, bar cookies yield the largest number of cookies with the least amount of effort.

Drop cookies can also be whipped out rather quickly if you arm yourself with one of my favorite cookie-making gadgets—a convenient 1¼- to 1½-inch diameter ice cream scoop with an automatic release lever (available at specialty kitchenware or gourmet shops or restaurant equipment supply stores), which releases the scooped-up dough easily with the pressing motion of a few fingers. I have different size scoops (they're a boon for shaping truffle candies as well) and couldn't live without them. Not only do the scoops speed up cookie making, but you'll have no sticky, messy fingers to contend with to boot.

The recipe collection that follows includes numerous flavors—orange, raspberry, and various nuts, to name a few—and texture options to suit all kinds of tastes. Even better, most are easily prepared. Most recipes use an electric mixer or food processor and the one-bowl method for mixing the ingredients. In most cases sifting isn't necessary.

To ensure cookie-baking success, keep these hints in mind. Always preheat the oven 10 to 15 minutes ahead and check the temperature with an oven thermometer. An oven that's calibrated 25 to 50 degrees incorrectly can mean the different between success and failure.

For best results, shiny, heavy-gauge aluminum

cookie sheets without sides are recommended for most cookies. (Of course if a recipe calls for a 10 x 15-inch jelly-roll pan, such a pan will have sides.) Cookie sheets should be two inches shorter and narrower than the oven. I have found a 14 x 17-inch cookie sheet the most practical size.

Follow recipe directions when it comes to greasing cookie sheets. Generally use solid vegetable shortening for greasing pans unless the recipe specifies otherwise. Strive to make all cookies in the same batch the same size, shape, and thickness for uniform baking results. For most even browning, cookies are best baked one sheet at a time in the center of the oven. Baking times in the recipes in this chapter are based on baking one sheet at a time.

Be sure to watch cookies carefully to avoid overbaking. Baking times in recipes are at best guidelines, so always check cookies three to four minutes before the minimum baking time suggested in the recipe; use a timer to avoid guessing. Use common sense in judging when cookies and brownies are done. If in doubt, underbake cookies and brownies rather than overbaking, as they continue to cook after removal from the oven and will harden upon standing.

Alternate cookie sheets between batches, so they have time to cool down, to avoid undesirable spreading and misshapen cookies. Let baked cookies cool completely before storing. Cookies are best stored in a cool place. Store crisp cookies in a jar or container with a loose-fitting lid and soft cookies in a tightly covered container. Chocolate cookies are best eaten fresh, but many can be stored in the freezer a month if wrapped airtight; any longer and they lose flavor and quality.

For those mad about brownies, we've included several delicious versions. There are several outstanding cookie variations on the bar theme including Chocolate Peanut Crisp Squares, Chocolate Florentine Triangles, Chocolate Turtle Cookie Squares, Chocolate Raspberry Streusel Crumb Bars, and White Chocolate Macadamia Bars.

In this chapter you'll find plenty of good ideas for filling the cookie jar, lunch boxes, cookie platters, and trays and for just plain good munching. So it's time to head to the kitchen, roll up your sleeves, and get baking some cookies.

307   DOUBLE CHOCOLATE BROWNIE COOKIES
Prep: 15 minutes   Cook: 10 to 12 minutes per batch
Makes: about 3 dozen

Loaded with chocolate, these are easily prepared with a little help from the microwave oven. Kids, young and old, love them.

2 **cups semisweet chocolate chips (12 ounces)**	1 **teaspoon vanilla extract**
4 **tablespoons butter**	¾ **cup sugar**
⅓ **cup firmly packed unsweetened cocoa powder**	¼ **cup flour**
	¼ **teaspoon baking powder**
2 **eggs**	1 **cup chopped pecans**

1. Preheat oven to 350°F. In a 2-quart glass bowl, combine 1 cup chocolate chips and butter. Heat in a microwave oven on High 1 to 1½ minutes, until chocolate is melted and smooth when stirred.

2. Stir in cocoa until blended. With a fork, beat in eggs, vanilla, and sugar until well mixed. Stir in flour and baking powder until well blended. Stir in pecans and remaining 1 cup chocolate chips.

3. Drop by rounded tablespoonfuls 2 inches apart onto foil-lined cookie sheets. Bake 10 to 12 minutes, or until tops are cracked slightly. Let cookies cool on pans 5 minutes, then remove to wire racks to let cool completely.

---

308   PEANUT BUTTER LACE-FILLED COOKIES
Prep: 20 minutes   Cook: 10 to 12 minutes   Makes: 3½ dozen

These are sensational. The cookies are delicious sandwiched together in twos with melted chocolate in between, or you can simply spread the bottom of each cookie with melted semisweet chocolate.

½ **cup light corn syrup**	½ **cup packed brown sugar**
½ **cup smooth or crunchy peanut butter**	¼ **cup flour**
5 **tablespoons butter**	¼ **teaspoon baking powder**
1 **cup quick-cooking or old-fashioned oats**	3 **to 4 ounces semisweet chocolate, melted**

1. Preheat oven to 300°F. In a 2-quart saucepan, bring corn syrup to a boil over medium heat. Add peanut butter and butter, reduce heat to low, and cook, stirring constantly, until butter is melted and mixture is well blended. Remove from heat. Stir in oats, brown sugar, flour, and baking powder.

2. Drop by level teaspoonfuls about 3 inches apart onto foil-lined cookie sheets. Bake 10 to 12 minutes, or until golden. Let cookies cool at least 2 minutes on pans before removing with a wide spatula to wire racks to let cool completely.

3. When cool, sandwich 2 cookies together with a little melted chocolate in between. Let stand at room temperature or refrigerate until chocolate is set.

309   FUDGY CHOCOLATE COOKIES
Prep: 20 minutes   Cook: 10 to 12 minutes   Makes: 20 to 22

These cookies are rich and chewy, designed for the most ardent chocolate fan.

2½ cups semisweet chocolate
    chips (15 ounces)
2 (1-ounce) squares
    unsweetened chocolate,
    broken up
3 tablespoons solid vegetable
    shortening

½ cup sugar
3 tablespoons light corn syrup
1 egg
1 teaspoon vanilla extract
⅔ cup flour
½ teaspoon baking powder
1 cup chopped walnuts

1. Preheat oven to 350°F. In a 2-quart glass bowl, combine 1½ cups chocolate chips, unsweetened chocolate, and shortening. Heat in a microwave oven on High about 1½ minutes, or until melted and smooth when stirred. Let cool slightly.

2. Add sugar, corn syrup, egg, and vanilla; blend well. Mix in flour and baking powder. Stir in remaining 1 cup chocolate chips and nuts.

3. Drop dough by rounded teaspoonfuls (or use a small ice cream scoop) 1½ inches apart onto lightly greased cookie sheets. With fingertips, flatten tops slightly.

4. Bake 10 to 12 minutes. Let cookies cool on pans 5 minutes, then remove to wire racks to let cool completely.

310   CHOCOLATE MOCHA CHIP COOKIES
Prep: 20 minutes   Cook: 10 to 12 minutes per batch
Makes: 4½ dozen

2 sticks (8 ounces) butter
1¾ cups sugar
2 eggs
1 teaspoon vanilla extract
4 (1-ounce) squares
    unsweetened chocolate,
    melted

1 tablespoon instant coffee
    powder dissolved in 1
    tablespoon boiling water
1¾ cups flour
    Dash of salt
2 cups chopped walnuts
    12 ounces semisweet
    chocolate chips (2 cups)

1. Preheat oven to 350°F. In a large bowl, beat butter and sugar with an electric mixer on medium speed until light and fluffy, about 2 minutes. Beat in eggs and vanilla and beat 1 to 2 minutes longer. Add melted chocolate and dissolved coffee and beat 1 minute, until thoroughly blended. Beat in flour and salt until well blended.

2. Stir in walnuts and chocolate chips. Drop by tablespoonfuls 2 inches apart onto ungreased cookie sheets.

3. Bake 10 to 12 minutes, or until barely set. Let cookies cool on pans 5 minutes before removing to wire racks to let cool completely.

311   CHOCOLATE COCONUT PECAN COOKIES
Prep: 10 minutes   Cook: 10 to 11 minutes   Makes: 3½ dozen

2   sticks (8 ounces) butter or
     margarine
2   cups sugar
2   eggs
2   tablespoons light corn syrup
2   teaspoons vanilla extract
2   cups flour

¾   cup unsweetened cocoa
     powder
1   teaspoon baking soda
1½ cups shredded or flaked
     coconut
1   cup chopped pecans

1. Preheat oven to 375°F. In a large bowl, beat butter and sugar with an electric mixer on medium speed until light and fluffy, 1 to 2 minutes. Add eggs, corn syrup, and vanilla and beat until well blended. Beat in flour, cocoa, and baking soda until thoroughly incorporated. Stir in coconut and pecans.

2. Drop by heaping tablespoonfuls onto ungreased cookie sheets. Do not flatten cookies. Bake 10 to 11 minutes. Do not overbake. Let cookies cool 1 to 2 minutes on pans, then remove to racks to let cool completely.

312   CHOCOLATE CHOCOLATE CHIP COOKIES
*Prep: 20 minutes   Cook: 10 to 12 minutes per batch
Makes: 34 (3-inch) cookies*

2   sticks (8 ounces) butter,
     softened
1½ cups granulated sugar
1   cup packed brown sugar
2   eggs
1   tablespoon vanilla extract
2¾ cups flour

1   teaspoon baking soda
1   teaspoon baking powder
½   cup unsweetened cocoa
     powder
12 ounces semisweet chocolate
     chips (2 cups)

1. Preheat oven to 350°F. In a large bowl, beat together butter, granulated sugar, brown sugar, eggs, and vanilla with an electric mixer on medium speed until light and fluffy, 3 to 4 minutes. Beat in flour, baking soda, baking powder, and cocoa until well blended.

2. Stir in chocolate chips. Drop dough by generous tablespoonfuls 2 inches apart on ungreased cookie sheets.

3. Bake 10 to 12 minutes, watching carefully, until set. Do not overbake. Let cookies cool on pans 3 to 4 minutes, then remove to racks to let cool completely.

Variation: **MOCHA CINNAMON COOKIES**

Add 1 tablespoon instant coffee powder and 2 tablespoons cinnamon to dough along with flour.

313   LACY ALMOND COOKIES
Prep: 20 minutes   Cook: 8 to 10 minutes per batch   Makes: 25

These delicate lace cookies, half-coated with chocolate, make a special holiday treat.

4 tablespoons butter	½ cup finely chopped
¼ cup light corn syrup	blanched almonds
⅓ cup packed brown sugar	¾ teaspoon vanilla extract
½ cup flour	4 ounces semisweet chocolate, melted

1. Preheat oven to 325°F. In medium saucepan, combine butter, corn syrup, and brown sugar. Heat to boiling over medium heat, stirring occasionally. Boil 1 minute. Remove from heat and quickly stir in flour, almonds, and vanilla until well mixed.

2. Drop mixture by teaspoonfuls at least 3 inches apart on ungreased foil-lined cookie sheets. Bake 8 to 10 minutes, or until golden. For easiest removal from pans, let cookies cool thoroughly on foil on pan. When cool, carefully peel foil from bottom of cookies.

3. Spread melted chocolate on half of each cookie, front and back. Place on wax paper-lined cookie sheets; refrigerate until chocolate is firm. Wrap air-tight and store in refrigerator.

314   CHOCOLATE WHAMMIE COOKIES
Prep: 15 minutes   Cook: 15 to 18 minutes per batch   Makes: 30

These cookies are the most chocolatey ever!

8 (1-ounce) squares semisweet chocolate, cut up	1 teaspoon baking powder
1 stick (4 ounces) butter	⅛ teaspoon salt
2 eggs	1½ cups coarsely chopped pecans
⅔ cup sugar	6 ounces semisweet
2 teaspoons vanilla extract	chocolate chips (1 cup)
½ cup flour	

1. Preheat oven to 325°F. In a 2-quart glass bowl, heat chocolate squares and butter in a microwave oven on High about 1½ to 2 minutes, or until melted and smooth when stirred.

2. Whisk in eggs, sugar, and vanilla until well blended. Whisk in flour, baking powder, and salt. Stir in pecans and chocolate chips.

3. Drop batter by tablespoonfuls 2 inches apart onto lightly greased cookie sheets. Bake 15 to 18 minutes, or until tops are shiny and cracked. Let cookies cool 10 minutes on pans, then transfer to racks to let cool completely. Store in a tightly covered container.

315 FUDGY WUDGY CHOCOLATE COOKIES
Prep: 10 minutes   Cook: 9 to 10 minutes per batch   Makes: 45 cookies

12 ounces semisweet
　　chocolate chips (2 cups)
2 tablespoons butter
¾ cup flour

2 teaspoons vanilla extract
1 (14-ounce) can sweetened
　　condensed milk
2 cups chopped pecans

1. Preheat oven to 350°F. In a 2-quart glass bowl, cook chocolate with butter in a microwave oven on High 1 to 2 minutes, or until melted and smooth when stirred. Mix in flour until well blended. Add vanilla and sweetened condensed milk and mix well. Stir in pecans.

2. Drop dough by tablespoonfuls 2 inches apart onto 2 greased foil-lined cookie sheets. Bake 9 to 10 minutes (cookies will be dull on top and soft). Let cookies cool on baking sheets. Carefully remove from foil.

316 PEANUT BUTTER MILK CHOCOLATE CHIPPERS
Prep: 15 minutes   Cook: 10 to 12 minutes per batch
Makes: 20 cookies

The combination of peanut butter and milk chocolate is irresistible in these cookies. Enjoy them warm for a special treat.

½ cup chunky peanut butter
1 stick (4 ounces) butter or
　　margarine, softened
¾ cup packed brown sugar
½ cup granulated sugar

2 teaspoons vanilla extract
1 egg
1½ cups flour
1 teaspoon baking soda
1 cup milk chocolate chips

1. Preheat oven to 350°F. In a medium bowl, beat peanut butter, butter, and sugars with an electric mixer on medium speed until light and fluffy, 2 to 3 minutes. Add vanilla and egg; beat until well blended. Add flour and baking soda; mix well. Stir in chocolate chips.

2. Drop dough by heaping tablespoons into mounds 2 inches apart in lightly greased cookie sheets. Flatten cookies slightly. Bake 10 to 12 minutes, or until golden.

3. Let cookies cool 5 minutes on cookie sheets before removing to wire racks to let cool completely.

317   TRIPLE CHOCOLATE COOKIES

Prep: 20 minutes   Cook: 10 to 11 minutes per batch   Makes: 4 dozen

These cookies are dotted with both semisweet and white chocolate pieces.

1½ cups quick-cooking oats
2½ sticks (10 ounces) butter, softened
2 cups sugar
2 eggs
1 tablespoon vanilla extract
   Dash of salt
¾ cup unsweetened cocoa powder

3 cups flour
1 teaspoon baking soda
1 teaspoon baking powder
1½ cups semisweet chocolate chips (9 ounces)
6 ounces imported white chocolate, broken into ½- to ¾-inch chunks (1 cup)

1. Preheat oven to 350°F. In a food processor, grind oats to a fine powder; set aside.

2. In a large bowl, beat butter and sugar with an electric mixer on medium speed until light and fluffy, 2 to 3 minutes. Beat in eggs, vanilla, and salt until well blended. Add cocoa, flour, ground oatmeal, baking soda, and baking powder and beat until well blended, 2 to 3 minutes. Mix in chocolate chips and white chocolate pieces. Batter will be stiff.

3. With a 1¼-inch ice cream scoop or with heaping tablespoonfuls, place batter 3 inches apart on lightly greased cookie sheets. With fingertips, press tops down slightly. Bake 10 to 11 minutes, or until set but still soft. Let cookies cool on pans 3 minutes, then remove to wire racks to let cool completely.

318   CHOCOLATE CHUNK COOKIES

Prep: 15 minutes   Cook: 12 to 14 minutes per batch   Makes: 32

These are buttery, rich, and flat with chunks of imported chocolate and pecans.

2 sticks (8 ounces) unsalted butter, softened
1 cup packed brown sugar
1 tablespoon vanilla extract
1 egg
1¾ cups flour

8 ounces imported bittersweet chocolate, cut into ½-inch pieces (such as Lindt or Tobler)
1½ cups coarsely chopped pecans or walnuts (6 ounces)

1. Preheat oven to 350°F. In a medium bowl, beat together butter and brown sugar with an electric mixer on medium speed until light and fluffy, 1 to 2 minutes. Add vanilla and egg and beat until well blended. Beat in flour. Stir in chocolate pieces and nuts, mixing well.

2. Drop by tablespoonfuls 3 inches apart onto ungreased cookie sheets. Bake 12 to 14 minutes, or until edges are slightly browned. Do not overbake. Let cookies cool on pans about 2 minutes before removing to wire racks to let cool completely.

---

319 CHOCOLATE CHIP COOKIE MIX

Marian Burros, a food writer for *The New York Times* and author of several cookbooks, shared this cookie mix recipe with me. Based on the original Toll House cookie recipe created in Massachusetts more than 50 years ago, it's been a favorite with her followers for years. When you have the mix handy in your kitchen, you can turn out a batch of cookies in no time flat.

9 cups unbleached
   all-purpose flour
1 tablespoon plus 1 teaspoon
   baking soda
2 teaspoons salt
3 cups packed dark brown
   sugar

3 cups granulated sugar
4 cups solid vegetable
   shortening*
4 cups chopped pecans
48 ounces semisweet chocolate
   chips (8 cups)

In a large bowl, combine flour, baking soda, salt, brown sugar, and granulated sugar; mix well. Using fingers, mix in shortening until mixture is crumbly. Stir in nuts and chocolate chips. Store in an airtight container in a cool, dry place up to 6 months. Mix will keep longer in the refrigerator or freezer. Keep on hand to use to make cookies. Makes about 28 cups.

Butter or margarine can be used instead of shortening, but mix must be stored in refrigerator or freezer.

CHOCOLATE CHIP MIX COOKIES
Prep: 10 minutes   Cook: 8 to 12 minutes per batch
Makes: 48 large or 64 small

2 eggs, slightly beaten
1 teaspoon vanilla extract

7 cups Chocolate Chip Cookie
   Mix (recipe above)

1. Preheat oven to 375°F. In a small bowl, beat eggs and vanilla until well blended. Place cookie mix in a large bowl. Add egg mixture and blend well. Dough will be heavy.

2. For large cookies, drop dough by heaping tablespoonfuls onto greased cookie sheets. For small cookies, drop batter by heaping teaspoonfuls. Bake 10 to 12 minutes for large cookies; 8 to 10 minutes for small cookies. For flatter cookies, pat cookies with back of spoon. Let cookies cool slightly on pans, then remove to racks to let cool completely.

320   MONSTER CHOCOLATE CHIP COOKIES
Prep: 15 minutes   Cook: 8 to 10 minutes per batch
Makes: 3½ dozen large cookies

2 sticks (8 ounces) butter,
    softened
1 cup packed dark brown
    sugar
¾ cup granulated sugar
2 eggs
2 teaspoons vanilla extract

3 cups flour
¾ teaspoon baking soda
½ teaspoon salt
12 ounces semisweet chocolate
    chips (2 cups)
1 cup chopped walnuts or
    macadamia nuts

1. Preheat oven to 350°F. In a large bowl, beat together butter and sugars with an electric mixer on medium speed until light and fluffy, 2 to 3 minutes. Beat in eggs and vanilla and continue beating 2 minutes. Beat in flour, baking soda, and salt until well blended, 1 to 2 minutes. Stir in chocolate chips and nuts.

2. Drop dough by generous tablespoonfuls 2 inches apart on foil-lined cookie sheets (about 12 to a pan). Flatten dough rounds slightly with fingertips. Bake 8 to 10 minutes, or until very light golden. Do not overbake or cookies will be too hard when cool. Let cookies stand 5 minutes, then remove to wire racks to let cool completely.

321   MACADAMIA COCONUT CHOCOLATE CHUNK COOKIES
Prep: 20 minutes   Cook: 10 to 13 minutes per batch   Makes: 3 dozen

For best results, use raw unsalted macadamia nuts in this recipe. Toast them, if desired.

1 stick (4 ounces) butter
½ cup solid vegetable
    shortening
1½ cups granulated sugar
½ cup packed brown sugar
2 eggs
1 tablespoon vanilla extract
    Dash of salt
3¾ cups flour
1 teaspoon baking soda

1 teaspoon baking powder
2 cups flaked or shredded
    coconut
1 cup macadamia nuts,
    coarsely chopped
6 ounces bittersweet or
    semisweet chocolate, cut
    into ½-inch chunks, or
    large chips

1. Preheat oven to 350°F. In a large bowl, beat together butter, shortening, granulated sugar, and brown sugar with an electric mixer on medium speed until light and fluffy, 2 to 3 minutes. Beat in eggs, vanilla, and salt until well blended, about 1 minute. Beat in flour, baking soda, and baking powder until thoroughly incorporated. Beat in coconut; batter will be stiff. Stir in nuts and chocolate chunks.

2. Using a small ice cream scoop or heaping tablespoon, form dough into large balls the size of golf balls. Place 3 inches apart on lightly greased cookie sheets. Flatten cookies slightly.

3. Bake 10 to 13 minutes, or until light golden. Do not overbake. Let cookies cool on pan 5 minutes, then remove to racks to let cool completely.

322   COCONUTTY-CHOCO-WALNUT BARS
Prep: 20 minutes   Cook: 35 to 40 minutes   Makes: 40 bars

This is an easy way to make lots of cookies in a hurry in a single pan. These are wonderful for party or holiday cookie trays.

2 cups flour
⅓ cup granulated sugar
2 sticks (8 ounces) plus
    1 tablespoon butter
4 eggs
1 tablespoon milk or water
⅔ cup packed brown sugar

1 cup dark corn syrup
2 teaspoons vanilla extract
1½ cups flaked coconut
1½ cups finely chopped walnuts
1 cup miniature semisweet
    chocolate chips (6 ounces)
¼ cup powdered sugar

1. Preheat oven to 350°F. To make butter crust, in a food processor, combine flour and granulated sugar. Cut 1½ sticks cold butter into pieces and add to processor. Process with 8 quick on-and-off turns. Mix together 1 egg and milk and with machine on, add through feed tube; blend just until dough forms a ball and leaves sides of bowl. Press dough into bottom and up sides of a foil-lined 10 x 15-inch jelly-roll pan.

2. Bake 10 minutes. Remove crust from oven; leave oven on.

3. Prepare topping. Melt remaining 5 tablespoons butter. In a large bowl, combine remaining 3 eggs, brown sugar, corn syrup, vanilla, and melted butter. Beat with a fork until blended. Mix in coconut, walnuts, and chocolate chips. Spoon evenly over prebaked crust.

4. Return to oven and bake 25 to 30 minutes, or until golden brown. Let cool before cutting into 40 (1½ x 2½-inch) bars. Before removing from pan, sift powdered sugar over top.

323   MUD BARS

Prep: 25 minutes   Cook: 25 to 30 minutes   Chill: 4 to 5 hours
Makes: 12 bars

A favorite with kids.

3 (1-ounce) squares
    unsweetened chocolate,
    cut up
1½ sticks (6 ounces) butter or
    margarine
3 eggs
1½ cups sugar
1½ teaspoons vanilla extract

¾ cup flour
1 cup chopped walnuts
1 cup shredded coconut
    (optional)
1 (7-ounce) jar marshmallow
    creme
Chocolate Mud Frosting
    (recipe follows)

1. Preheat oven to 350°F. In a 2-quart glass bowl, combine chocolate and butter. Heat in microwave oven on High 1½ to 2 minutes, stirring once or twice until smooth.

2. With a fork, beat in eggs, sugar, and vanilla until well blended. Add flour and mix well. Stir in walnuts and coconut. Spread mixture in a well greased 7 x 11-inch baking pan.

3. Bake 25 to 30 minutes, until set around edges. Brownies should be moist in center. Do not overbake.

4. Remove from oven and immediately drop spoonfuls of marshmallow creme all over warm brownies. Let stand 5 minutes. Spread marshmallow topping evenly. Refrigerate until completely cooled, 3 to 4 hours.

5. Spread Chocolate Mud Frosting over marshmallow topping. Refrigerate at least 1 hour, or until set, before cutting into 12 (3½ x 2-inch) bars. Bars can be cut smaller, if desired.

CHOCOLATE MUD FROSTING

¾ cup semisweet chocolate
    chips
3 tablespoons milk

½ teaspoon vanilla extract
1 tablespoon light corn syrup

In a 1- or 2-cup glass measure, heat together chocolate chips and milk in a microwave oven on High 45 to 50 seconds, or until chocolate is melted and smooth when stirred. Add vanilla and corn syrup and blend well. Refrigerate, stirring occasionally, until thickened to frosting consistency.

324   OATMEAL PEANUT CHOCOLATE SQUARES

Prep: 15 minutes   Cook: 17 to 19 minutes   Chill: 30 to 40 minutes
Makes: 25

1 stick (4 ounces) butter or margarine, melted
1 cup flour
½ cup packed brown sugar
1 cup quick-cooking oats
1 teaspoon vanilla extract

6 ounces semisweet chocolate chips (1 cup)
⅓ cup chunky or smooth peanut butter
½ cup chopped peanuts

1. Preheat oven to 350°F. In a medium bowl, combine butter, flour, brown sugar, oats, and vanilla; mix until blended. Press evenly over bottom of a buttered 8-inch square baking pan. Bake 16 to 18 minutes, or until golden around edges. Let cool.

2. Meanwhile, in a 2-cup glass measure, combine chocolate chips and peanut butter. Heat in microwave oven on High about 1 minute, or until melted and smooth when stirred.

3. Spread chocolate mixture over baked crust. Sprinkle peanuts on top. Refrigerate until topping is almost firm, 30 to 40 minutes. Cut into 25 squares. Store, covered, in refrigerator.

325   CHOCOLATE COCONUT BARS

Prep: 15 minutes   Cook: 28 to 30 minutes   Makes: 40 bars

Loaded with coconut, these easy bar cookies are reminiscent of a popular candy.

1 stick (4 ounces) butter or margarine, melted
2 cups chocolate wafer or chocolate chip cookie crumbs
2 cups flaked or shredded coconut

1 (14-ounce) can sweetened condensed milk
12 ounces semisweet chocolate chips (2 cups), melted

1. Preheat oven to 350°F. In a medium bowl, combine melted butter and cookie crumbs; mix well. Press into bottom of an ungreased 9 x 13-inch baking pan. Bake 10 minutes.

2. Remove crust from oven. Sprinkle coconut over crust. Pour sweetened condensed milk evenly over all. Return to oven and bake 18 to 20 minutes, or until coconut begins to brown lightly around edges of pan. Let cool in pan.

3. Spread melted chocolate evenly over top. Let stand until set or refrigerate until firm. Cut cooled cookies into 40 (1¾ x 1½-inch) bars.

326 CHOCOLATE RASPBERRY STREUSEL CRUMB BARS

Prep: 25 minutes   Cook: 30 to 35 minutes   Makes: 48

The favorite combination of raspberry and chocolate is hard to resist in these sensational bar cookies. They're a wonderful cookie offering any time of year.

1½ cups flour	½ cup seedless raspberry jam
½ cup sugar	1¼ cups semisweet chocolate
1 stick (4 ounces) butter, cut	chips (7½ ounces)
into pieces, softened	Crumb Topping (recipe
3 tablespoons heavy cream	follows)
1 teaspoon vanilla extract	

1. Preheat oven to 350°F. To make shortbread base, in a food processor, combine flour and sugar and process a few seconds until mixed. Add butter, cream, and vanilla and process until mixture holds together.

2. Press evenly over bottom of a foil-lined 9 x 13-inch shallow baking pan. Bake 12 to 15 minutes, or until very light golden.

3. Place spoonfuls of jam on top of warm crust. Spread evenly with a table knife. Sprinkle chocolate chips evenly over jam. Then top with Crumb Topping, sprinkling evenly over all. Return pan to oven and bake 18 to 20 minutes longer, or until crumb topping is golden. Cool completely, then cut into 48 bar cookies.

CRUMB TOPPING

¾ cup flour	⅓ cup sugar
5⅓ tablespoons butter, cut into	1 teaspoon vanilla extract
pieces, softened	½ cup chopped walnuts

In a food processor, combine flour, butter, sugar, vanilla, and walnuts. Process with quick on/off motions until mixture resembles coarse crumbs.

327 WALNUT CHOCOLATE CARAMEL BARS

Prep: 20 minutes   Cook: 32 to 40 minutes   Makes: 48 bars

2 cups flour	½ cup heavy cream
1 cup granulated sugar	½ cup light corn syrup
1½ sticks (6 ounces) butter, cut	2 teaspoons vanilla extract
up, softened	3 cups chopped walnuts or
¾ cup packed brown sugar	pecans (about 12 ounces)
½ cup unsweetened cocoa	
powder	

1. Preheat oven to 350°F. In a food processor, combine flour and ½ cup granulated sugar. Process a few seconds to blend. Add butter and 2 tablespoons water. Process in short, then longer, on-and-off turns until mixture clings together and forms a dough.

2. Press dough into a foil-lined 10 x 15 x 1-inch jelly-roll pan. Bake 12 to 15 minutes, or until crust is light golden.

3. Meanwhile, in a large bowl, combine remaining ½ cup granulated sugar, brown sugar, cocoa, cream, corn syrup, and vanilla. Stir until well blended. Stir in walnuts.

4. Carefully spoon mixture over crust. Spread evenly with knife. Return to oven and bake 20 to 25 minutes longer, or until bubbly all over. Let cool in pan 1 hour or longer before cutting into 48 bars.

---

328 LAYERED CHOCOLATE NUT BARS
Prep: 20 minutes   Cook: 43 to 48 minutes   Makes: 40 bars

A trio of layers—cookie crust, solid chocolate, and nutty topping—stacks up to something mighty delicious in these bar cookies that are mixed and baked in a single pan.

1   **stick (4 ounces) plus 5⅓ tablespoons butter or margarine, softened**
1¼   **cups flour**
⅔   **cup plus 3 tablespoons granulated sugar**
1   **teaspoon baking powder**
2   **tablespoons heavy cream**
2   **eggs**

2   **cups chopped walnuts (about 8 ounces)**
2   **tablespoons grated orange zest (optional)**
2   **teaspoons vanilla extract**
12   **ounces semisweet chocolate chips (2 cups)**
   Powdered sugar

1. Preheat oven to 350°F. To make crust, in a food processor, combine 1 stick butter, flour, 3 tablespoons granulated sugar, and baking powder; process until well blended. With machine on, add cream through feed tube and process until dough clings together in a stiff ball. Press dough evenly over bottom of an ungreased 9 x 13-inch baking pan. Bake 10 minutes.

2. Meanwhile, melt remaining 5⅓ tablespoons butter. In a medium bowl, beat together eggs and remaining ⅔ cup granulated sugar with an electric mixer on medium speed until light, about 2 minutes. Beat in melted butter. Stir in nuts, orange zest, and vanilla. Set nut topping aside.

3. Remove crust from oven; leave oven on. Immediately sprinkle chocolate chips over crust. Return pan to oven and bake 2 minutes to melt chocolate. With a knife, spread chocolate evenly over crust. Carefully spread nut topping over chocolate.

4. Return pan to oven. Bake 30 to 35 minutes longer, or until light golden brown. Let cool in pan several hours or overnight. Carefully cut cooled cookies into 40 (1¾ x 1½-inch) bars. Sift powdered sugar over top.

329   LAYERED NUTTY CHOCOLATE SQUARES
Prep: 20 minutes   Cook: 17 to 19½ minutes   Chill: 2 to 3 hours
Makes: 45

These are yummy—part cookie, part candy.

1½ sticks (6 ounces) plus 1
    tablespoon butter or
    margarine, softened
¾ cup packed brown sugar
1 egg
1½ teaspoons vanilla extract
1½ cups flour

9 ounces semisweet chocolate
    chips (1½ cups)
⅓ cup light corn syrup
2 cups salted peanuts or
    coarsely chopped salted
    pecans

1. Preheat oven to 350°F. In a medium bowl, combine 1½ sticks butter and brown sugar. Beat with an electric mixer on medium speed until light and fluffy, 2 to 3 minutes. Beat in egg and 1 teaspoon vanilla until blended. Add flour and beat until well blended. Press dough evenly in bottom of a foil-lined 9 x 13-inch baking pan. Bake 16 to 18 minutes, or until light golden. Let cool 10 to 15 minutes.

2. Meanwhile, in a 1-quart glass bowl combine chocolate chips and corn syrup. Heat in microwave oven on High 1 to 1½ minutes, stirring until smooth. Stir in remaining 1 tablespoon butter and remaining ½ teaspoon vanilla until blended.

3. Spread chocolate mixture evenly over baked crust. Sprinkle nuts over top; press in gently. Refrigerate until set, 2 to 3 hours. Cut into 45 squares.

330   CHOCOLATE MACAROON BARS
Prep: 25 minutes   Cook: 37 to 42 minutes   Makes: 48

These European-style bars have a layer of raspberry filling sandwiched between a chocolate crust and a ground almond macaroon-like topping.

1 stick (4 ounces) butter
3 (1-ounce) squares
    unsweetened chocolate
2 cups granulated sugar
2 whole eggs
2 teaspoons vanilla extract
1 cup flour
½ cup seedless red raspberry
    or boysenberry jam

1 tablespoon Cointreau or
    orange-flavored liqueur
1½ cups finely ground almonds
4 egg whites
¼ teaspoon salt
    Powdered sugar

1. Preheat oven to 350°F. Line a 9 x 13-inch baking pan with aluminum foil. Grease foil.

2. To prepare crust, in a 1-quart glass bowl, heat butter and chocolate in a microwave oven on High 1½ to 2 minutes, or until melted and smooth when stirred. Whisk in 1 cup granulated sugar, whole eggs, and 1 teaspoon vanilla until blended. Beat in flour. Spread in prepared pan.

3. Bake 15 minutes. Remove crust from oven. Increase oven temperature to 375°F.

4. In a small bowl, mix together jam and Cointreau until smooth. Spread over chocolate crust. In a food processor, combine almonds, egg whites, remaining 1 teaspoon vanilla, remaining 1 cup granulated sugar, and salt. Process until well blended. Carefully spoon over jam, spreading evenly to cover completely.

5. Bake 20 to 25 minutes, or until top is golden. Let cool, then cut into 48 bars 1⅝ x 1½ inches. Sift powdered sugar over top.

---

331 BITTERSWEET CHOCOLATE WALNUT SQUARES

Prep: 15 minutes   Cook: 25 to 30 minutes   Makes: 25

1 cup flour
1 stick (4 ounces) plus 2 tablespoons butter or margarine, cut up, softened
3 tablespoons brown sugar
1½ teaspoons vanilla extract
½ cup heavy cream
3 ounces bittersweet or semisweet chocolate, cut up

1 egg
1 teaspoon instant espresso powder
⅓ cup granulated sugar
1½ tablespoons cornstarch
1 cup chopped walnuts
Powdered sugar

1. Preheat oven to 375°F. To prepare crust, in a food processor, combine flour, 1 stick butter, and brown sugar. Process until blended. Add vanilla and process until dough clings together in a ball. Press evenly into bottom of an ungreased 8-inch square baking pan. Refrigerate while preparing topping.

2. In a medium saucepan, combine cream, chocolate, and remaining 2 tablespoons butter. Heat over low heat, stirring occasionally, until chocolate melts and mixture is smooth. Remove from heat; let cool slightly. With wire whisk, beat in egg, espresso powder, granulated sugar, and cornstarch until well blended. Stir in walnuts.

3. Pour chocolate mixture over chilled crust. Bake 20 to 25 minutes, or until set. Let cool in pan. Cut into 25 squares. Sift powdered sugar over top. Store in refrigerator.

332   CHOCOLATE PEANUT CRISP SQUARES
Prep: 20 minutes   Cook: 30 to 34 minutes   Makes: 5 dozen

1 **stick plus 7 tablespoons unsalted butter, softened**	½ **cup packed light brown sugar**
⅓ **cup granulated sugar**	⅓ **cup corn syrup**
⅓ **cup unsweetened cocoa powder**	⅓ **cup heavy cream**
1¾ **cups flour**	2 **cups dry-roasted unsalted peanuts**
1 **egg**	6 **ounces semisweet chocolate chips (1 cup)**
1 **teaspoon vanilla extract**	

1. Preheat oven to 350°F. To make crust, in a food processor, combine 1 stick plus 3 tablespoons butter, granulated sugar, and cocoa. Process until blended. Add flour and process until incorporated. Add egg and vanilla and process until dough clings together.

2. Press dough evenly in bottom and up sides of a foil-lined 10 x 15-inch jelly-roll pan. Prick dough all over with fork. Bake 12 to 14 minutes, until dry and set.

3. Meanwhile, make topping. In a medium saucepan, combine remaining 4 tablespoons butter, brown sugar, corn syrup, and cream; mix well. Heat to boiling over medium heat, stirring occasionally. Stir in peanuts. Spread evenly over partially baked crust.

4. Bake 13 to 15 minutes, or until bubbly. Sprinkle chocolate chips on top, but do not spread. Let cool in pan before cutting into 60 (1½-inch) squares with a sharp knife.

333   CHOCOLATE PECAN PIE SQUARES
Prep: 20 minutes   Cook: 41 to 48 minutes   Makes: 54

These are just plain delicious and a festive addition to any dessert tray.

2 **cups flour**	6 **ounces semisweet chocolate chips (1 cup)**
1¼ **cups granulated sugar**	⅔ **cup packed light brown sugar**
2 **sticks (8 ounces) butter, cut into pieces, softened, plus 3 tablespoons butter, melted**	½ **cup heavy cream**
	⅓ **cup light corn syrup**
1 **egg**	3 **cups chopped pecans**
3 **teaspoons vanilla extract**	

1. Preheat oven to 350°F. To make crust, in a food processor, combine flour and ½ cup granulated sugar. Add 2 sticks softened butter and process until mixture is in fine crumbs. With machine on, add egg and 2 teaspoons vanilla through feed tube. Process just until dough leaves sides of bowl and masses together.

2. Press dough evenly over bottom of a foil-lined 10 x 15-inch jelly-roll pan. Bake 15 to 17 minutes, or just until golden.

3. Remove from oven and sprinkle evenly with chocolate chips. Return to oven 1 to 2 minutes to melt chips. Spread melted chocolate over crust.

4. In a large bowl, combine remaining ¾ cup granulated sugar, brown sugar, cream, corn syrup, melted butter, and remaining 1 teaspoon vanilla. Mix well. Stir in pecans. Carefully spoon pecan topping over chocolate on crust.

5. Bake 25 to 30 minutes, or until golden. Let cool in pan 1 hour before cutting into 54 squares.

---

334 WHITE CHOCOLATE MACADAMIA BARS
Prep: 15 minutes   Cook: 26 to 29 minutes   Makes: 40

The combination of white chocolate, macadamia nuts, and coconut is outstanding in these extravagant cookie bars.

1 **(9-ounce) package chocolate wafer cookies**
1 **stick (4 ounces) unsalted butter**
1¼ **cups flaked or shredded coconut**
1 **(7-ounce) jar macadamia nuts (about 2 cups), coarsely chopped**

9 **ounces imported white chocolate, cut into ½-inch chunks**
1 **(14-ounce) can sweetened condensed milk**

1. Preheat oven to 350°F. In a food processor, grind cookies until crushed to fine crumbs. Place butter in a 9 x 13-inch baking pan. Heat in oven until melted, watching carefully, about 3 to 4 minutes. Remove pan from oven; stir in crumbs until thoroughly moistened. Spread evenly in pan, pressing gently with back of a fork or spoon to form crust.

2. Sprinkle coconut evenly over crumb mixture; then sprinkle nuts and white chocolate chunks on top. Drizzle sweetened condensed milk evenly over all.

3. Bake 23 to 25 minutes, or until golden brown. Let cool in pan. Cut into 40 (1½ x 1¾-inch) bars.

Variation: **BITTERSWEET MACADAMIA BARS**

Substitute 1½ cups (about 9 ounces) bittersweet chocolate chunks for white chocolate chunks. Proceed with recipe as directed above.

335   CHOCOLATE ALMOND CRUNCH COOKIES
Prep: 10 minutes   Cook: 20 to 22 minutes   Makes: 5 dozen

These chocolate cookies are brittle and tasty with almonds on top.

2 sticks (8 ounces) butter or margarine	¼ cup unsweetened cocoa powder
1 cup sugar	1¾ cups flour
2 tablespoons instant espresso powder	6 ounces semisweet chocolate chips (1 cup)
1 teaspoon vanilla extract	⅔ cup sliced or coarsely chopped almonds
Dash of salt	

1. Preheat oven to 375°F. In a medium bowl, beat together butter, sugar, espresso powder, vanilla, and salt with an electric mixer on medium speed until fluffy, about 2 to 3 minutes. Beat in cocoa and flour until well blended.

2. Stir in chocolate pieces. Spread mixture in foil-lined 10 x 15-inch jelly-roll pan. Sprinkle almonds over top; press in lightly with fingertips.

3. Bake 20 to 22 minutes, until cookie is set and almonds are golden brown. Let cool before cutting into 60 (1½-inch) squares.

---

336   CHOCOLATE TURTLE COOKIE SQUARES
Prep: 20 minutes   Cook: 22 to 26 minutes   Makes: 4 dozen

1¾ cups flour	1½ cups pecan halves
1 cup granulated sugar	½ cup packed brown sugar
2 sticks (8 ounces) plus 3 tablespoons butter, softened	¾ cup semisweet chocolate chips
⅓ cup unsweetened cocoa powder	

1. Preheat oven to 350°F. To make crust, in a food processor, combine flour, granulated sugar, 1 stick butter, and cocoa. Process until mixture forms a dough ball. Press into an ungreased, foil-lined 9 x 13-inch baking pan. Arrange pecan halves, flat side down, evenly over dough; press in slightly.

2. To make topping, in a small heavy saucepan, combine remaining stick plus 3 tablespoons butter and brown sugar. Cook over medium heat, stirring occasionally, until mixture begins to boil. Boil 1 minute, stirring constantly. Pour over pecans and crust.

3. Bake in center of oven 18 to 22 minutes, or until topping is bubbly. Remove from oven and sprinkle chocolate pieces on top; do not spread. Let cool on wire rack before cutting into 48 squares.

337 CHOCOLATE SAUERKRAUT BARS

Prep: 20 minutes   Cook: 25 to 30 minutes   Makes: 48 bars

No one will ever guess the secret ingredient in these moist, dark bars.

2 sticks (8 ounces) butter or margarine, softened
2 cups granulated sugar
1 teaspoon vanilla extract
¼ cup firmly packed unsweetened cocoa powder
4 (1-ounce) squares unsweetened chocolate, melted
3 eggs
2½ cups flour

1 teaspoon baking powder
1 teaspoon baking soda
¼ teaspoon salt
1 cup buttermilk
1 (16-ounce) jar sauerkraut, rinsed well, drained, and finely chopped
½ cup currants or raisins
½ cup chopped pecans
1 (11.5-ounce) package milk chocolate chips (2 cups)

1. Preheat oven to 350°F. In a large bowl, beat butter and granulated sugar with an electric mixer on medium speed until light and fluffy, about 2 minutes. Add vanilla, cocoa, and melted chocolate; beat well. Add eggs, one at a time, beating well after each addition.

2. Stir together flour, baking powder, baking soda, and salt to mix. Add to chocolate mixture alternately with buttermilk, beating just until combined. Stir in sauerkraut, currants, pecans, and chocolate chips.

3. Spread batter in a greased 12 x 18-inch sheet cake pan. Bake 25 to 30 minutes, or until a cake tester inserted in center comes out clean. Let cool before cutting into 48 (1½ x 3-inch) bars.

338 BROWNIES

Prep: 10 minutes   Cook: 32 to 38 minutes   Makes: 36 to 40

5 (1-ounce) squares unsweetened chocolate, cut up
2 sticks (8 ounces) butter or margarine
1¾ cups sugar
¼ cup light corn syrup

2 teaspoons vanilla extract
4 eggs
¼ teaspoon salt
1 cup sifted flour
¾ cup chopped pecans
6 ounces semisweet chocolate chips (1 cup)

1. Preheat oven to 350°F. In a 2-quart glass bowl, combine unsweetened chocolate and butter. Heat in a microwave oven on High 1½ to 2½ minutes, or until chocolate is melted and smooth when stirred.

2. With a fork, beat in sugar, corn syrup, vanilla, and eggs until well blended. Mix in salt and flour until well mixed.

3. Spread evenly in a greased, foil-lined 9 x 13-inch baking pan. Sprinkle nuts and chocolate chips over top. Bake 30 to 35 minutes, or until set. Do not overbake. Let cool before cutting into bars.

339   CHOCOLATE SYRUP BROWNIES

Prep: 20 minutes   Cook: 35 to 40 minutes   Makes: 36

This tried and true recipe was given to me by my sister, Tammie. It's one she makes often.

1 stick (4 ounces) plus 5⅓ tablespoons butter or margarine, softened	1 cup flour
	1 cup chopped walnuts
	6 tablespoons milk
2⅓ cups sugar	½ cup semisweet chocolate chips
4 eggs	
1 (16-ounce) can chocolate-flavored syrup	

1. Preheat oven to 350°F. In a medium bowl, beat 1 stick butter and 1 cup sugar with an electric mixer on medium speed until light and fluffy. Add eggs, one at a time, beating well after each addition. Beat in chocolate syrup and flour until well blended, 3 to 4 minutes.

2. Stir in nuts. Spread batter evenly in a greased 9 x 13-inch baking pan. Bake 30 to 35 minutes, or until set. Do not overbake.

3. Meanwhile, prepare frosting. In a small saucepan, combine remaining 5⅓ tablespoons butter, remaining 1⅓ cups sugar, and milk. Heat to boiling over medium heat, stirring often. Boil 1 minute. Remove from heat and add chocolate chips. Beat until frosting is smooth and of spreading consistency.

4. Spread frosting evenly over hot brownies. Let cool to room temperature before cutting into 36 bars 2⅛ x 1½ inches.

---

340   CARAMEL CHOCOLATE BROWNIES

Prep: 20 minutes   Cook: 32 minutes   Chill: 1 hour   Makes: 36

These rated at the top of my son's list of favorites.

8 ounces walnut pieces	⅔ cup plus ¼ cup flour
1 stick (4 ounces) plus 1 tablespoon butter, softened	1 (12.25-ounce) jar caramel topping
	12 ounces semisweet chocolate chips (2 cups)
1 cup sugar	
2 eggs	¼ cup heavy cream
2 teaspoons vanilla extract	½ cup flaked coconut
3 (1-ounce) squares unsweetened chocolate, melted	

1. Coarsely chop walnuts. Measure out 1 cup and set aside. Finely chop remaining walnuts.

2. Preheat oven to 350°F. In a medium bowl, beat together 1 stick butter, sugar, eggs, and vanilla with an electric mixer on medium speed until light and fluffy, 2 to 3 minutes. Beat in melted chocolate. Add ⅔ cup flour and beat until well blended. Stir in finely chopped nuts.

3. Spread batter evenly in greased, foil-lined 9 x 13-inch baking pan. Bake 10 minutes.

4. In a small bowl, mix together caramel and remaining ¼ cup flour until blended. Drizzle over partially baked brownies. Sprinkle coarsely chopped nuts over top. Return to oven and bake 20 minutes longer, or until bubbly.

5. Meanwhile, in a 1-quart glass bowl, heat chocolate chips with cream and remaining 1 tablespoon butter in a microwave oven on High 1¼ to 1¾ minutes, or until smooth when stirred. Set glaze aside.

6. Let brownies cool 15 minutes. Spread glaze over brownies. Sprinkle coconut on top. Refrigerate 1 hour, until glaze is set. Carefully cut into 36 (1½ x 2⅛-inch) bars. Return to refrigerator until serving time.

---

341 CREAM CHEESE 'N' CANDY TOPPED BROWNIES

Prep: 15 minutes   Cook: 32 to 37 minutes   Makes: 25

When you want a cross between a cheesecake and a brownie, this is the recipe to try. Top with any type of chopped candy that appeals to you or your children: English toffee, Butterfinger, peanut butter cups, Snickers bars.

1½ sticks (6 ounces) butter or margarine	⅛ teaspoon salt
3 (1-ounce) squares unsweetened chocolate, cut up	¾ cup flour
	1 (8-ounce) package cream cheese, softened
1½ cups granulated sugar	⅔ cup powdered sugar
3 eggs	⅔ cup chopped candy (see headnote)
2½ teaspoons vanilla extract	

1. Preheat oven to 325°F. To make brownies, in a 2-quart glass bowl, combine butter and chocolate. Heat in microwave oven on High 1½ to 2 minutes, until melted and smooth when stirred. Whisk in granulated sugar, eggs, 1½ teaspoons vanilla, and salt until well mixed. Whisk in flour until combined.

2. Spread batter evenly in a buttered 8- or 9-inch square baking pan. Bake 30 to 35 minutes, or until set. Do not overbake. Brownies should still be moist. Let cool in pan.

3. In a medium bowl, mix together cream cheese, powdered sugar, and remaining 1 teaspoon vanilla until smooth. Spread over cooled brownies. Sprinkle candy on top. Refrigerate until set, 1 hour or longer. Cut into 25 squares. Keep refrigerated.

NOTE: *These brownies are also great without the topping. Prepare as directed, adding 1 tablespoon instant espresso powder along with sugar to brownies. Stir in 1 cup chopped walnuts or pecans before spreading in pan. Proceed and bake as directed above.*

342   WHITE CHOCOLATE BROWNIES
Prep: 15 minutes   Cook: 22 to 27 minutes   Makes: 24

These white chocolate brownies are dotted with bittersweet chocolate chunks. Be sure to use imported European white chocolate for the best flavor.

6 ounces imported white chocolate, cut up
¾ cup sugar
1 stick (4 ounces) butter
2 eggs
1½ teaspoons vanilla extract
1 cup flour

½ teaspoon baking powder
Dash of salt
6 ounces semisweet or bittersweet chocolate, cut up
½ cup chopped walnuts

1. Preheat oven to 350°F. In a 2-quart glass bowl, combine white chocolate pieces, sugar, and butter. Heat in microwave oven on High about 1½ minutes, or until melted and smooth when stirred.

2. With a whisk or fork, beat in eggs and vanilla until well blended. Add flour, baking powder, and salt and stir until well mixed. Stir in bittersweet chocolate and walnuts.

3. Spread evenly in a buttered, foil-lined 7 x 11-inch baking pan. Bake 20 to 25 minutes, or until golden brown. Do not overbake. Let cool, then cut into 24 pieces.

343   NO-BAKE RUM BROWNIES
Prep: 10 minutes   Cook: 2 minutes   Chill: 1 to 2 hours   Makes: 25

1 (9-ounce) package chocolate wafer cookies
12 ounces semisweet chocolate chips (2 cups)
⅔ cup heavy cream or milk
1½ teaspoons rum extract

⅛ teaspoon salt
½ cup powdered sugar
2 cups miniature marshmallows
1 cup chopped pecans or walnuts

1. In a food processor or blender, process chocolate cookies into fine crumbs; set aside.

2. In a 2-quart glass bowl, combine chocolate chips and cream. Heat in a microwave oven on High about 2 minutes, until chocolate is melted and smooth when stirred. Stir in rum extract and salt; remove ½ cup and set aside.

3. Stir powdered sugar into remaining chocolate mixture until blended. Add reserved chocolate cookie crumbs, marshmallows, and nuts. Mix well.

4. Turn into a buttered 8-inch square baking pan; spread evenly. Spread reserved ½ cup chocolate mixture over top. Refrigerate until set, at least 1 to 2 hours. Cut into 25 squares.

344   TWO-TONE CHOCOLATE BROWNIES
Prep: 10 minutes   Cook: 25 to 30 minutes   Makes: 16

Add white chocolate candy pieces to dark chocolate brownies in this taste-tempting treat.

1 **stick (4 ounces) butter or margarine, softened**
1 **cup sugar**
2 **eggs**
1 **teaspoon vanilla extract**
3 **(1-ounce) squares unsweetened chocolate, melted**
¾ **cup flour**

1 **(4-ounce) creamy white candy bar with almonds (Alpine White), cut into ½-inch pieces, or 4 ounces imported white chocolate, broken into pieces (about 1 cup)**
⅓ **cup chopped roasted almonds**

1. Preheat oven to 350°F. In a medium bowl, beat together butter, sugar, eggs, and vanilla with an electric mixer on medium speed until light and fluffy, about 2 minutes. Add melted unsweetened chocolate and beat 2 minutes, until well incorporated. Add flour and beat 1 minute to blend well.

2. Stir in candy bar pieces and almonds. Spread evenly in a greased 8-inch square baking pan. Bake 25 to 30 minutes. Brownies will be soft; do not overbake. Cool completely, then cut into 16 (2-inch) squares.

345   RASPBERRY SWIRL BROWNIES
Prep: 10 minutes   Cook: 35 to 40 minutes   Makes: 32

1 **stick (4 ounces) butter**
4 **(1-ounce) squares unsweetened chocolate, cut up**
3 **eggs**
1 **teaspoon vanilla extract**
1½ **cups sugar**

⅔ **cup flour**
Dash of salt
½ **cup semisweet chocolate chips**
½ **to ⅔ cup seedless raspberry jam**
½ **cup chopped walnuts**

1. Preheat oven to 350°F. In a 2-quart glass bowl, combine butter and unsweetened chocolate. Heat in microwave oven on High 2 to 2½ minutes, stirring once or twice until melted and smooth.

2. With a fork beat in eggs, vanilla, and sugar until blended. Mix in flour and salt. Stir in chocolate chips.

3. Turn mixture into a greased 8-inch square baking pan. Drop spoonfuls of jam over brownie batter. Using a knife, swirl jam around and through batter. Sprinkle nuts over top.

4. Bake 35 to 40 minutes, or until top looks set. Let cool in pan, then refrigerate. When cold, cut into 32 (2 x 1-inch) bars.

346   LAYERED BROWNIE NUT BARS

Prep: 15 minutes   Cook: 33 to 39 minutes   Makes: 54

A nutty brownie-like topping is layered on a shortbread crust for a tasty bar cookie. Cut into bars or triangles as desired.

2 cups flour	¼ cup granulated sugar
2 sticks (8 ounces) butter, cut up and softened	2 eggs
½ cup powdered sugar	⅛ teaspoon salt
2 teaspoons vanilla extract	1 cup chopped pecans or walnuts
12 ounces semisweet chocolate chips (2 cups)	

1. Preheat oven to 350°F. To make shortbread crust, in a food processor, combine flour, butter, powdered sugar, and 1 teaspoon vanilla. Process until mixture forms a cohesive dough. Press mixture evenly over bottom of a foil-lined 10 x 15-inch jelly-roll pan. Bake 18 to 22 minutes, or just until very light golden.

2. Meanwhile, make brownie-nut topping. In a 1-quart glass bowl, melt chocolate in microwave oven on High 1½ to 2 minutes, stirring once, until melted and smooth when stirred. With a fork, beat in granulated sugar, eggs, remaining 1 teaspoon vanilla, and salt until well blended. Stir in nuts. Spread evenly over crust.

3. Bake 13 to 15 minutes, or until set. Let cool. Cut into 54 bars.

---

347   BUTTERSCOTCH BROWNIES

Prep: 10 minutes   Cook: 25 to 30 minutes   Makes: 25

These light brownies dotted with chocolate pieces are rich in butterscotch flavor.

1 cup packed brown sugar	1½ cups flour
6 ounces butterscotch-flavored chips (1 cup), melted	1½ teaspoons baking powder
	¼ teaspoon salt
	¾ cup chopped walnuts
4 eggs	6 ounces semisweet chocolate chips (1 cup)
1 teaspoon vanilla extract	

1. Preheat oven to 350°F. In a large bowl, combine brown sugar and melted butterscotch chips; mix well. Add eggs and vanilla and beat until well blended. Stir in flour, baking powder, and salt; mix well. Stir in walnuts and chocolate chips.

2. Spread batter evenly in a greased 9-inch square baking pan. Bake 25 to 30 minutes, or until golden and set. Let cool in pan. Cut into 25 (1½-inch) squares.

348 CHOCOLATE SHORTBREAD WEDGES

Prep: 15 minutes   Cook: 30 to 32 minutes   Makes: 10 to 12

1 stick (4 ounces) butter	Dash of salt
½ cup powdered sugar	1 teaspoon vanilla extract
⅓ cup unsweetened cocoa	1 cup flour
powder, preferably	2 teaspoons grated orange zest
Dutch-processed	(optional)

1. Preheat oven to 325°F. In a medium bowl, beat together butter, powdered sugar, cocoa, and salt with an electric mixer on medium speed about 1 minute, until well blended. Beat in vanilla, flour, and orange zest until well blended. Mixture will be slightly crumbly.

2. Turn dough into an ungreased 9-inch springform pan. Pat evenly and firmly over bottom of pan, pressing bits of dough together. Using a knife, score dough into 10 to 12 wedges, cutting about three quarters of way through dough. Press tines of a fork against outside edge of dough to create a decorative rim. Prick dough all over with fork.

3. Bake 30 to 32 minutes, or until shortbread is set and feels almost firm to touch. Shortbread should not brown. Let cool in pan 5 to 10 minutes, then cut through marked wedges. Let cool completely before removing sides of pan.

349 CHOCOLATE SHORTBREAD COOKIES

Prep: 20 minutes   Cook: 45 minutes   Makes: 24

After I tasted this shortbread at Stars Cafe in San Francisco, chef Jeremiah Tower generously gave me the recipe. The cookies are tender and practically melt in your mouth. Be sure to bake them at a low temperature as directed.

2 sticks (8 ounces) unsalted	½ cup unsweetened cocoa
butter, softened slightly	powder
½ cup sugar	Dash of salt
1½ cups flour	

1. In a medium bowl, beat together butter and sugar with an electric mixer on medium speed 30 seconds. Add flour, cocoa, and salt. Beat at medium-low speed until dough comes together, about 2 to 3 minutes.

2. On a floured board, roll dough out about ¼ inch thick. With a lightly floured 3-inch star cookie cutter (or other desired shape), cut dough into cookies. Place 1 inch apart on ungreased or foil-lined cookie sheets. Refrigerate 1 hour if time allows.

3. Preheat oven to 250°F. Bake cookies 45 minutes, or until firm. Let cookies cool on pans 5 minutes, then remove to racks to let cool completely.

350 BLACK AND WHITE SHORTBREAD SQUARES

Prep: 15 minutes   Cook: 18 to 22 minutes   Makes: 54 squares

2 cups flour
½ cup powdered sugar
2 sticks (8 ounces) butter, cut up and softened
1 teaspoon vanilla extract
6 ounces semisweet chocolate chips (1 cup), melted

8 to 10 ounces imported white chocolate, chopped
1 cup diced roasted lightly salted almonds

1. Preheat oven to 350°F. In a food processor, combine flour, powdered sugar, butter, and vanilla. Process until crumbly. Add melted semisweet chocolate and process until dough leaves sides of bowl and forms ball.

2. Press dough evenly over bottom of a foil-lined 10 x 15-inch jelly-roll pan. Bake 17 to 20 minutes, or until set.

3. Sprinkle cut-up white chocolate evenly over top. Return to oven 1 to 2 minutes, or until white chocolate melts. Remove from oven and let stand 2 to 3 minutes.

4. With a table knife, spread melted white chocolate evenly over top. Sprinkle almonds on top, pressing in slightly. Let stand 45 minutes, then cut into 54 squares about 1½ inches; cookies will still be warm. Let cool in pan. Refrigerate to set up white chocolate. Store, covered, in refrigerator.

351 CHOCOLATE COCONUT MACAROONS

Prep: 10 minutes   Cook: 18 to 22 minutes   Makes: 15 cookies

These are delicious, chewy, and easy to prepare. Eat them "as is," or use them to make Sarah Bernhardts (above).

2 cups flaked or shredded coconut
⅓ cup sugar
1 tablespoon light corn syrup
2 tablespoons flour

3 tablespoons unsweetened cocoa powder
1 teaspoon vanilla extract
2 egg whites
Dash of salt

1. Preheat oven to 325°F. In a medium bowl, mix together coconut, sugar, corn syrup, flour, and cocoa until blended. Stir in vanilla, unbeaten egg whites, and salt until well mixed.

2. Using a small 1½-inch diameter ice cream scoop or a generous tablespoonful, place 15 small mounds of coconut mixture 1½ inches apart on a greased, foil-lined cookie sheet. Bake 18 to 22 minutes, until just set. Let cool on pan. When cool, carefully separate cookies from foil.

352   SARAH BERNHARDTS
Prep: 25 minutes   Cook: 1 to 1½ minutes   Makes: 14 cookies

To make these sensational cookies easily, buy bakery coconut macaroons to use for the base.

¾ cup heavy cream
14 ounces semisweet or
    bittersweet chocolate,
    cut up
 5 tablespoons unsalted butter
14 coconut macaroons 1½ to
    2 inches in diameter
    (10-ounce package of moist
    bakery-style macaroons
    or 1 recipe Chocolate
    Coconut Macaroons
    (below)

 1 tablespoon light corn syrup

1. In a 1-quart glass bowl, heat cream to boiling in a microwave oven on High, 2 to 2½ minutes. Stir in 8 ounces chocolate and 2 tablespoons butter, mixing until completely melted and smooth. Refrigerate, stirring occasionally, until cold and thickened, but not set, 3 to 4 hours.

2. In a medium bowl, beat chilled chocolate mixture with an electric mixer on high speed about 1 minute, or until mixture becomes stiff enough to hold its shape and lightens slightly in color. Do not overbeat, or mixture will become grainy.

3. Place chocolate mixture in a large pastry bag fitted with an open star or a plain ¾-inch diameter decorating tube or tip, filling bag half to three quarters full. Pipe a 1½-inch-high chocolate mound on top of each macaroon. Place on a wax paper-lined baking pan. Refrigerate until firm, 1 to 2 hours.

4. When firm, prepare glaze. In a 2-cup glass measure, combine remaining 6 ounces chocolate, corn syrup, and remaining 3 tablespoons butter. Heat in a microwave oven on High 1 to 1½ minutes, until melted and smooth when stirred. Let cool 10 minutes, or until lukewarm.

5. Holding one cookie filling-side down, dip carefully but quickly into glaze to cover chocolate filling completely and almost all of cookie. Quickly place cookies upright on wax paper-lined baking pan. Refrigerate until set, 1 to 2 hours. Store in a tightly covered container in refrigerator.

353   MINI CHOCOLATE PISTACHIO CUPS
Prep: 25 minutes   Cook: 8 to 10 minutes   Makes: 3½ dozen

These little brown bites are baked in paper-lined mini-muffin pans. Frosted with chocolate and topped with pistachio nuts, they are ideal to add interesting diversity to cookie trays.

6 ounces semisweet chocolate chips (1 cup)	½ cup flour
6 tablespoons unsalted butter	½ teaspoon baking powder
2 eggs	1⅓ cups chopped pistachio nuts
⅓ cup sugar	Chocolate Frosting (recipe
1 teaspoon vanilla extract	follows)

1. Preheat oven to 375°F. In a 2-quart glass bowl, combine chocolate chips and butter. Heat in a microwave oven on High 1 to 1½ minutes, or until melted and smooth when stirred. Stir in eggs, sugar, and vanilla until well mixed. Then stir in flour and baking powder until well blended. Mix in 1 cup pistachios.

2. Line 42 mini-muffin cups (1¾ inches in diameter) with paper bon bon cups. Spoon batter into cups, filling three quarters full. Bake 7 to 8 minutes. Do not overbake. Let cool in pans. Frost with Chocolate Frosting and sprinkle remaining ⅓ cup pistachios on top. Wrap tightly and refrigerate up to 5 days, or freeze and use within 2 months.

CHOCOLATE FROSTING

¾ cup semisweet chocolate chips	3 tablespoons heavy cream
	1½ tablespoons butter

In a 1-cup glass measure, combine chocolate chips and cream. Heat in microwave oven on High 45 to 60 seconds, or until smooth and melted when stirred. Stir in butter until melted and smooth. Let stand until cooled and thickened, 10 to 15 minutes, before using.

354 CHOCOLATE WALNUT PIZZELLES

Prep: 15 minutes   Cook: 30 to 45 seconds per pizzelle   Makes: 22

You'll need an electric pizzelle iron to make these crisp Italian cookies. They're great for dipping in coffee or just on their own.

1 cup chopped walnuts
1 cup sugar
¾ cup flour
¼ cup unsweetened cocoa
   powder
2 teaspoons baking powder

1 tablespoon vanilla extract or
   2 teaspoons brandy
   extract
3 eggs
5⅓ tablespoons butter, melted

1. Preheat electric pizzelle iron with 2 (5-inch) round grids according to manufacturer's directions.

2. In a food processor, grind nuts until consistency of fine crumbs. Add sugar, flour, cocoa, and baking powder and process until well blended, 30 to 45 seconds. Add vanilla, eggs, butter, and 2 tablespoons water. Process until well blended, 45 to 60 seconds. Batter will be sticky and stiff.

3. Drop a generous spoonful of batter in center of each heated grid. Immediately close iron, squeezing handles together gently. With a sharp knife, scrape off any batter that flows out around edges. Cook in electric iron 30 to 45 seconds, or until set and cooked through. (Pizzelles crisp up upon cooling.) Loosen pizzelle with fork or point of knife and carefully remove to a rack to let cool. Repeat with remaining batter. Store pizzelles in a tightly covered container. Use within 1 to 2 weeks.

355 MOCHA CINNAMON BALLS

Prep: 25 minutes   Cook: 16 to 18 minutes per batch
Makes: 4½ dozen

Instant espresso powder gives these fragile chocolate balls pizzazz.

2 sticks (8 ounces) butter or
   margarine, softened
½ cup granulated sugar
2 teaspoons vanilla extract
⅓ cup unsweetened cocoa
   powder
1 tablespoon instant espresso
   powder

½ teaspoon cinnamon
¼ teaspoon salt
1¾ cups flour
¾ cup miniature semisweet
   chocolate chips
1 cup finely chopped pecans
   or walnuts
   Powdered sugar

1. Preheat oven to 325°F. In a large bowl, beat together butter and granulated sugar with an electric mixer on medium speed until creamy, about 2 minutes. Beat in vanilla, cocoa, espresso powder, cinnamon, and salt; mix well. Add flour; beat until blended. Stir in chocolate chips and pecans.

2. Shape dough into 54 (1¼-inch) balls. Place 2 inches apart on ungreased cookie sheets. Bake 16 to 18 minutes. Remove to wire racks to let cool. While balls are warm, sift powdered sugar over tops. Store in an airtight container.

356   CHOCOLATE-DIPPED ALMOND PRETZELS
Prep: 25 minutes   Cook: 10 to 12 minutes   Makes: 40

If you love the combination of almond and chocolate, this cookie is made to order for you.

5 tablespoons plus 1 teaspoon butter or margarine, softened	1 egg
	1 cup flour
⅓ cup sugar	8 ounces bittersweet or semisweet chocolate, melted
⅓ cup almond paste, at room temperature	

1. In a medium bowl, beat together butter, sugar, almond paste, and egg with an electric mixer on medium speed, until well blended, about 2 minutes. Add flour and beat until a dough forms. If dough is too soft to roll, cover and refrigerate ½ hour.

2. Preheat oven to 325°F. Divide dough into 2 equal portions. Pat each portion into a 4 x 5-inch rectangle. Cut each portion into 20 (1-inch) squares. On a sheet of wax paper, roll each square of dough with fingertips into a 6½- or 7-inch-long rope. Twist into pretzel shape and place 1½ inches apart on ungreased cookie sheets.

3. Bake 10 to 12 minutes, or until edges are just golden. Pretzels will be pale. Let stand on pans 5 minutes, then remove to racks to let cool completely.

4. Dip top sides of cooled pretzels in melted chocolate. Let dry on racks.

357   JIFFY COCONUT MACAROONS
Prep: 10 minutes   Cook: 8 to 10 minutes per batch   Makes: 44 cookies

These chewy cookies couldn't be easier to whip up.

1 (14-ounce) package flaked or shredded coconut	2 teaspoons vanilla extract
	6 ounces semisweet chocolate chips (1 cup)
1 (14-ounce) can sweetened condensed milk	

1. Preheat oven to 350°F. In a large bowl, mix together coconut, sweetened condensed milk, and vanilla until well blended. Stir in chocolate chips.

2. Drop by teaspoonfuls onto 2 well-greased, foil-lined cookie sheets. Bake 8 to 10 minutes, or until golden around edges.

3. Carefully remove from cookie sheets immediately to avoid sticking.

358 GIANT ALMOND FLORENTINES
Prep: 25 minutes   Cook: 12 to 16 minutes
Chill: 3 hours 15 minutes   Makes: 6 cookies

This is one of my all-time favorite recipes from my "Cookies" cookbook (HP Books). These large 6½-inch diameter candy-like confections have become one of my trademarks. I give them for holiday as well as hostess gifts. Use melted chocolate-coating wafers, which are available at cake decorating and candy supply stores, to spread on the bottoms for best results, since this type of chocolate will stay shiny.

2   sticks (8 ounces) butter
1   cup sugar
⅓   cup honey
⅓   cup heavy cream
4   cups sliced blanched
      almonds (about 1 pound)

½   pound chocolate-coating
      wafers (compound
      coating), melted

1. Preheat oven to 375°F. Grease six 8-inch foil pie pans. Foil pans must be used for easy removal of baked florentines in 1 piece.

2. In a medium-large heavy saucepan, combine butter, sugar, honey, and cream. Heat to boiling over medium heat, stirring frequently. Cook 1½ minutes, stirring constantly. Remove from heat. Stir in almonds.

3. Divide mixture evenly among greased pie pans. Using back of wooden spoon, pat evenly into bottom of pans. Bake pans, 3 at a time, on a single oven rack, 10 to 14 minutes, or until a rich golden brown. Rotate pans during baking, if necessary, to avoid overbrowning. Let cool completely in pans. Refrigerate 10 to 15 minutes for ease in unmolding.

4. With fingers, carefully press in pan bottoms from underneath and pop florentines out in 1 piece. Refrigerate florentines, stacked between layers of wax paper until thoroughly chilled, about 3 hours.

5. Spread melted chocolate coating over bottoms of chilled florentines. Let stand until chocolate is set. Wrap each florentine separately in plastic wrap. Store in refrigerator.

359   CHOCOLATE MINT CRINKLES

Prep: 30 minutes   Chill: 1 hour   Cook: 9 minutes per batch
Makes: 50

1 stick (4 ounces) butter,
   softened
1⅓ cups granulated sugar
4 eggs
2 teaspoons vanilla extract
4 (1-ounce) squares
   unsweetened chocolate,
   melted

2 cups flour
2 teaspoons baking powder
¼ teaspoon salt
1 (10-ounce) package mint
   semisweet chocolate
   chips
1 cup sifted powdered sugar

1. In a large bowl, combine butter, granulated sugar, eggs, and vanilla. Beat with an electric mixer on medium speed until light and fluffy, 2 to 3 minutes. Add melted unsweetened chocolate and beat until well blended. Add flour, baking powder, and salt; beat to mix well. Stir in mint chocolate chips. Cover and refrigerate 1 hour or longer to firm up dough.

2. To bake cookies, preheat oven to 350°F. Shape dough into 50 (1¼-inch balls). Roll balls in powdered sugar to coat. Place 2 inches apart on greased cookie sheets.

3. Bake 9 minutes. Do not overbake. Cookies will be soft, but will firm up as they cool. Let cookies cool 2 minutes on pans, then remove to wire racks to let cool completely.

360   CHOCOLATE BISCOTTI

Prep: 20 minutes   Cook: about 32 minutes   Makes: 24

This chocolate version of the twice-baked Italian cookie, biscotti, is crisp and delicious. Coated on the bottom with melted bittersweet chocolate, it is reminiscent of a pricey commercial counterpart. Try it dipped in coffee or tea.

2 eggs
¾ cup sugar
1 teaspoon baking soda
⅓ cup unsweetened cocoa
   powder
1½ cups flour

¾ cup chopped slivered
   blanched almonds
6 ounces bittersweet or
   semisweet chocolate,
   cut up
2 teaspoons vegetable oil

1. Preheat oven to 350°F. Line a cookie sheet with foil. Generously grease foil. In a medium bowl, beat eggs and sugar with an electric mixer on medium speed until light, about 2 minutes. Beat in baking soda, cocoa, and flour until well blended. Stir in almonds. Batter will be stiff and slightly sticky.

2. With floured hands, shape dough into 2 flat logs, 12 inches long and 2½ inches wide, on cookie sheet.

3. Bake 20 minutes. Remove from oven and let stand 2 to 3 minutes; leave oven on. With a sharp knife, carefully cut each log diagonally into 12 pieces. Let stand 5 minutes, then turn pieces on their sides. Return to oven and bake 10 minutes longer. Let biscotti cool completely.

4. In a small glass bowl, melt semisweet chocolate with oil in a microwave oven on High 1 to 1½ minutes, or until chocolate is melted and smooth when stirred. With a flexible spatula, spread a little chocolate on bottom and partway up one side of each cookie. Place on unfrosted side on wax paper-lined baking pan until dry and set. Biscotti will keep up to 2 weeks in an air-tight container.

---

361   WHITE CHOCOLATE-TOPPED FRUIT PIZZA
Prep: 25 minutes   Cook: none   Chill: 3 to 4 hours   Serves: 10 to 12

This pizza showcases fresh fruits. For the base, bake a brownie mixture in a pizza pan. Top with a white chocolate-cream cheese mixture and then the best fruits of the season.

4 ounces imported white chocolate, melted	Brownie Pizza Crust (recipe follows)
1 (8-ounce) package cream cheese, softened	3 to 4 cups sliced fresh fruit and/or whole berries
2 tablespoons powdered sugar	2 tablespoons apricot jam, melted
1 teaspoon vanilla extract	

1. Combine melted white chocolate, cream cheese, powdered sugar, and vanilla; stir until smooth. Spread evenly on baked and cooled Brownie Pizza Crust. Top with an attractive assortment of sliced or cut-up fresh fruit. To glaze, brush with apricot jam.

2. Refrigerate until white chocolate mixture is set, about 3 to 4 hours. Cut into wedges to serve.

BROWNIE PIZZA CRUST

2 (1-ounce) squares unsweetened chocolate	1 cup sugar
1 stick (4 ounces) butter	1½ teaspoons vanilla extract
2 eggs	½ cup flour

1. Preheat oven to 350°F. In a 1-quart glass bowl, combine chocolate and butter. Heat in a microwave oven on High 1 to 1½ minutes, or until melted and smooth when stirred. With a fork, beat in eggs, sugar, and vanilla until thoroughly blended. Add flour and blend well.

2. Spread batter evenly in a buttered 12-inch round pizza pan. Bake 10 to 12 minutes. Brownie crust should be moist. Do not overbake. Let cool.

362   CHOCOLATE RUGELACH

Prep: 20 minutes   Chill: 3 hours   Cook: 15 to 17 minutes per batch
Makes: 48 pieces

1 (8-ounce) package cream
  cheese, softened
2 sticks (8 ounces) butter,
  softened
3 tablespoons unsweetened
  cocoa powder
¼ cup granulated sugar
1 teaspoon vanilla extract

1¾ cups flour
¾ cup miniature semisweet
  chocolate chips
½ cup chopped walnuts
¼ cup packed brown sugar
1 teaspoon cinnamon
Powdered sugar

1. To make chocolate pastry, in a food processor, combine cream cheese, butter, cocoa, granulated sugar, and vanilla. Process until smooth. Add flour. Process until well blended and dough begins to cling together in a ball. Cover and refrigerate several hours or overnight.

2. Preheat oven to 350°F. In a medium bowl, combine chocolate chips, walnuts, brown sugar, and cinnamon.

3. Divide chilled dough into 3 equal portions. On a floured work surface, roll each portion into an 11- or 12-inch circle. Spread a third of nut-chocolate chip mixture over each circle of dough. Cut each circle into 16 equal wedges. Roll up wedges, beginning from wide end. Press tips to secure. Place rugelach point side down on ungreased cookie sheets.

4. Bake 15 to 17 minutes, or until set. Let rugelach cool 5 minutes on pans, then remove racks to let cool completely. While warm, sift powdered sugar over tops.

363   CHOCOLATE FLORENTINE TRIANGLES

Prep: 25 minutes   Cook: 20 to 25 minutes   Makes: 60 to 70

A chocolate cookie-type base sports an almond-and-candied-fruit topping in these cookies made in a jelly-roll pan.

1¼ cups flour
⅔ cup plus ½ cup sugar
½ cup unsweetened cocoa
  powder
2½ sticks (10 ounces) butter,
  softened
⅔ cup heavy cream
1½ tablespoons grated orange
  zest

1 cup sliced blanched or
  natural almonds (about 4
  ounces)
½ cup chopped red candied
  cherries
½ cup chopped green candied
  cherries
½ cup chopped candied
  pineapple

1. Preheat oven to 375°F. To make chocolate crust, in a food processor, combine flour, ⅔ cup sugar, cocoa, and 1 stick butter. Process until blended. With machine on, add ⅓ cup cream through feed tube, processing until dough begins to cling together in a ball. Press dough evenly over bottom of a foil-lined 10 x 15-inch jelly-roll pan. Refrigerate while preparing topping.

2. In a medium saucepan, combine remaining 1½ sticks butter, remaining ½ cup sugar, and remaining ⅓ cup cream. Cook over medium heat, stirring often, until mixture boils. Boil 2 minutes, stirring constantly. Stir in orange zest, almonds, candied cherries, and candied pineapple. Spread evenly over chilled crust.

3. Bake 15 to 20 minutes, or until top is bubbly and golden. Let cool in pan before cutting into 60 triangles or squares. Store in refrigerator.

---

364 FILO BITTERSWEET FRUIT TRIANGLES
Prep: 30 minutes   Cook: 20 minutes   Makes: 32

These individual filo triangles filled with dried fruits, chocolate, and nuts are perfect for snacks, picnic desserts, or party pick-ups.

¾ **cup chopped bittersweet chocolate (about 4 ounces)**
½ **cup dried apricots**
½ **cup golden raisins**
¼ **cup diced roasted almonds**
2 **tablespoons dark or amber rum**

16 **filo dough sheets (thawed in refrigerator if frozen)**
1 **stick (4 ounces) unsalted butter, clarified (see Note)**

1. Preheat oven to 350°F. In a food processor, combine chocolate, apricots, raisins, almonds, and rum. Process until mixture is chopped into very small pieces.

2. Unwrap filo dough sheets and place on a large sheet of wax paper. Cover with wax paper and a damp towel. Remove 1 filo dough sheet to another large sheet of wax paper; brush with some clarified butter. Top with a second filo sheet. Cut lengthwise into 4 equal strips.

3. Place about 1 teaspoon chocolate-fruit filling in 1 bottom corner of each strip. Fold 1 corner of dough strip over filling to opposite side to make a triangle. Continue folding strip as in a flag fold, keeping triangle shape until all dough is folded. Place seam side down on ungreased baking sheets. Repeat with remaining filo, more clarified butter, and remaining filling. Brush tops with more butter. Bake 20 minutes, or until golden brown. Serve warm or at room temperature.

NOTE: *To clarify butter, in a small skillet melt butter over low heat. Let stand a few minutes. Skim off and discard white foam that rises to top and do not use any milky residue that sinks to the bottom of the skillet. The clear yellow liquid is clarified butter.*

365   CHOCOLATE RUM BALLS
Prep: 15 minutes   Cook: none   Makes: 8 or 9

If you don't have cake crumbs on hand, purchase a store-bought chocolate cake to use in making this recipe. The recipe can easily be doubled.

2 cups stale chocolate cake
   crumbs
1 tablespoon butter, melted
1 tablespoon light rum
1½ teaspoons rum extract

1½ to 2 tablespoons light corn
   syrup
⅓ to ½ cup chocolate shots
   (chocolate-flavored
   decors)

1. In a medium bowl, combine cake crumbs, melted butter, rum, and rum extract. Mix well. Add 1½ tablespoons corn syrup and blend until mixture holds together. Add remaining ½ tablespoon corn syrup if needed to bind.

2. Form into 8 or 9 (1¾-inch) balls by rolling mixture between palms of hands. Then roll balls in chocolate shots to coat completely. Store in a tightly covered container in refrigerator. Serve in paper candy cups.

Index

Note: In this index, "c." is used as an abbreviation for "chocolate." When it appears at the beginning of a subentry, it is ignored for purposes of alphabetizing: e.g., under the main heading "Apricot(s)," the subentry "c.-dipped" is alphabetized under "d."

About the Author

Natalie Haughton graduated from the University of California at Davis with a degree in home economics. Her talents for writing, recipe development, and food styling for photography have been honed at jobs in advertising and public relations as well as with major food companies and consumer education organizations.

Haughton is the author of *365 Easy One-Dish Meals* (HarperCollins) and *Cookies* (HP Books). Desserts are her admitted passion, chocolate her lifetime love, and her husband and two children her most devoted taste-testers.